BORG
LIKE ME

& OTHER TALES OF ART, EROS, AND EMBEDDED SYSTEMS

D1291010

BORG
LIKE ME

& OTHER TALES OF ART, EROS, AND EMBEDDED SYSTEMS

GARETH BRANWYN

FOREWORD BY MARK FRAUENFELDER

Sparks of Fire Press

For more info, additional content and book formats, and for other works by
Gareth Branwyn, visit **Sparks of Fire Press:**
www.sparksoffirepress.com

ISBN-10: 0692233237
ISBN-13: 978-0692233238

Book design and production by Michael Lee.
Preliminary book design by Katie Walker Wilson.
Editing by Gillian BenAry.
Icon designs by Blake Maloof.
Cover design by Katie Walker Wilson.
Cover art by Jeremy Mayer.

For Blake.

Your love, support, inspiration,
hard work, and patience
throughout this project, and in general,
mean the world to me.

CONTENTS

FOREWORD

Gareth Branwyn and I have been friends for almost 25 years. We discovered each other in the early 90s through the pages of *Factsheet Five*, a fat catalog printed on newsprint, that served as the Yahoo! of the zine (small magazine) world. My wife, Carla, and I were living in Boulder, CO at the time, publishing a zine called *bOING bOING*, and Gareth was in Virginia with his own zine, *Going Gaga*. The names and subject matter (cyberpunk, comics, pranks, subversive art) seemed to resonate, so we exchanged copies. I invited Gareth to contribute to *bOING bOING*, and Carla and I loved his contributions so much, we asked him to become our senior editor. We communicated by sending each other letters and postcards, customized with rubber stamp art and magazine cut-out collages, as well as the occasional (and expensive!) long-distance phone calls. We had so many things to talk about: virtual reality, smart drugs, post-modernism, hypermedia, indie comics, robot and cyborgs. (Speaking of cyborgs, the title of his book is no idle boast. Gareth is the most "borged" person I know. While others write a lot about post-humanism, cyborgs, and other *Six Millon Dollar* subjects, Gareth has been busy getting joints replaced, his heart rebuilt, and being regularly injected with cutting-edge biological drugs. When he writes about the merging of technology and humans, he does so from first-hand experience!)

Eventually, Gareth convinced me to sign up for The Well, a dial-up virtual community founded by *Whole Earth Catalog* creator Stewart Brand, where interesting people hung out online to discuss all kinds of topics. It also offered email, and Gareth and I ramped up our dialog there. The Well served as our online collaboration space, and we embarked on a number of projects there, including our mutual involvement in *Mondo 2000, Wired, Industry Standard, STIM,* several early dot-coms, several Japanese cyberculture magazines neither of us can remember the names of anymore, and finally, MAKE magazine.

The more I've worked with Gareth, the more I've come to appreciate how truly special he is. There are many reasons I love and admire him, but the overwhelming reason is that he's such an extremely warm and empathetic person. That would be enough, but just having a caring heart is not really that rare. Everyone close to me does, more or less. I treasure that, and I frankly keep my distance from people who don't embody these qualities.

But what makes Gareth so special is his ability to couple his generosity of spirit with an insatiable interest in people and the world around him. No matter what you bring up in conversation — the latest AI research, the physiological effects of spicy foods, 50s architecture and design, the impact of light pollution on human culture, the pagan origins of Easter — Gareth will dive into the subject with relish, offering illuminating, often bizarre and humorous insights. Colorful stories from his past frequently provide surprisingly apt anecdotes. Countless times, I've witnessed Gareth have a conversation with someone about a subject I would've dismissed as deadly dull, only to see Gareth light up and enthusiastically launch into a fascinating discussion.

Because of Gareth's boundless curiosity, he is constantly trying on different hats in his life and career (which are one and the same for him). He's a broad-spectrum, whole systems enthusiast. Over the course of his life, he's been a commune-dwelling hippie, a hammock weaver, a Wiccan/occultist, an offset printer, a zine publisher, a cyberpunk, a mail artist, a tabletop game geek, a robot builder, a DIYer, an amateur William Blake scholar, an academic, a non-profit administrator, a book and magazine publisher, and much more. And he never seems to switch hats - he stacks one on top of the other as they're acquired. That stack has grown impressively tall, and it just keeps growing!

But throughout all of this, Gareth has been, first and foremost, a writer. He is a master at taking his seemingly inexhaustible interests and writing about them in ways that make his fascinations as interesting to others. He has an impressive ability to study a subject, discard the bullshit, penetrate the impenetrable, identify the gist, and then present it in a way that's extremely clear, honest, and eye-opening. It's his superpower. I love reading (or hearing) Gareth's take on something, because it frequently allows me to see it with fresh eyes.

Gareth has written for dozens of print and online publications, and I've probably read everything he's published, at least once. It's been a great treat to read his oeuvre once again in *Borg Like Me* and to get some of the backstory on these essays. A few highlights include his wonderful "Borg Like Me" and "Tears in the Rain" essays, which I had the pleasure of hearing him read at SXSW 2014 (to wild applause), "Mindfucking Since 1976," a tribute to one of our mutual heroes, Robert Anton Wilson, originally written for *Boing Boing*, "Into the Future: The Making of Beyond Cyberpunk!," about the groundbreaking HyperCard stack he co-created (and I contributed to), which was like a World Wide Web on your desktop years before the Web existed, "The Internet is Punk Rock!," on his surreal collaboration with pop punk rocker Billy Idol, and what he calls his "Patron Saints of Makers," series which he originally wrote for MAKE (covering the lives and maker spirits of artist William Blake, rocketry pioneer Jack Parsons, and early robotics experimenter W. Grey Walter).

In Borg Like Me, we all get to watch Gareth as he deftly balances that impressive stack of hats. As wonderful and broad-ranging as the collection of essays, ideas, and personal reminiscences is here, this is really only the tip of the Gar-berg. I'm confident that he will continue to voraciously absorb the world, chronicle his journey —stackin' those hats— and generally make the world a far more interesting place, for a long time to come.

—Mark Frauenfelder
Somewhere over America, April 25, 2014

Morning Invocation of the Muses

Daughters of Beulah! Muses who inspire the Poets Song

Record the journey of immortal Milton thro' your Realms

Of terror & mild moony lustre, in soft sexual delusions

Of varied beauty, to delight the wanderer and repose

His burning thirst & freezing hunger! Come into my hand

By your mild power; descending down the Nerves of my right arm

From out the Portals of my Brain, where by your ministry

The Eternal Great Humanity Divine, planted his Paradise

[Come into my hand!]

Inspired several years ago by a passage in Steven Pressfield's *The War of Art* (where he suggests saying a prayer each morning to whatever forces inspire you), I began saying the above before beginning my work each day. It's adapted from the preface to William Blake's prophetic long-form poem, *Milton* (the same preface which includes the "And did those feet in ancient time…" verse that's become a British national hymn). Every morning, I brew my coffee. Then I sit at my computer with my left hand on my keyboard and my right hand on my mouse — my softwired connection to the Big Giant Head of the Internet — and I recite (out loud) these words. I try and really rattle the rafters with the thing, call DOWN those muses! Then I drink coffee until steam shoots out of my neck bolts. Suitably caffeinated, musically uplifted, I whistle my way on down, deep into the datamines.

INTRODUCTION

YOU MAY ASK YOURSELF, HOW DID I GET HERE?

When I was a teen, growing up in a small town outside of Richmond, VA, I knew I wanted to be a writer. OK, I wanted to be a lot of things. I also wanted to be an aerospace engineer, an architect, an oceanographer... and a demonologist. Oh, and for a time, I also wanted to be a fashion designer. I loved art and design almost as much as I was in love with, and in awe of, women, so I figured a career in fashion was the personal-professional perfect storm. But my hippie-redneck friends (see "Chapter Zero") convinced me that a straight man could never be a fashion designer, and foolishly, I listened. I still snuck clothing designs into my sketchbooks, alongside occult symbols, heavy metal band logos, and plans for rocketships, underwater habitats, and solar-powered art colonies.

But being a writer was my deepest, most persistent fantasy. The kind of writer I imagined was the dangerous sort, the kind whose words are wielded as weapons — of truth, enlightenment, and the (un)American way. Hunter S. Thompson wasn't on my radar yet to crystalize this image of the guerrilla scribe, so at first it was people like Edward R. Murrow and Rod Serling who sketched the outlines of the archetype. Then, in my later teens, it was Lester Bangs (*Creem*), Raymond Mungo (creator of the Liberation News Service), and Richard Fairfield (editor of *The Modern Utopian*). Then came Hunter.

With these writers to inspire me, I invoked the romantic Jini of a chain-smoking, whiskey-belting *l'enfant terrible* holed up in some dusty and dimly-lit publishing office or seedy motel. My iconic writer could forever be found at his desk, hunched over a well-lubricated Olivetti or Smith-Corona, feverishly firing its type-arms into paper-pulp. Like the machine was some sort of synaptic Gatling gun hellbent on pulverizing every injustice and mundanity caught in the writer's sights.

For all of my boyish wishing and exaggerated writer-as-superhero fantasies, my career in writing has been a bit less revolutionary and melodramatic. Writing about decentralization and community, DIY media and technology, hacker and maker culture, and so-called "reality hacking" (subverting consensus reality), I think I've made at least some humble contribution to what sci-fi author Rudy Rucker has semi-seriously dubbed "The Great Work." (As of this writing, I am not aware of having mowed anyone down with the words fired from my keyboard... but I ain't done yet.)

After graduating high school, I headed for the hills of rural Virginia, to the Twin Oaks commune. Throughout my teen years, I was terrified that hippies would become extinct before I was old enough to become one. It seemed like a dying subculture in the mid-70s and I wanted to jump on that gypsy bandwagon before the caravan came to a halt. It was by kismet that I found out that Twin Oaks Community, one of the hardiest surviving tribes of hippiedom, was close-by in Louisa, VA. I was on their doorstep as soon as I'd graduated.

I had taken journalism and vocational printing classes in high school. And with my printing, graphic arts, and basic journalism skills, I quickly found myself co-managing Twin Oaks' print shop. There, I learned the day-to-day printing trade, graphic design, and soon found myself working on *Communities*, the bi-monthly magazine that Twin Oaks produced. *Communities* was my gateway drug to established magazine writing. From there I got a job writing a column for *The Futurist* in Bethesda, MD. And I just kept bootstrapping to bigger and better venues from there. Each time, I'd take writing more seriously and it began taking over more of my work cycles.

I'VE NEVER BEEN ALL THAT INTERESTED IN TECHNOLOGY

Because of my time at such high-exposure publications as *Esquire* (where I covered tech), *Wired*, *Mondo 2000*, and *MAKE*, and seminal indie projects like *Beyond Cyberpunk!* and *bOING bOING*, I'm mostly known as a tech writer. But, in truth, it is human beings that fascinate me – their ingenuity, imagination, and creativity, how they live, how they love, the stories they tell themselves, and the art and poetry they create (and I count religion within that) in trying to make sense of their world. It just so happens that in this grand and accelerated age of technology, a lot of that human story is mediated, magnified, and potentially imperiled by technology. So, I've frequently found myself standing on that particular street corner, marveling at the traffic, dutifully taking notes.

And here's an admission I need to make, especially to those who think of me as that tech writer and perhaps expect this to be a tech book. I'm not *really* a geek. I just play one on the internet. I've never really been all that interested in technology in and of itself, at least not as much as I'm interested in the people who use (and creatively abuse) it. I first got into early personal computers, which served as my portal to the entire world of science and technology that I've been chronicling ever since, through William Gibson's *Neuromancer* (and the other books in his so-called "Sprawl" series). Within these books, Gibson proclaimed: "The street finds its own uses for things." Well, I've always been more interested in the street than the things.

Over the years, I've actually written on all sorts of subjects, from music and art, to sex and romance, geek humor to spirituality. And, of course, fringe and DIY media and culture. At 20, I even wrote a series of travel dispatches for a Wiccan newsletter during a trip to ancient ceremonial sites in the UK. It was because of these pieces that I got my first writing assignment for *Esquire*. (But that's a long, strange story best left for another time.) The point is that over the long arc of my career, I've covered many diverse categories of human endeavor. And this book includes core samples from that range.

BORG LIKE US

In this saturated age of high-technology, we have all become part human, part machine. We are constructs, mediated networks of relationships; meat and machinery. I like to tell people that I am a cyborg and a chimera. And I'm not exaggerating. I am literally part man, part machine (see "the Borg Like Me" essay), and part mouse. For the spinal arthritic condition that I've had since my teens, I get infused with a biological drug every six weeks that's engineered from tweaked mice proteins. And part of my leg is in my chest. I've had triple-bypass heart surgery (see "Boating the Abyss") and they used a major vein from my left leg to graft into my coronary arteries.

And lest you think I'm a special case, a majority of you reading this will be some combination of glasses/contact lens wearers, hearing-aided, and/or you regularly use some other sophisticated medical device(s). You have likely been implanted or reconstructed in one way or another, take sophisticated modern medicines, and so on. Sure, a lot of this isn't terribly recent technology, but the extent, sophistication, and numbers of repairs, augmentations, and assists have increased to the point where the term "post-human" no longer resides exclusively within the realm of science fiction. We're 3D printing organs now, and looking at a near future where this could become commonplace. And nearly all of us are cyborgs in the sense that we daily sit at a computer and softwire ourselves (hand-to-mouse, fingers-to-keys, fingers-to-touch-screen) into a globally-connected human brain annex and communications system (see "Radio Days of Cyberspace").

Over the years, a lot of my work has been about that border area where machines and humans are leaking into one another (which we're doing with abandon these days). In my writing, I've always tried to help the technologically faint-of-heart feel more comfortable and empowered by technology (and to not be afraid to figure out how to use it to ones advantage, to ask critical questions about it) and to make engineers and their machines more accountable to us human users. You will see a lot of my flirtation with this human-machine membrane within these pages.

IS THIS GOING TO BE PAINFULLY PERSONAL?

The short answer? "Aw hell, yes." I've always tried to live my life as honestly and openly as possible. Frequently I think I've fallen far short in this regard. Chickened out. People who know me well probably think of me as being the reigning king of the overshare (e.g. during my Kickstarter campaign, my editor, Gillian BenAry, referred to me on Facebook as "the progenitor of iTMI"), but honestly, I wish I had the courage to be even *more* open, honest, and unfiltered.

As I struggled over this issue at the beginning of working on this book, and was talking to a friend online about it, she wrote something so perfect in response that it stopped me in my tracks:

Stop slowing down to take everyone's temperature. This is old-fashioned fear and you can conquer it. In terms of venturing into "territories that make people uncomfortable: spirit, sex, death." Look at it this way: We might be uncomfortable, but we're also intrigued. We'll jump on board and take the trip, but only with a confident, courageous tour guide (that would be you). Go for it!

And so I did.

—Gareth Branwyn
Arlington, Virginia, April 11, 2014

CONVENTIONS AND ICONS USED IN THIS BOOK:

We use two icons throughout the text. They are both derived from works by William Blake. (That name will crop up a lot in this book. You can't really know a lot about me and not end up knowing about Blake.) Both icons were rendered by *my* Blake, my son, Blake Maloof (see, I even named my son after him).

Los — This image is a stylized version of William Blake's piece dubbed "Los Entering the Grave," the opening image in his prophetic long-form poem *Jerusalem*. In Blake's mytho-poetic symbolism, graves are portals to other worlds, especially to Beulah (his land of dreams, imagination, and Eros), and into Eternity. In *Jerusalem*, he uses the image as the portal through which the reader enters the imaginative world of the text. Some even believe that Blake himself is the night watchmen opening the door in the image. It is most certainly Los, Blake's representation of one's genius/inner poet. Blake also saw the Gothic archway as a feminine symbol (you do the math), so placing the image at the beginning of *Jerusalem* acts as an invocation of his female muses. In my text, I use it as the transition between the newly written introductions to the essays and the original content. So, throughout the book, everything before this graphic is a new introduction, everything after is either reprinted (with published sources indicated) or an original book essay (also pointed out in the intro).

Orc — Orc is the son of Los and represents the raw, unbridled creative impulse, the untamed "holy fire." He is the spirit of revolution, creative and otherwise. The icon Blake Maloof created here is based on an image of Orc found in William Blake's poem, *Urizen*. In *Borg Like Me*, the Orc icon is used as incidental art. He was orginially created for a "reality hacking" how-to series in the book that I decided to hold back for another project.

IMMERSIVE MEDIA NOTES

Music is critically important to me (as I'm sure it is to many of you). Music has been so intimately associated with some of the pieces in this collection, I decided to include "Immersive Media Notes" so that you can queue up the music in question and invoke that "fourth wall" to hopefully further appreciate the piece.

bOING bOING vs Boing Boing

I was the Senior Editor of the print zine cum magazine (and later the extremely popular website) *bOING bOING*. When it was a zine/magazine, we styled it *bOING bOING*. I have retained this convention whenever I'm referring to the print publication. At some point in the life of the popular blog, created by Mark Frauenfelder (later joined by David Pescovitz, Cory Doctorow, and Xeni Jardin), they began using the more conventional *Boing Boing*. When referring to the website, I use this convention.

CHAPTER ZERO:
THE LAUNCH PARTY

I originally wrote this piece as the opening chapter for my memoirs. People kept telling me that I told great stories, have had interesting, often hilarious, life experiences, and should be writing everything down. So, in the 80s, I started doing just that.

Calling this "Chapter Zero" was probably an overly negative assessment of my childhood. I didn't think that I had much to say about my life experience before I left the small Southern Baptist town of Chester, VA (at least that I couldn't fold into successive chapters). Somehow, summarizing that childhood by writing a pre-chapter about the night before I left town seemed like the right note to sound, albeit a harsh one. I worked on successive chapters on and off for a few years before running out of steam for the project. Maybe one day...

In 1993, when I saw Richard Linklater's *Dazed and Confused*, it almost spooked me by how much that movie *was* my senior year of high school. I graduated in 1975 (skipping the 11th grade); the movie takes place in 1976. Several of the male characters wear exact shirts, pants, and a belt that I owned. The way they talked, the music they listened to, the crusin' and boozin' — it was all too familiar. The movie became seriously unnerving when they also drive to a hilltop overlooking town to party after graduation, as my story recounts here. In truth, the "hill outside of town, the highest point in Chester" that I describe was more of a hump than a hill and its attraction was not a commanding view of our little pokey town, but rather, its seclusion and dramatic view of the sky (which is how it'd gotten its reputation as a place to spot comets and UFOs — which somehow became eminently easier to do once we were all suitably baked).

I posted this piece on garethbranwyn.com years ago but only ever shared the link with friends. This is the first time it's been published. Apologies to Carl and Weston (not their real names). Gareth wasn't my name at this point either, so we're all in disguise here.

Immersive Media Note: To get the most out of this essay, listen to Deep Purple's *Made in Japan* before, during, or after reading it.

We have our heads poked into the Milky Way. Carl, Weston, and I have parked on something of a hill outside of town, the highest point in Chester — yeah, that's right — Chester. Chester, Virginia, my home, at least for the next few hours. The hill, part of a long-exhausted tract of farmland, looks out over part of the town — mostly, it looks into the sky. Sitting on the hood of Weston's forest green Galaxie 500, the night sky dominates. It's a surprisingly cool and still late spring night. The stars are in brilliant focus, the planets winking hints of color, the spiral arm of our parking spot in the Milky Way, a spew of soft dust overhead. Billions of immense nuclear furnaces reduced to mood lighting at this distance. It's a magical night, the perfect stage for a grand exit. Mine.

Weston has rummaged around beneath the front seat and produced a black vinyl zippered case. As he unzips it, Deep Purple's "Made in Japan" blares from the open doors of the car. Please, not "Smoke on the Water" again! I've lost track of how many times we've heard that fucking song tonight. Let's see: it was playing when Weston and Carl picked me up, it was playing as we ate our Friday night chickens (every Friday, we go to the Safeway and each get a deli-cooked chicken), it was probably playing while we waited for over an hour at Skaggies Grocery before convincing some redneck to buy us an 8-pack of Miller. Ian Gillan's high-pitched wail on "Child in Time" reminds me that "Smoke" will soon be here again.

Inside Weston's zipper case is our coveted instrument of self-destruction: the SuperToker. Not the proletarian Toker, not the gimmicky Mini-Toker, this is the pinnacle of stoner technology: the SuperToker. Strapped down to the inside walls of the case, the SuperToker (and its various tools and accessories) looks like a piece of serious labware, something to load up with the raw materials of the primordial ooze and zap them with jolts of electricity in an attempt to trigger primitive life. We're loading it up with something far less grandiose (but no less primordial): round-town brown, the only weed that ever seems to blow towards Chester.

"Smoke on the water, fire in the sky …" We smoke-ring our own fire into the sky as Deep Purple recounts for the umpteenth time tonight what happened when they were in Montreux (something about a flare gun, Frank Zappa, and a big-ass fire is all I ever get from intense scrutiny of this song).

I'm afraid. I'm filled with anticipation. For the UFOs. Other friends claim they've seen them out here at the edge of town. It's that kind of night tonight where you half expect a whispery silver craft to glide out over the tree line and tattoo your face with radiation you can show off to the local news team as evidence of your encounter. I want a visitation, an abduction. I *need* an abduction, a dramatic escape. If almond-headed, fetal aliens don't do it, my parents will, tomorrow morning, in that embarrassing Nile barge they drive, the powder blue Buick Electra. Carl and Weston know I'm leaving tomorrow morning (my parents are driving me to a commune I want to visit), but they have no idea to what extent they've acted as propellant, or how far I hope the fuel I've stored up will carry me. If all goes according to plan, I will never see this town nor Weston and Carl again (it does and I don't). It's a disappearing act I've been rehearsing for years. In the top drawer of my desk at home are calendars for the last year and a half. Every day of every week of every month has a big "X" stabbed into it. Every night that I carve that "X," a little piece of this town and these people wink out of existence. I went ahead and "X"ed out today before I left. In my mind, I'm already gone, this night already a half-forgotten memory.

I've read too many books on UFOs — every one in the tiny Chesterfield County library. I've vividly imagined the encounters as I've read them: the scorched earth, the missing time, the cosmic sunburns. Some nights, I wake from sleep, with dreams overlaying reality. I swear that I can see those penetrating alien eyes and bulbous gray heads outside my window. I'm often afraid to open my curtains, sure that I'll find an unearthly presence staring back at me. Sitting on Weston's hood, constantly gurgling away at the water pipe to keep the round-town brown psychoactive, I realize that I'm the fetal alien. I'm the monster I don't want to face in the black glass of my bedroom window. I've never been a part of this place or these people. It's not that I don't like Weston and Carl. We've spent most of our time together since elementary school. It's just that I've never felt like we were members of the same species, let alone the same community. Our friendship has been a placeholder for something not yet available to me, a convenience born of proximity. I've been a drag-friend, someone who does a pretty good job of dressing up and play-acting friend, but it's all surface. The really sad thing is that they've never noticed because surface is depth to them. They don't go any deeper than cruising and smoking and drinking and trying their best to get laid (which they're miserable at). Naive or not, I think I'm onto something, that I've been in training for a mission, a mission to save myself and to help rid the world of ignorance and mediocrity. My mission begins in a few hours.

The constant ignition and ingestion of low-grade marijuana shake is giving me a headache and second thoughts about my pending embarkation. I'm dreading the trip with my parents, I'm dreading the tedium of leaving. The option of UFO abduction seems much more desirable at this point. But they'd want to take Weston and Carl, too. How could I convince my spindly space buddies that I'm the only one they want to suck up into their big silver seed and silently zip off with, leaving these two hayseeds with nothing but an unbelievably tall tale that no one in Chester will buy? I think of those redneck fishermen in the south who claimed in one of my library books that they were taken up into a spacecraft and returned. Maybe they had a misfit buddy too, with delusions of grandeur, who convinced his space bros to take him and him alone, leaving the other guys to shit their overalls back in the bass boat.

"Hey, let's go!" Weston is rousing me from my staring contest with the high heavens. "I need to start the car before we drain the batteries." As I stuff myself into the backseat and we test the mettle of Weston's shock absorbers on the hard clodded earth of the field, "Space Trucking" rumbles from the Galaxie's speakers. The timing is not lost on me as we jet into the darkness down the pitch-black country road. I crane my head into the back window in one last vain hope that we're being tailed from above and I won't be forced to take the long road on my journey. The Milky Way offers up nothing but silence, and inexhaustible distance.

"Frank Zappa and the Mothers were at the best place around, till some stupid with a flare gun burned the place to the ground."

Art: William Barker

ATLANTIC SD 8236

LED ZEPPELIN II

STEREO **ONE**

1. WHOLE LOTTA LOVE (5:33)
   Page-Plant-Jones-Bonham
2. WHAT IS AND WHAT SHOULD NEVER BE (4:47)
   Jimmy Page-Robert Plant
3. THE LEMON SONG (6:20)
   Page-Plant-Jones-Bonham
4. THANK YOU (3:50)
   Jimmy Page-Robert Plant

(ST-A-691671RI)

MFG. BY ATLANTIC RECORDING CORP., 1841 BROADWAY, NEW YORK, N.Y.

THE LEMON SONG

I wrote this a few years ago after a female friend messaged me a photo of her thigh. Okay, she was showing me her new thigh tattoo, but her lovely thigh came along as the canvas. I looked, responded to the tattoo. "Nice!" And then, minutes later, I looked again. And again. I couldn't stop looking and I felt pervy about it. Repeatedly stealing looks at it quickly reminded me of exactly why this particular piece of female anatomy held such mojo for me. Cavorting through that memory, I decided to write it down and share it with her. Here it is in print, my first little Kodak moment with a lady thigh, now forever tattooed onto my libido.

Immersive Media Note: To get the most out of this essay, listen to side one of *Led Zeppelin II*.

I was 13 years old and visiting my grandparents in Florida for the summer. The family next door appeared to be my grandparent's main source of entertainment. From the back porch they reprovingly watched and commented on the neighbors' comings and goings. My family, my grandparents, were conservative, repressive, Catholic. Marilyn, the young divorcee neighbor and her two kids seemed wildly free and cool to me by contrast. Almost feral. They quickly captivated my attention and I took special notice of the teenage daughter who, with her younger brother, spent a lot of time in their backyard kiddie pool.

Bobby, the son, was a year or so younger than I was, and Sharon, the daughter, maybe 16. Marilyn was a bit of a wild woman, bringing home sketchy guys at all hours, most recently Bill, a barrel chested fellow with Navy tattoos and a vintage baby blue Cadillac. Daughter Sharon regularly snuck booze from the liquor cabinet and claimed she smoked pot. Bobby was a dead ringer for Eddie Munster and was fond of fireworks and blowing up and breaking things. My sister and I at the time listened to The Beatles, the Stones, R&B, and a lot of mainstream pop music. Sharon listened to Dylan, The Doors, The Mothers of Invention, Black Sabbath, and Led Zeppelin. Sharon was also interested in art and had painted murals all over her bedroom walls, including her own re-creations of album art and logos from her favorite bands. I remember being gobsmacked by that alone — she was allowed to freely paint on the walls of her room! I couldn't even fathom that rather tame transgression, let alone the boozing, the weed, and all of the other craziness I imagined they indulged in. And given the boredom of summers with my grandparents, from the den couch where I slept and read my dime store sci-fi, I did plenty of imagining.

Sharon had silky jet-black hair and luscious, tan skin. She reminded me of a young Cher, with long, straight hair and a longer, lean body. She seemed to enjoy the sexual jitters she generated in me whenever she paraded around their house or the yard in her bathing suit. One day, she and I were in the house alone. I had gone over there to see Bobby and had timidly wandered into her room to say hi. As usual, she was playing music and I nervously asked if I could flick through her modest stack of LPs. I knew she listened to a lot of music I'd never heard (or even heard of) and I was curious to know more. I couldn't really relate to The Doors or The Mothers (that would come later), but I was immediately taken with Led Zeppelin. And she, probably for lack of anything better to do, began to introduce me to them and their music. We ended up sitting on her bed, precariously jack-knifed around fanned-out record jackets, band photos, and music magazines. Led Zeppelin II blasted noisily from the small speakers of her cheap stereo console, which was basically a hinged portable on spindly wooden legs. At one point, she rearranged herself on the bed to get more comfortable and she unceremoniously stretched her legs straight out in front of me. She had on little cut-off shorts and a bathing suit halter top. From where I leaned on one elbow, her thighs were suddenly right in front of my face, inches away. I was awestruck by them, seeing a part of a woman's body this close for the first time. I was so close I could make out the peach-fuzzy hairs on her thighs, smell her suntan lotion. The texture of her skin, the caramel color of it, the shapeliness of her legs — it was all unfathomable to me and it made me suddenly feel desperate and funny-headed. I tried to imagine how soft her inner thighs must feel. And I could not get over those tiny body hairs, how they seemed to wick up the sunlight in the room, creating an almost imperceptible halo around her, an aura of sensual mysteries.

As we sat there, me swimming inside my forbidden revelry, "The Lemon Song" came on. It sounded so unashamedly sexual, bump and grind nasty. My God, were they actually talking about juice running down legs — as I stared helplessly into the endless pair in front of me? I felt altered, like I could actually feel, for the first time in my life, my sexuality as a presence, a gatherable and directable power. And I realized that same power could be encoded in music, that a lot of music was an overt expression, an invocation of it. In that moment, I caught my first intoxicating whiff of the sexual voodoo of rock n' roll. Like some Sunday morning TV preacher, I remember thinking "How can this even be allowed on the radio?," "This sort of thing should be spoken OUT LOUD!, like there was some inherent danger to organized society in this music and the feelings it aroused.

Maybe Sharon could sense my growing … confidence because when the side was over, she basically told me to scram. Not surprisingly, I became obsessed with Led Zeppelin after that. And thighs shot to the top of my list of worship-worthy parts of the female body.

What's astounding is that trying to imagine what thighs felt like that day, I didn't even come close. The first time I actually smoothed my hand along a girl's thighs — a preacher's daughter in high school — I damn-near fainted. With all of my powers of imagination, trying to imagine what thighs actually felt like that day, I didn't even come close. Her thighs were so impossibly silky, it was like there was nothing there — like there was no friction beneath my fingertips. I couldn't get over it. I still can't. And in that magical moment, I must have thought back fondly to Sharon's thighs, and that lazy summer-afternoon Zeppelin ride over Pompano Beach, Florida. So close I could smell the Coppertone. The brimstone. And the lemon juice.

ILLUMINATUS!

PART II

The Golden Apple

DELL 4591-1.50

by Robert Shea and Robert Anton Wilson

MIND-FUCKING SINCE 1976

In January of 2012, *Boing Boing* dedicated a week to the memory of writer, "guerrilla ontologist," high weirdo, and Saint of Discordianism, Robert Anton Wilson. I was thrilled when *Boing Boing* founder and co-editor Mark Frauenfelder invited me to participate. There are many things that originally cemented Mark's and my friendship when we met in the early 90s. One of these was a mutual love of Robert Anton Wilson. We both loved Bob's polymathic intellect, his penchant for absurdism, and his impressive mixing of science and metaphysics, skepticism and open-mindedness, silliness and a serious desire to figure out what the hell we human beings are up to and what we're capable of.

RAW, as his fans frequently call him, was one of the original "reality hackers," a results-based approach to human development, or "programming and meta-programming the human biocomputer" (to steal a phrase from fellow proto-reality hacker, John Lily). Reality hackers like RAW believe in using any form of technology, spiritual practice, chemical, or mind hack that can create the desired state-change in the individual doing the "hacking." Wilson and his long-time collaborator Timothy Leary also dubbed this practice "hedonic engineering." Mark and I were (and remain) fascinated by this very inclusive and experimental approach to individual self-transformation. It still informs most everything I do and lurks just underneath the surface of much of what *Boing Boing* is involved with.

"It's not true unless it makes you laugh, but you don't understand it until it makes you weep." —Illuminatus!

I first discovered Robert Anton Wilson when I was 18 years old. I'd just moved to Twin Oaks, the famous commune in the tobacco fields of central Virginia, and was working for *Communities*, the magazine the commune published. Wilson and Bob Shea's *Illuminatus!* trilogy had just been published and I sent off for a review copy on *Communities* letterhead. I was shocked when Dell actually sent me all three volumes of the books. I had no idea what *Illuminatus!* was; I thought I was getting free, trashy sci-fi to kill some time time down on the farm.

The first few chapters in and I knew I wasn't reading science fiction, at least not a kind I recognized. Reading the first book, *The Eye in the Pyramid*, then the second, *The Golden Apple*, and then the third, *Leviathan*, was like going on an endless acid trip, complete with that oscillating delirium of humor and the absurd, flashes of diamond clarity and frequent *a-ha* moments, awkward sexual arousal, plenty of cartoonery, fear, paranoia, and a little out-and-out terror. (It's no coincidence that these books are divided up into ten "Trips.") There is so much going on in *Illuminatus!*, an almost infinite density, that you have to unhinge your mind (like a serpent would its jaw) to fit it all in. I read the trilogy, and then read it again. (When my late-wife and I first started dating, we read the books out loud to each other, and after Bob died, I read them for a fourth time.)

There are few works of art or pieces of media that have altered my nervous system to the extent that *Illuminatus!* has (even using the phrase "altering my nervous system," is a Wilsonian "tell"). In 1976, I was this awkward, alienated Wiccan teen, a restless seeker. But I was also a science and space nerd. I could never reconcile these two and constantly switched between them, rejecting one for the other, at least for a time. But here was a world where these points of view were not mutually exclusive, a playfully plastic world where open curiosity, creativity, absurdity, and skepticism leavened all explorations, whether religious/

mystical, artistic, or scientific. It was Robert Anton Wilson who turned me onto the concept of "hilaritas" (see "Seek Ye the Hilaritas"). *Illuminatus!* (and all of RAW's oeuvre) is steeped in that spirit.

The trilogy, and all of the Robert Anton Wilson books that I read after that (which is all of them), have formed an amazingly steady through-line to my life. I've gone through many intense changes since that 18-year-old kid scammed free reading material, and my belief systems (or "BS" as RAW called them) have changed dramatically, but most of my takeaways from Wilson have remained steady. His basic approach of being "open to anything, skeptical of everything" is how I've tried to live my entire adult life. This allowed me to finally embrace both parts of myself, the part that wanted to be open to magick and the unseen, the poetic, and the part of me that requires extraordinary evidence for extraordinary claims.

In recent years, I'd somewhat fallen out of touch with RAW's unique brand of "guerrilla ontology." A few years before Wilson died, *Beyond Cyberpunk!* co-creator, Peter Sugarman and his wife, Colleen, were on their honeymoon, traveling through the deserts of Utah., when they happened upon the 5-volume set of audio interviews that Bob had done called *Robert Anton Wilson Explains Everything: Or Old Bob Exposes His Ignorance*, in the bargain bin of a truck stop (I kid you not). They aren't particularly into this sort of thing, but perhaps more based on my interest than theirs, they bought the set. They listened to them on their honeymoon and enjoyed them so much, they bought me a copy. I now listen to the series regularly and can't recommend it highly enough.

At one point in *Robert Anton Wilson Explains Everything*, Michael Taft, the interviewer, asks Bob why he's so into conspiracy theories. He'd spent the better part of his life studying them, writing about them, but he doesn't seem to actually believe in any of them. So, why the intense interest? Bob thinks about it for a second and replies: "Keeps the mind supple."

So, thank you, Mr. Wilson, for pulling an uptight, over-thinking teen out of his constrictive reality tunnels and for a lifetime of helping to keep my mind supple.

BY THIS RIVER

In 2003, *McSweeney's* began a series of "Short Essays on Favorite Songs, Inspired by Nick Hornby's Songbook." I discovered the series in late 2005, soon after my wife Pam's death, and decided to write an ode to Brian Eno's "By This River," the song that had served as the soundtrack to our courtship, and in many ways, continued to play in the background throughout our relationship. As soon as the draft was finished, I knew I'd never send it. It was too painful, too personal, the emotions still too raw. Over the years, I've returned to this composition numerous times, twiddling its textual knobs, bringing some aspects higher up in the mix, dialing down others. Then I've "played it back," and still feeling unsettled, unsatisfied, I've filed it away again. For this collection, I've decided to finally release it. Like some little newspaper sailboat, or flaming Viking funeral barge, I want to set it down into the river of time and let it float away. It's time to let it go.

In finally finishing the piece, I did some research and discovered more about this song and its origins. What I found has shed a little more light on why the track held such a powerful charge for Pam and myself. Although it's on an Eno record (1977's *Before and After*

Science), it's actually a Cluster & Eno track (Cluster being the German electronic duo Hans-Joachim Roedelius and Dieter Moebius with whom Eno released a record earlier in that same year). Many people don't realize that *Before and After Science* is basically a grab bag of material from Eno's various musical projects of the time – (his nascent ambient series, leftovers from his previous "rock" record, *Another Green World*, and his collaborations with Roedelius, Moebius, and other German electronic artists, like Conny Plank). The record was also an opportunity for him to continue experimenting with chance operations during the recording process, principally through the use of his *Oblique Strategy* cards, a deck of aphoristic instruction cards developed by Eno and artist Peter Schmidt.

"By This River" was recorded in the mid-70s when Eno, Roedelius, and Moebius were living communally in a farmhouse in Germany. According to several accounts, the group would go for long walks through the German countryside and then head back to the studio to try and sonically interpret some impressions from their strolls. "By This River" definitely feels like the "englobing" of a mood and place. Eno says that he walked in on Hans Roedelius noodling the melody on piano and the lyrics just came out of him; he found himself spontaneously singing along (Eno is known for his extemporaneous lyrical inventions). And he also says that while the song has a melancholiness to it, he never conceived of it as miserable or sad. "It's a little like you're describing another world that doesn't quite exist, but you really wish it did," he told Roedelius' now-grown daughter, Rosa, in a 2011 interview.

I say in the piece that my wife and I chose this song as our wedding processional and never really told anybody why. Hearing Eno describe its intent, I finally think I know the answer. We desperately wanted to make that dreamy other-world a reality. I'd like to think we managed to do that, for a satisfyingly sustained length of time, before a very dark and ugly sky finally fell down upon us.

Immersive Media Note: To get the most out of this essay, listen to "By This River" while you're reading it.

In 1979, I was an undeodorized hippie living on a commune in the foothills of the Blue Ridge Mountains. As a teenager, I'd listened to many streams of rock and roll, from The Beatles, to Black Sabbath and Led Zeppelin, to the fiddly prog rock of Yes and King Crimson, but once I got down on the farm, it was all about the Grateful Dead. It was into this jam band stoner world that a life-changing record arrived on our doorstep in the form Brian Eno's *Before and After Science.*

It came in a wooden crate, on a dolly being pushed across the commune's parking lot by a new member named Kent. The boxes he muscled towards his room were filled with albums from some strange, parallel rock universe I didn't even know existed. I'd never heard of Brian Eno, or Robert Wyatt, Matching Mole, Hatfield and the North, Gong, or Magma, and I didn't even know there was a "Berlin period" for Bowie and Iggy. From his U-Haul, he also hefted boxes of extremely high-end audio equipment, including a gigantic quadraphonic sound system. I may have been all about tie-dyed T-shirts and Garcia solos, but I knew the experience-enhancing potential of tweaky hi-fi audio. I quickly started helping him unload his stuff.

Kent was one of the weirdest people I'd ever met, and coming from a Deadhead living on a commune, that's saying something. He'd just graduated from Cornell with a degree in Astrophysics. Talking to him was like trying to play pinball with a blob of quicksilver. You'd say something, from the mundane to the more profound, and you could almost see the thoughts bouncing around his neural pathways, splitting off in a million different directions, lighting up brain regions. His reactions were often bizarrely incongruous with the input and any expected output, like he'd teased out some hidden meaning in your statement, or what you'd said had been so profoundly stupid, it had blown out brain circuits. He would reel back on his heels, like he'd literally been struck by what you'd said, and he'd snicker, his whole body vibrating. It was rarely clear what the exact nature of the impact was, but after awhile, you didn't care. You thought: "That's Kent." Kent, and maybe a tab of acid, or too much weed, or the final resolution to a some logical paradox that'd been plaguing him for years. Or perhaps all three.

That first night, after the boxes were neatly stacked in his room, and the stereo all wired up before anything else had been unpacked (priorities being what they were), we fired up the massive tube amp, and an equally colossal doobie. My first question, and I cringe to admit it now, was did he have any Dead. He did, but he wanted me to hear something else. I was content to hear any soundwaves undulating their way out of that sleek and ungodly expensive system. What I heard next would shatter my sonic universe, and eventually redirect the course of my life.

As a dying sun was laid to rest in the cornfields beyond Kent's room, the funky, metallic guitar struts that open *Before and After Science* began slicing through the smoky haze of the room. I'd never heard anything like it, this type of music or the sound system that was unwinding it from its pristine vinyl platter. While the music played, Kent was not content to simply listen; he busied himself by adjusting the sliders on the mixer and twiddling the knobs on various twinkling components. He had a device on his stereo rack that allowed him to add a delay, in milliseconds, to each speaker, altering the spatial dimensions of the sound.

As the album played on, the room grew dusky, then dark, causing my focus on the music to intensify. It was as if I could feel my aesthetic DNA being re-sequenced with the revelations of each track. An indescribable, ecstatic feeling began to wash over me. Part of me could tell that this music was somehow opening a window onto my future, a life that, within a decade, would be filled with technology, science (and science fiction), electronics, artistic experimentation, and an emerging cut and paste cultural aesthetic. It was all somehow compressed within this music. The feeling was so intense, it was almost frightening. I felt as though I was literally listening to music from the future. I began my drift away from hippiedom that day, although it would be three more years before I actually left the farm.

While the entire record entranced me, it was the track "By This River" that cast the first irreversible spell, maybe because it was one of the most conventional in structure. Apparently Eno's idea of a love song, "By This River" is a simple, melancholy mood-piece about two people standing on a riverbank. The instrumentation and lyrics are minimal, with processed vocals, an electric piano, a few flute-like synth lines, and a bell. The song is swollen with atmosphere, suggesting far more than it actually contains. Perhaps because we had a little lazy Southern river bordering our commune, I equate the song with that river – humid-heavy summer heat and dappled, sleep-inducing sunlight. It's lethargic, muddy river water. And opiates. It feels like you're listening to the soundtrack to a dream state. As the atmosphere makes you picture a river scene slowed to a crawl, the vocals imply cataclysmic events, the river of time swelling its banks, space collapsing in on itself, all dispassionately witnessed by the two characters in the song.

Here we are, stuck by this river, you and I, underneath a sky that's ever falling down, down, down, ever falling down.

About a year after Kent moved to the farm—and I'd been schooled in half a dozen subgenres of new music (Canterbury prog rock, experimental electronica, "kraut rock," punk, new wave, no wave)—he went home for a vacation and lent me his room while he was gone. It was time for me to pass The Good News on to another sonic seeker.

I'd become friends with Pam Bricker, a former commune member, herself an astoundingly talented musician, who'd recently returned to the farm. She'd left years earlier to "go to Boston to become a rock star"(her words to me the night before she'd left). She'd gained some measure of stardom there, but unable to handle the pressures of birthing that star, and a music industry that couldn't decide whether they wanted to invest in her or not, she'd suffered a nervous breakdown. She'd tried to kill herself and had now returned to the commune hoping to put herself back together. She didn't talk to anybody for the first few months back, but slowly, she began working her way out of her shell.

As she slowly became more social, Pam and I had begun a casual friendship, mainly around listening to and discussing music. One early Fall night, I walked up to her and said: "Hey, you wanna go upstairs and listen to some REALLY weird shit?" She laughed, widening her eyes in mock anticipation of mischief, and off we went. Thus began her journey into the new music universe I was now deftly navigating. She loved it all as much as I did. Soon we were spending successive evenings after dinner listening to music. We'd usually get stoned and spin a few sides, sitting together in the dusky silence, our eyes often closed, immersing ourselves as deeply as possible in the music. Like me, she was particularly taken with Brian Eno.

One night, in the middle of *Before and After Science*, we were having one of our regular grandiose conversations about life, the universe, and everything. She was sitting on the stairs to the loft bed. Feeling a growing physical closeness between us, I had my hand on the stairs next to her head, leaning in so we could hear each other over the music. We were talking about the semantics of the word "love," how it had so many shades of meaning that could shift as circumstances change (agape – spiritual love, philia – "brotherly" love, eros – romantic love, storge – familial love or romantic love that develops from friendship). As the opening piano lines of "By This River" cascaded from the speakers, I was saying: "It's like, I tell you that I love you all the time now, 'cause we're friends, but if our feelings changed, saying 'I love you' would suddenly take on a whole different meaning."

She caught my eyes, held my gaze in a way she never had before. Her look was clear; the meaning had just changed; the sky had fallen, only to reveal another, brighter one on the other side. As in the song, time and space began to elastify, and to work on us like an intoxicant. We lingered in that gaze of altered intent for a moment, then continued on with our conversation. But neither of us was present anymore, we'd skipped ahead to a new meaning of things.

You talk to me as if from a distance and I reply with impressions chosen from another time, time, time, from another time.

When the record was over, I gave her a hug goodnight. As she walked out of the door, I said, "I love you" (as I always did). But this time, I loaded it up with a different meaning. She stopped, looked over her shoulder, weighed the words, then smirked mischievously. "I love you, too," she said. "Good night." I could hear the smile on her face as she walked away.

A few nights later, we slept together for the first time and continued to do so for the next twenty-two years. We used "By This River" as the processional for our wedding in 1984. We never bothered to tell anybody why. When the pianist struck those opening chords, the ones that had first opened that portal onto our dream world, I was instantly transported back to that moment by the loft stairs. As a teen romantic, I'd dreamed of falling in love with a smart, talented, and beautiful woman; living a charmed and artistic life, one for the storybooks. My two decades with Pam did not disappoint.

But the sky fell again. And this time, there was no spiritual sun on the other side. In 2003, shockingly. Pam got up one morning, announced that she'd been cheating on me, and walked out of my life. She'd finally found some measure of success in her musical career, becoming one of the singers in the band Thievery Corporation, and she'd been touring the world with them. The freedom, temptations, and excesses of rock n' roll were taking their toll. I thought she'd have to be crazy to leave what we had. She got crazier.

Pam had spent a lifetime battling clinical depression. She would frequently say that, even though she was happy with her life, she couldn't seem to shake the inner demons of depression, addiction, and crippling self-doubt. The truly sad thing is that, actually, heroically, she did just that. Every damn day that Pam Bricker got up and fully lived her life, raised our son, managed her career, and dealt with a handicapped husband, was a victory for her. For 50 years, she won that fight, slew those demons. Every day.

But the sky was not done falling. On February 20th, 2005, the darkest regions of Pam's nature finally got the better of her. In the predawn hours, in her chilly little Takoma Park apartment, Pamela Carroll Bricker took her own life.

Through the day, as if on an ocean, waiting here, always failing to remember why we came, came, came. I wonder why we came.

The Radio Days of
CYBERSPACE

by Gareth Branwyn

I am a strange loop...

THE RADIO DAYS OF CYBERSPACE

This little essay from my zine *Going Gaga* represents a real turning point for me as a writer. It was published in GG No. 6, the "Pocket Universes" issue, which explored virtual reality, online subcultures, and fantasy worlds. While I was already five issues into *Gaga*, and had been writing for several commercial magazines, I've always looked back on this piece as when I started feeling like a writer, not because the content is particularly elevated or better than anything I'd written, but because it was the point where I stopped roleplaying being a writer, and actually became one. I had a moving experience that I thought expressed something universal (about how all of our nervous systems were leaking into cyberspace) and I was able to effectively capture that idea without too much compositional struggling.

Up until this point, writing had frequently been more pain than pleasure. I struggled with the structure, the voice, the vocabulary. There's something sublime about being in that zone as a writer, feeling the pleasure and the seduction of the writing process. There's a flirtation that sometimes happens, between you and the content, and with you and your imagined readers. I finally discovered the full-on feeling of that sass while writing this piece and I've been chasing that feeling across my keyboard ever since.

It's amazing to read this piece now and think about how crude all of this technology actually was in 1991. I talk about a future personal tech singularity that will come and combine our computers, phones, answering machines, stereos, and video equipment. I'm not even sure I would've been able to conceive of all of things that today's smart phones— the realization of that desire—can do and how small they've become. On my mid-late 90s personal tech hardware site, Street Tech, we used to talk about the "unconscious carry," a theoretical personal tech super-device that was so small, lightweight, and cheap that it could easily get lost in your pocket (and inevitably end up in the laundry). Today, we live with that technology (and sure enough, my smart phones have ended up in the hamper more times than I'd care to admit).

In this piece, I talk about the very cyberpunk/90s cyberculture notion of the body, the surface of our skin, as becoming a target-site for technology, a membrane that will soon be pierced as the tech disappears inside of us. This hasn't happened yet (advanced joint and organ implants notwithstanding), but given our current unconscious carries, our Google Glass, and our other wearable technologies, we're sure getting extra personal with our gear. It's only a matter of time now before we fully consummate the cyborgian nuptials.

"Cyberspace. A consensual hallucination experienced daily by billions of legitimate operators, in every nation, by children being taught mathematical concepts... A graphic representation of data abstracted from the banks of every computer in the human system. Unthinkable complexity. Lines of light ranged in the nonspace of the mind, clusters and constellations of data. Like city lights, receding."
—William Gibson, Neuromancer

"You might very well be a mountain range or a galaxy or a pebble on the floor. Or a piano... I've considered being a piano....

"You can't really ask what the purpose of virtual reality is because it's just too big. You can ask what the purpose of a chair is, because it's a small enough thing to have a purpose." —Jaron Lanier, Virtual reality inventor

I AM A STRANGE LOOP, MY COMPUTER, MY MOUSE, AND ME

I am a technophile. This is a recent realization for me. I tried for years, with Neo-Luddite stubbornness, to ward off the forward migration of technology towards the borders of my very being. To no avail.

I had an experience the other night that illustrates this point. As I was whizzing around the networks, I glanced over at the thick tangle of gray cords that sprout from the back of everything on my crowded computer table. The mouse, the keyboard, the CPU, the phone, the modem, the printer, my coffee warmer —everything has a cable—all "Macintosh gray." I was thrilled by the sight and the knowledge that I was part of this wiring too, via my "mouse hand." With that thought, something clicked and I felt my mind spill out from my head, down the nerves in my arm, onto my mouse, and into that cascade of wires. I felt, viscerally for the first time, physically connected to a computer-mediated network of hundreds, even thousands, of people thinking at the same time, all softwired together through a similar set of wires, computer hardware, and software.

And then it hit me. I remembered that, maybe five years ago, several weeks after getting my first computer, I'd had the exact opposite thought. I'd looked at a similar bundle of wires and stacks of hardware in drab plastic boxes and I had felt ashamed. I'd felt as though I'd given myself over to The Machine and it was going to transfigure me in some grotesque way. That computer and its language (CP/M) was foreign, unforgiving. I spent weeks trying to serve its needs, so that it might serve mine. It never offered me any help. Its only prompt was a single period staring back at me from a green screen. I spent my days being reprimanded by the computer's error messages.

But my machines are no longer my adversaries. They've become useful and powerful augmentation; they extend my range, expand my capabilities. I am a cyborg with a digital brain annex and an international computer network built into me. No fits of Spockian logic have hobbled my humanity. I dare say I'm better now that I've grown into my new machine parts (or they've grown into me).

I AM A STRANGE LOOP, MY TV, REMOTE CONTROL, AND ME

I have more than just computer augmentation. I also have a copy machine, a TV/VCR (our group house has 6 TVs and 4 VCRs), a phone and answering machine (6 phones on 4 lines), banks of stereos, sound, and video equipment, and miscellaneous Walkmen, boom boxes, and various other electro-toys. This stuff will soon converge into a point of singularity. Computers are now stereos, video players, and telephones; while TVs are getting computerized and phones get video. Sooner or later this will all end up in one box and continue to shrink till it disappears inside of us. At the same time we experiment with cybernetic gizmos in our home, the planet itself is being covered by its own thickening web of cables and talking beams of light.

These are the radio days of cyberspace. We are gearing up to enter a new world of our own creation that has been slowly installing itself since the days of the telegraph, the radio, and the telephone. Our brains are daily being taught to deal with the pace and surrealism of this new reality, through our television. Your average commercial or MTV video provides the toddler training for the speed of this new signal. Time and space are elastic, images rush by like the stargate in 2001, electronically edited to cuts-by-the-second.

Your local movie theater probably has a new bumper that starts each feature film. You travel, in split seconds, inside the theater chain's logo, through fields of computer-generated shapes, landscapes that explode and are reconstituted to read "Feature Presentation." Hundreds of distinctly different "scenes" and ideas compressed into ten seconds of Technicolor mindfuck. That's the trailer for the cyberspace to come.

I AM A STRANGE LOOP, MY VIRTUAL WORLD, MY DATA SUIT, AND ME

"Virtual Reality" (VR) is sure to be a big buzzword for the early nineties. The technology that it names, all hyperbole aside, could be as important as any of the techno-toys mentioned above.

Simply put, VR is a 3D computer-generated world that an individual can enter with the aid of stereoscopic goggles and position-sensing clothing. A computer is programmed with an environment that is fed to the user via the goggles. As the person in VR turns their head, the computer generates the view, such that the illusion of actually being in a Tron-like world is achieved. Fiber-optic sensors fitted into gloves and even full-body suits provide the computer with enough information to create a simulation of the user. If you hold out your hand, you see a computer-rendered hand. If you look down at your body, you see a computerized version of it. Another person can don a similar suit and climb into "cyberspace" with you. And neither of you need to look like your real-world selves. You can recreate yourself in a new image and interact with a new rendering of your partner. You can play Roger Rabbit to someone else's Jessica. Or you can slip out of humanoid forms altogether and be race cars or trees or Kafka's cockroaches. There are few limits.

A recent demo of this type of dual-VR system had two architects designing a daycare center over the phone, from two different locations. They were able to scale themselves down to kid-size and enter their design as children. Doors, windows, walls, and other design elements could be picked up and moved around. Eventually, virtual reality will spill over, like my mind did the other night, through the phone system and onto The Net. The houselights will come on and William Gibson's cyberspace matrix will finally be open for business.

Things will get very interesting in this world outside of realspace. People will be able to generate facsimiles of their dreams and nightmares and crawl into them. Cybernaut gangs will meet in the matrix to fight Valhallan wars in which any atrocity exhibition is possible. But no one will get physically hurt. You'll be able to meet a friend in c-space and playback your latest hallucinations. They'll counter with theirs. You'll try to out-trip each other. Megacorps will hold board meetings and seminars in virtual reality. Lonely guys will hump virtual sex dolls. Lots of people will have VR phobia and will never venture beyond their biological eyeballs. Psychologists will scramble to answer questions about virtual addiction and fantasy/reality confusion. Things will get infinitely weirder.

Everybody wants to know what will happen with virtual reality. Will it be used for good, as a way of communicating better and learning more about the world, the nature of consciousness, non-ordinary reality, and the imagination, or will it be trivialized, commercialized, and co-opted to extend the reach of Big Brother? The answer is easy: it will, like all technology before it, be used for both.

I AM A STRANGE LOOP, MY ETERNAL OPTIMISM, MY ANGRY CYNICISM, AND ME

THE ELECTRONIC COTTAGE: A FLASHFORWARD

In 1997, I published a book called *Jamming the Media: A Citizen's Guide to Reclaiming the Tools of Communication*. In the same odd way that *Borg Like Me* is a sort of lazy-person's memoir – collecting existing material and writing new introductions to create a biographical meta-narrative, that book was a way for me to summarize my decade-plus deep personal immersion into various forms of DIY media, sharing what I'd learned, profiling some of the amazing amateur media-makers I'd discovered and befriended, and attempting to make some sense of what it all meant. It was basically a scrapbook of my 90s media exploits. And it heralded a coming age of pervasive personal media that I (and others) could see dawning in a big and dramatic way. I was heavily involved in computer networking and BBSes (bulletin board systems), zine publishing, HyperCard and hypermedia, mail art, fax networking, cassette culture, shortwave radio (listening to pirates), and I was hanging out with folks involved in cable access TV and no-budget filmmaking. I was also helping my musician wife record and produce her own cassettes and LPs. I had even started dabbling in robot building and hardware hacking. I covered all of this activity in *Jamming the Media* (minus the electronics), and of course, all of these discrete, single-cell media organisms quickly coalesced into the multimedia/hypermedia Hyrda of the web-driven internet that we know today.

As William Gibson once famously said: "The future is here, it's just not evenly distributed yet." This snippet from the introduction to *Jamming*, circa 1997, was my attempt at offering a glimpse of the not-yet-distributed future I was living with in the mid-90s. All of the communications, multimedia, and publishing capabilities I was braying on about here, which then filled a room, now live inside a device no bigger than a chocolate bar that we carry around forgotten in a pants pocket.

My four-year-old son, Blake, and I had just finished a father and son project. He'd created a picture on our Mac, using a paint program that he already knew better than I did. We printed the art out on our laser printer and he decided that he wanted to make some additions to it. He didn't want to make the changes in the paint program, he announced, he wanted to make multiple copies of the art at various sizes and collage them together. With my permission, he fired up our desktop copier and waited patiently for the green ready light. After reducing and enlarging the image several times and cutting and pasting, he presented the finished art to me. After my obligatory parental praises and head pats, he announced, "I want to fax it to someone." I racked my brain trying to think of a suitable recipient who knew Blake and had a fax machine. I scribbled down a number on a piece of paper and handed it to him as he confidently padded towards the fax machine. He fed the paper in properly, dialed the number and sent the fax as he obnoxiously mimicked the high-pitched fax tones. Later, when I was tucking him into bed and telling him how much fun I'd had, I casually added: "By the way, did you know that all that stuff we used tonight—the computer, the laser printer, the copier, the fax machine—didn't exist just a few years before you were born? It's all new technology." He looked genuinely stunned, his eyes darting back and forth, trying to grasp the thought. He managed a distant "Really?" as he rolled over, his big, expressive eyes still wide and blinking in bewilderment. "My God, I think I just blew his mind," I thought as I turned off the light and left the room.

The central image of James Dreyden's 1981 book *The Electronic Cottage* is of a home wired into a global, interactive data environment. In the antiquated Apple II and TRS-80 world of the time, these projections seemed fantastic, verging on sci-fi. I now live in such an electronic cottage, one that is far beyond the technology explored in Dreyden's book. The back bedroom of our small brick colonial house, built right after World War II, is now crammed with digital technology. Two computers (one with a built-in TV) are wired into the Internet with high-speed modems. Laser printers, a copier, a fax machine, a headset telephone, a digital camera, three CD players (one audio, two computer), a professional portable tape recorder, a shortwave radio receiver, and other devices clutter tables that skirt the room. Cast-off and forgotten old tech gathers dust in corners and on shelves. Hundreds of floppy disks and CDs, offering libraries worth of information and entertainment, are everywhere stacked into twisting towers of plastic.

The rest of our house is similarly choked with 80s and 90s "personal tech:" more computers, a portable phone, a personal data assistant, sound mixing equipment, TVs, VCRs. While my work as a technology writer and my insatiable techno-lust makes our house somewhat of an exception, a survey of middle class American homes would probably find a similar cache of high techery, albeit in less obscene quantities.

Sometimes, in the middle of the night, when I get up to go to the bathroom, I stop in the doorway of my office and peer in. The cosmic screen-savers are cruising along at warp speeds and the green, red, and yellow lights on all the hardware twinkle in the darkness, making the room look like the cockpit of a work-a-day spaceship. I wonder what the original owners of the house would think if they had a similar vision in the night ... a flashforward on their way to the bathroom. For them it would be incomprehensible, science fiction.

Let's take their hand for a moment, pull them into the Twilight Zone, and show them what we've done with the back bedroom.

OUR MEDIA HACK SHACK

Over the years, my wife and I have put together this little home media studio. Living on a rather tight budget (being flaky artist types), we've built our global media hack shack with mainly mid-priced and used techno-toys. Using this cobbled-together technology, and lots of sweat equity, we've so far produced:

> two highly-regarded print zines
> two software packages
> seven professional recordings on tape, vinyl, and CD
> the text for seven books
> the research and text for countless magazine and newspaper articles
> the print materials for dozens of art and cultural events
>four World Wide Web sites and other Net-based publications
>All of the graphics, PR, and media materials to support all of these projects

And, that's not counting our work for years as freelance graphic artists, cranking out other people's newsletters, annual reports, proposals, stationery, ads, logos, and signage. It also does not count the daily global communication that goes on over the Internet to make all the above possible. Between my wife's self-managed career as a jazz artist and my octopus-like existence as a DIY publisher and freelance writer, our house hums all day long like a teeny cable newsroom.

This list of personal accomplishments is not meant as a boast, but simply to show what an "average human intelligent unit" (to quote Buckminster Fuller) can accomplish, given these available technologies, a passion to communicate, and…oh yeah….no sleep! And, all of it was done on less money than most yuppies blow on the mommy van.

Art: Danny Hellman

BELOW THE CLOWN

T his piece is how I came to finally work with Mark Frauenfelder and *bOING bOING*. It was 1991 and Mark and I had been trading our zines, my *Going Gaga* and his bOING bOING, for a few issues and had given each other exuberant thumbs up in our respective publications. But I finally chose the contest announced in *bOING bOING* #5 — to share a story of your strangest true encounter on a bus, train, or subway — to submit something. I'd had this bizarre experience on the New York subway system a few years earlier while attending "Steps to an Ecology of Love," a workshop with Mary Catherine Bateson (basically about working with her father, Gregory Bateson, on his last book, *Angels Fear: Towards An Epistemology Of The Sacred*). I'd written a rough of this piece after the experience it details but hadn't done anything with it. I decided to polish it up and send it off to Mark and see what happened. I won! OK, mine was the only submission, but still ... I did get a post card from science fiction author Paul Di Filippo praising the piece. I was thrilled by this acknowledgement by someone I truly admired and it did a lot to egg on my writing.

This was also the first time one of my pieces had ever had an original illustration commissioned for it, by the amazing Danny Hellman. I was knocked out by how perfectly I thought his art complimented the unsettling weirdness, the underlying chaos and violence of this experience. And this modest little submission led to a life-long collaboration and friendship with Mark and his wife (and *bOING bOING* co-editor) Carla Sinclair.

One funny thing I discovered in digging up this piece. In the original introduction, Mark says that my prize for winning the contest was the original cover art for *bOING bOING* #6 (this piece appeared in #7). I don't remember ever getting my prize! Maybe I did and just forgot where I put it. I was getting so much mail in those heady zine and mail art days, so who knows? I'd certainly like to find it now. It's probably worth some dough! Or at least a nice frame and a place of pride on my wall.

"Behind our backs, but before our grinning faces, the clown continues to do what has kept him a significant force for morality. By keeping man in perspective with his times, the clown acts as a powerful connective; he points out the breed of animal that lies under our hypocritical hides. Clowns point up frustrations, failure, ineptitude." —Bill Ballantine, *Clown Alley*

Several years ago, I travelled to New York City to attend a workshop with Mary Catherine Bateson (daughter of cyberneticist Gregory Bateson and cultural anthropologist Margaret Mead). Having no place to stay in the city, I commuted from my mother-in-law's in New Jersey. Each day, I would take the bus to Port Authority, then the subway to the workshop at Teachers College at Columbia University. This was only my second trip through the Big Apple's lower intestines, and let me tell you, I was none too excited about making the descent. The subway ride back to the train station on the first day started out like the ride in — frantic scrambling and shoving for seats, bars, poles, anything that would stabilize passengers from the anticipated train-launching whip lash. I sat on my hard, red plastic extrusion, trying not to look too bewildered (take your television's advice: "Never let 'em see you sweat"). The train, now filled to capacity with a clinging, jostling barrel o' monkeys, entered phase two of peer-approved subway behavior: Phase 1: Kick, gouge, shove for seat or pole; Phase 2: Cease all eye contact — deploy invisible psychic forcefield and spell out in body language: "Touch = Die!"

Just as the doors were about to snap shut (in that brutal meat-slicer way that only NYC subway doors do), one last passenger slipped through.

Nobody looked up. Nobody moved. Nobody screamed.

He was dressed in full-on clown regalia. His shoes were once white, with red heels and bulbous red toes. He wore a cheap, synthetic clown jumper striped blue, yellow, and red with fuzzy gray-white buttons and a ruffly collar. His wig was one of those cheesy synthetic afros, originally red, now aged to a shabby, anemic pink. His make-up was Barnum and Bailey standard-issue, minus the clown-white foundation. But, this guy was no ordinary circus clown, he was a street clown … no … a street person in a clown suit, A REAL street clown. Emmett Kelly on a career binger. He obviously lived in that suit. Everything was dirty, wrinkled, smelly, and lumpy. His wig was flattened on one side where he obviously slept on it. His make-up was smeared with dirt and shaded by days of beard growth. He wore torn white gloves, now two-tone: gray on top, black in the palm. Most unsettling of all, he carried a bullhorn, a painfully loud "you're under arrest," battery-operated bullhorn! An overturned box-lid from a case of Campbells' Chicken Noodle hung from ropes around his neck making him look like some cigarette hostess from hell. This he apparently used to collect donations.

Nobody looked up. Nobody moved. Nobody screamed.

He steadied himself just inside the train door, spreading his legs in police-like fashion as the car lurched forward. He clacked the button on the bullhorn:

"Homelessness is a crime against vampires," he incomprehensibly blabbled. "The Tri-Lateral Commission has pulled the rug over all your eyes. International banking has got to go!" And then I think he said: "The Bible says 'thou shall not suffer from which to live.' Many people you meet on the street nowadays aren't actually people, they're reptiles from outer space. THEY used to show them on TV, but THEY don't want to anymore, so STOP IT! STOP THEM! Please HELP me! I need your help!!"

A crumpled show card, which desperately clung from the front of his soup box, summarized his main points. Periodically he would tip the bullhorn down towards the list in a gesture of emphasis. The last lines "Please HELP me! I need your help!!" were delivered with genuine desperation and fear, like he was about to be tortured. It sent shivers through me.

Nobody looked up. Nobody moved. Nobody screamed.

He started to make his way through the car as it shot through the darkness beneath New York. The lights flickered and the train pitched, but everyone sat (or stood) perfectly rigid, ignoring the "clown." He went from seat to seat, aiming the bullhorn, point-blank, towards each person's face, (clack):

"Captain Kirk's not REALLY the captain. He's not Lost in Space."

"I'M the captain!," he added, menacingly. "The lizards can't get ME. Nixon knew what they were talking about. Please help. Thank you. Help the homeless."

This "Please help" was remote, recited. There was no pain in it like the first time. "Help the homeless" seemed like someone else's line, maybe a homeless advocate he'd heard. The alien rap probably wasn't very successful at generating cash, so he tacked "Help the homeless" on the end to improve his odds, although he apparently wasn't doing very well in the fundraising department. As he bent down to blow another passenger away with his naked, cosmic truth, I saw that his box lid contained a grand total of two soda pop tops, one bubble gum wrapper, a cigarette butt, a dime or two, and several large grease stains. I swear something moved in his wig.

Nobody looked up. Nobody moved. Nobody screamed.

Nobody even seemed to be with us in the car anymore. They'd all disappeared inside the pages of a book, *The Times*, or they'd crawled out of their skins on the invisible beams they'd created through laser-like forward stares. No one even flinched as the bullhorn came upside their heads and a high-decibel blast rattled their eardrums:

[Singing] "… the hairs of her dicky-di-doe, the hairs of her dicky-di-doe … Come on … sing! Everybody LOVES to sing!"

He was a few seats away from me now and I was starting to panic. I wasn't trained in NYC herd-approved subway behavior. I was weak, I couldn't turn off my humanity. God forbid, I CARED about this poor, crazy clown! What was I going to do? Would I give him money? Would I wince at the volume, the pain? Would I look up? Would I move? Would I scream? The scream in my head turned into a mechanical one as the subway fought its forward motion, brakes full-on into the station.

The pillar outside read: "Port Authority." I sprang from my seat and was many cars down the platform before I even had time to register the fact that I was in motion. I didn't bother to look back and see what had become of our alien homeless clown. The chaotic swirl of the terminal allowed me to forget everything until I was safely on the bus to Jersey. I looked around, half expecting another clown to be working this crowd. All was dark and quiet and air conditioned inside the bus. I didn't even care that the driver was barreling through city traffic and negotiating looping on-ramps without using his hands on the wheel as he did his fare accounting. He drove with elbows and knees.

I quickly fell asleep and had a dream:

I'm back on the subway, again below the clown. He pulls out a big knife and starts to skin himself alive. He's writhing in pain, crying "Help me, HELP ME!" The reptile that is revealed under his skin flicks its tongue and hisses (hey, it's the Gorn from *Star Trek*!). He keeps cutting, shedding skin after skin, laying bare layer-upon-layer of human suffering. I'm watching this utterly horrifying scene from above, unable to speak or to respond. Distant.

Nobody looks up. Nobody moves. Nobody screams.

Art: Mark Frauenfelder

JOURNEY TO KOOKTOPIA
(WITH MARK FRAUENFELDER)

For this piece, Mark Frauenfelder and I wanted to capture some of the surreal insanity we were encountering along the sci-tech fringes as we covered emerging and DIY technologies for *Mondo 2000* and *bOING bOING*. We were aghast as we talked to some of these kooky inventor-types, the high-weirdness they professed with a straight face. We'd get on the phone with each other afterwards and laugh our asses off. A great skepticism and snarky tone definitely comes through. We couldn't help it. The AIDS virus being beamed by the commies on "scalar waves," a real Krell helmet from the movie *Forbidden Planet* that magnified the wearer's intelligence (and libido), bandages in hospitals that spread disease, not through contact with other patients, but through contact with other bandages (that then infect the person who originally wore them!) — it just pegged our absurdism meters to the point where we couldn't take any of it seriously anymore.

Lest anyone think, from reading this, that I'm closed-minded about all such fringe science and technology, I am not (nor is Mark). As previously mentioned, it is my desire for cerebral flexibility, the lila-play of the mind, that has attracted me to a lot of fringe thought

(Robert Anton Wilson's bit about keeping the mind supple). And as Old Bob was also fond of pointing out, most things are not Aristotelean and binary, but there are degrees of truth in them (Wilson dubbed this "Maybe Logic"). So, just as modern chemistry grew out of the fool's errand that so-called "outer alchemy" (as opposed to the inner, spiritual kind) turned out to be, who knows what nubbins of truth might be found within the land of the tinfoil hats?

Mark and I originally wrote this piece for *Mondo 2000*, Number 6. It was some of the most fun I've ever had working on an article and it's always a treat working with Mark. I think this is the only feature we ever wrote together. We collaborated on the *Beyond Cyberpunk!* Kata Sutra comics, and another comic series, in 2003, called the "Digital Living Handy Reference Cards" (for a site I was editing called *Digital Living Today*). This piece also appeared in 1995's *Happy Mutant Handbook* put together by us *bOING bOING* editors.

"And they knew not their hole from an ass on the ground." —Firesign Theatre *The Book of Holes*

The Church of the SubGenius uses the term "bulldada" to refer to "that which is good because it has no idea how bad it is." While most people might immediately think of outsider art or the Home Shopping Network as primary sources of bulldada, we recently stumbled upon a whole universe of do-it-yourself inventors who put kitsch media and all the art-school surrealists to shame. Imagine this:

You live in a world caught up in an interdimensional/intergalatic war being fought on an infinite number of battlefronts. A golden age of super-science and psychic wonders — our birthright — has been stolen from us, and only a handful of weekend warriors have discovered the truth and are brave enough to fight for it. The very laws of physics (among other things) are at stake. Free energy, immortality, space-time travel, and the ability to hack the very laws of thermodynamics should all be available to us. So what's gummed up the perpetual engine of progress?

In this bulldada universe next door, the enemy goes by many names: The Elite, the Men In Black, the Illuminati, the Shadow Government, the Gnomes of Zurich. Whatever they're called, you can blame them for the gravity dump we currently live on. They're the ones who've bought or stolen Utopia's blueprints and shelved them in the dusty safes of old government buildings, or sold them to the Russians, or slipped them to bug-eyed monsters through gaping holes in spacetime. Composed of a villainous alliance between corrupt humans and evil space aliens, the Elite is hell-bent on keeping the working stiffs of the world (that's YOU) addicted to petroleum, pesticides, and pharmaceuticals — all products of greedy global corporations who've signed pacts with the Shadow Empire.

The Russkies are key players in this unholy alliance, too. For years, the Russians have been blasting massive doses of electromagnetic energy into our noggins with enormous transmitters. These waves are eating away at our brains, corrupting our morals, and preventing us from realizing what's really going on (please see above). Recently, the world-dominating shadow-elite-alien-commie-government conspiracy has us believing that they aren't the same one-world-and-we'll bury-you-freaks they've always been. And now that our guard is down, they're about to initiate Phase Two of their dastardly plan — triggering cyclopean earthquakes across North America by resonating geomagnetic polarity bands.

As if all this wasn't enough, we've also got the "independents" to deal with, the Deros, a race of sinister dwarves living in honeycombed tunnels throughout the Earth's crust, and bee-like Martians with Mensa-level IQs who buzz their tiny saucers over our sleepy Spielbergian neighborhoods. Some of the Earth's quixotic protectors believe that the Earth and its inhabitants are actually owned by an alien race that has "a legal right to us, by force, or by having paid out analogues of beads for us to former, more primitive owners." (Charles Fort).

But fear thee not! For there is amassing, in the garages and foreclosed farmlands of America, a fearless army of self-educated stalwarts standing at the gates of the Elite's citadel. They have designed and built awesome weapons and bewildering gizmos to fight (or at least puzzle to death) the shadowy forces that threaten us. Armed with glass bulbs filled with exotic Tesla gases, gyroscopes, redesigned AC generators, polar negative discs run by vibratory circuits of sympathetic polar attraction drawn directly from space, and ether pumps, they are going to demolish the tyrants who have turned the human race into a bunch of slaves and mind-mutilated cattle.

They are the kook-tech inventors/salesmen and this is their story. So snuggle up in the Orgone blanket, fix yourself a mug of hydrogen peroxide, crank up the UFO detector, and read on!

FRY ME THE MOON
"Curiosity is a sighn [sic] of intelligence" —Al Fry

Al Fry, who lives in a one-payphone town in Idaho, is the proprietor of Fry's Incredible Inquiries, a mail-order business of DIY kook-tech manuals and books on UFOs and the coming new age. As an expert on suppressed inventions and the owner of "probably the largest selection of time travel publications ever put together," Fry told us that some of his customers "go backwards and forwards in time using these machines." Fry hesitated to give us much information about time travel: "I only go so far in most of my interests and dealings in such areas due to the dangers involved. Big Brother keeps tabs on the really high-tech geniuses around and I prefer to remain just enough of the country boy to slow such problems." Fry claims that the most advanced high-tech gadgetry has been around for ten thousand years, but the common folk have lost access to it. "The government & 'elite' front men have technology that is pretty mind-boggling but I can't get any deeper into that than I am," said a cautious Fry.

Fry is more willing to discuss Project Phoenix, which began as a government-run weather balloon program that unleashed a Pandora's box of psychic disaster upon the citizens. The most benign function of the balloons was to transmit a Wilhelm Reich-discovered radio frequency that reduced the intensity of storms by attracting Orgone, and disrupting DOR (Deadly Orgone). But the transmissions were also "pulsed and cycled" in such a way as to control the minds of people living under the influence of the balloons. The same signals, when intensified, were used to generate time warp vortices large enough to send an automobile and its hapless occupants careening through time. The scientists continued to increase the strength of the Reichian waves until giant mental constructs were unleashed and could not be contained. Around 1983, the constructs coalesced and took the form of a 25-foot-tall Bigfoot monster, wreaking havoc and terrorizing project scientists. Some feel that the monster was created by a renegade faction of the government who wanted to sabotage Project Phoenix for their own wicked purposes.

Fry is an authority on everything from the dangers of ice cream ("Smelly, chemical-laden poison that we wouldn't even feed our dog. In its frozen form with its artificial 'taste foolers' it gets spooned right down our gullets.") to proper living for trailer park denizens ("The aluminum sends deleterious rays inward which is unhealthy and draining. Polarity devices and such are of some benefit. One self-made device consists of a pan of sand that is charged up under a properly-made pyramid. Set in a corner this works for around a week, at which time some cold unpolluted water should be poured over the sand & its wood container to cleanse it"). Fry also offers a correspondence course in Human Functioning Secrets that makes this modest claim: "Once you have taken the full course, you should be able to mind read, stop your mental and physical pain as well as showing others how to do so, have total memory recall, share beauty in relationships, talk a new communication, know the answers to hate, pride, prejudice and hostility, have a true knowledge of world peace and a serenity never known before. You will have answers to miracles, the beginning of time, what infinity is, how it happened and what you really are. You will have a new communication with nature and all living beings."

ELECTRONIC WITCHCRAFT

John Ernst Worrell Keely, born in 1827, was a guy who gave garage inventors a bad name. He claimed to have discovered a new physical force that resulted from the intermolecular vibration of ether. This sympathetic vibratory action could be used to drive an engine. After Keely demonstrated a prototype of his motor, he was able to obtain investors and the Keely Motor Company was born. Subsequently, Keely was unable to perfect his motor or patent the device. He continued to get funding for his projects even though none of his devices ever worked outside of his physical presence. Devotees even claim that he had the devices tuned to his body so that only he could operate them. When he died, officers of the Keely Motor Company had his workshop thoroughly examined. They found numerous trapdoors, air and hydraulic lines, and other sideshow trickery. Keely was summarily denounced as a fraud.

But Jerry Decker and the folks at Vanguard Sciences are not deterred by such discoveries and dismissals. They run KeelyNet (a popular bulletin board in Kooktopia), host conferences, and put out a newsletter, all devoted to Keely and such related voodoo-tech as levitation, radionics, anti-grav machines, and UFOs. They say Keely was one of the great scientists of our age and that he was the victim, like all free energy crusaders, of greed, power, and ego. "It always boils down to these three things," says Decker. "Keely was so far ahead of his time, they haven't even begun to figure out what he was about. Read your quantum physics and you'll see how right Keely was." When asked about the 1884 *Scientific American* article that revealed the workshop scam, Decker makes light of it, chalking it up once again to ego, power, and greed. We ask him the obvious question of why no free energy device has ever been found to withstand the test of time (or close examination). If any of this were real, wouldn't greed, power, and ego also compel a corporation to want to get there first, corner one of these discoveries, and bring it to market? And, doesn't the radionic pendulum swing both ways? Wouldn't ego, power, and greed just be a teensy-weensy reason why the inventors tinker with this stuff in the first place?

He freely admits that lots of the free energy inventors are "a bit crazy, paranoid, egotistical, and greedy," but he refuses to suspect the integrity of their ideas.

As we talk, Decker gets more and more excited. We ask him about Scalar Beam weapons (see earlier reference to those damn Russkies electromagnetically hammering away inside our heads), and in seconds he's leapt back to the Middle Ages, to something posited then called "first issue," a clear fluid that leaks out of you when your skin is first broken. He goes into frenzied detail about how this substance continues to have a sympathetic relationship with you after it leaves your body. He suggests an experiment. The next time someone cuts themselves, put the "first issue" on a swab and take it to another room. Don't tell your now profusely bleeding subject what you're doing. If you, from the other room, pour alcohol onto the swab, the person will feel it on their wound. Decker is off on the next subject before we can ask him if he's ever tried it. He seems genuinely startled by the question. No, he hasn't. Does he know anyone who has? Several of his friends did and nothing happened. But, let him tell us about this other neat thing he read [all of this is available on KeelyNet, by the way] that says iatrogenic diseases in hospitals can be explained by this sympathetic ooze theory. All the bandages in the hospital are thrown in the same hamper where your diseased ooze oozes all over everybody else's first issue. These icky mutant disease vibes are then beamed backed to you, and all viral hell breaks loose. Bulldada!

From here, Decker careens off into the fourth dimension with some nonsense about taking snapshots of scalar waveforms of various diseases and then beaming the disease pattern into other people. He says some papers, on KeelyNet, describe how the Soviets were doing this for years, aiming their deadly scalar waves toward Oregon. And then AIDS, the ultimate disease of paranoids, enters the conversation. Yup … you guessed it … scalar beams.

KeelyNet's piece de resistance is Decker's own essay on the Krell Helmet. Remember the movie *Forbidden Planet* and the long-dead Krells, whose engines of progress still hummed in immense canyons of steel beneath the planet? The Krell Helmet was a device that the civilization had built to pump up their big alien brains. Decker claims a friend of a friend of a friend (no fooling) has built such a device and that this "engineering genius" now has mental muscle to spare. He can enter into other people's brains to read their thoughts or to seed them. He can extend his "cerebellic fields" to control mass for "genetic transmutation, levitation, and a host of other unknown possibilities." "I can't really tell you any more than that. I know a lot more, but I'm not at liberty to divulge. [He starts giggling.] I can tell you the guy is kinda kinky [more giggling]. He almost killed his girlfriend with the helmet. They had sex while he was wearing it and … ya know … it amplifies everything! [Snicker snicker.]"

HURLER OF LIGHTNING

If Keely is the mischievous angel of Kooktopia, Tesla is its risen god. His research and inventions in electricity and radio are fundamental to much of our technology today. Many of his speculations about satellites, microwaves, robotics, and his "world system of intelligence transmission" (interconnected radio, telephone, personal communications and information services) have proven to be very prescient. Even so-called Star Wars weapons, tele-robotic wars of science fought in space, was a Tesla prediction. His personal eccentricities, his strange working methods (he allegedly prototyped in his mind and troubleshot in his dreams) and his penchant for making outrageous claims (such as stating that he could split the Earth in two like an apple and that he spoke with ETs) have made him a primary object of worship in kook circles. Those who study him and his inventions mix his scientifically-sound discoveries with his wackier speculations. They seem to make very little attempt to critically evaluate his work. If Tesla thought it, it must be true.

Enter Steve Elswick and his magazine *Extraordinary Science*, the official publication of the International Tesla Society. This quarterly publication reports on the doings of the society and their Colorado Springs Tesla Museum. *Extraordinary Science* also publishes papers which cover the gamut of Tesla-tech, from the practical to the downright daffy. Recent issues spend a lot of time discussing electro-healing therapies, with many of the references cited being from turn-of-the-century publications! Kirlian photography, Rife Plasma Beams, and other "light therapies" are uncritically discussed. Evaluative data is given short shrift over anecdotal comments such as this from an article on the Violet Ray healing device: "We use it, and we've noticed that the problems seem to clear up for us faster than people who don't use the device." The author notes that the most dramatic effect is on the family dog and his stiff back: "We apply the electrode to his back for less than thirty seconds, and within an hour, the stiffness always disappears." Other themes in *Extraordinary Science* include UFOs, free energy systems, and various speculative theories about the nature of natural forces.

STRANGE LOOPS

When we started on our journey through Kooktopia, we used dada and surrealism as convenient signposts. Now that we're done looking at the map, it looks more like a work of deconstructionism. To these wacky tinkerers, science is a story, a collection of good cosmo-conceptions buttressed by a few anecdotes and some saucy rumors. If it sounds good, it is good. The sketches, the diagrams, and the patents do not refer to anything, they are the thing itself. The more complex-looking and arcane the drawing, the more ancient the knowledge, the more powerful the "discovery." Experimentation becomes performance (to lure in other scientists and investors). Several people we talked to even suggested, in answer to questions of fraud, that their colleagues might sometimes need to fake a demo due to the sensitive nature of their device and the pressures of making the tech work on cue. It's not surprising that a number of well-known kook inventors worked in the circus or vaudeville before they went into *serious* science.

There is a logic applied in this world of funhouse science that defies self-criticism. It is very similar to the Mobius-looped philosophy of fringe science's big sister, the New Age. If something goes wrong with the technology, it's because of some outside force (weather conditions, faulty parts, sabotage, Men In Black). It's never the fundamental principles on which the design is based or the design itself that's at fault. And if the U.S. Patent Office rejects an application, it must be because there is a suppressive conspiracy at work. Countless individuals experimenting with etheric forces or Keely's vibratory physics and making no appreciable headway have not dissuaded new generations of kook-techs from trying all over again. The fact that it doesn't work has only magnified its attractiveness — this is a magical world and these people are questing for philosopher stones.

Of course, in the end, the last laugh may be on those of us who hold onto such stuffy notions as the laws of thermodynamics and the scientific method and who are reflexively skeptical of etheric forces, free energy devices, and build-your-own UFOs. After all, science is not immutable. New ways of looking at things, new discoveries, can radically change our thinking. Recent studies in chaos and dynamical systems are a case in point. And if one of these contraptions does pan out, we'd be more than happy to parade around with "pyramid energizers" on our heads and confess the wrongs of our dismissive skepticism. Maybe you have to be as crazy as Tesla (who allegedly puked at the sight of round objects) to come up with the AC generator, or as whacked as Newton (who couldn't stand the sight of female pubic hair) to invent calculus, or as tweaked as Edison (who named his kids Dot and Dash) to invent the light bulb and the phonograph. Maybe it's not such a bad idea to be tolerant of even the goofiest techno-whoey. Remember, one of today's kooks could turn out to be tomorrow's hero of science. Maybe.

PASSPORT TO KOOKTOPIA

We barely visited a modest barrio of the vast Kooktopian kingdom. Contact these travel guides for the full tinfoil hat packaged tour:

Most of the resources we listed in the original piece have long gone out of business. We suspect government operatives, or more likely, alien reptilian agents wearing the meat-suits of government operatives. Al Fry's *Incredible*

Inquiry Catalog, which sported such endearing typos as "sighns of intelligence" is long gone. The International Tesla Society and their *Extraordinary Science* magazine went bankrupt.

Klark Kent's *Super Science*, which we described as the go-to source for "bulldada objets d'art" is still around, now under the name of Zephyr Technology (*zephyrtechnology.com*). And it still doesn't disappoint. For $1400, you can get a really cool-looking ELF (Extremely Low Frequency) Generator — now with TrackBall Tuning (think an Ed Wood movie prop if Wood had enjoyed a budget). For an additional $277, you can get an extra "anti-beaming antenna" that can be used to remove "unwanted voices in your head" (We shit you not).

When we did the piece, Keelynet was a honest-to-goodness, old-school BBS. Now they can be found at *keelynet.com* and *vanguardsciences.biz*. They're still promoting and selling a lot of the same or similar material that the BBS offered in 1992. I guess since this is "science" that's never subjected to any sort of experimental scrutiny, there's not a lot of updating of the technologies that needs to happen.

These days, the media mecca for Kooktopians is, of course, *Coast to Coast AM* (*coasttocoastam.com*), the late-night paranormal and conspiracies talk show that's, amazingly, broadcast (and net-streamed) seven nights a week, from 1am–5m ET. I love having this on in the background while I work, like bulldada audio wallpaper.

Then, of course, there's talk show uber-whacko Alex Jones (*infowars.com*), on the occasions when his spittle-flecked rants turn from political conspiracies to the clockwork elves, the Elites smoking DMT, and aliens being responsible for having the Large Hadron Collider built to open up a hyper-dimensional portal for them to travel into our spacetime continuum. Do yourself a favor and search on "Alex Jones, DMT and the Clockwork Elves." You can't make this stuff up. Oh, wait, yes you can.

WHY I HATE THE NEWAGE
(AND THE NEWEDGE)

Being something of a life-long seeker, I've traveled some strange and serpentine paths. I lived on a hippie commune for 6-1/2 years, practiced Wicca, communed with nature spirits at Findhorn Community in Northern Scotland (or at least revelled in the gorgeous landscapes where they were purported to reside). I've tried nearly every form of meditation, mind-altering substance, and consciousness-altering technology (tarot cards, deprivation tanks, brain machines) known to modern psychonauts. While I have to report, sadly, that most of it has been big smoke, little fire, I'm glad to have made the journey, undertaken the investigation. Some of these experiences and practices have impressed me and I still use them, namely meditation and some ritual practices.

I've also suffered from an extreme form of spinal arthritis most of my life. Western medicine can do little to help, besides killing the pain and reducing inflammation (at great health risks with long-term use). So, like many, I've sometimes turned to non-Western, non-traditional forms of healing. And again, I've found mostly smoke and little fire – OK, in my case, NO fire.

Given the travels of my youth through the spiritual and medical marketplaces of the new age, I was not seduced when rave culture and the so-called "new edge" came along and began to trade in many of the same goods and services. Dressing up the same ol' new age in glow sticks, cybernetic rhetoric, and electronic music at 135 beats per minute did little to impress me. "New age" or "new edge," it sounded the same to me. And I was rather shocked and disappointed when *Wired* bought into the nonsense and published their infamous "Here Come the Zippies!" cover story in 1994 (now generally considered one of *Wired's* greatest blunders).

"Zippies" were a movement within rave/new edge culture promoted in the U.K. as a left-brain balancing of right-brain hippie tendencies. The idea was that by combining hippie beliefs and practices with networked computer technologies, designer drugs (Ecstasy), and electronic dance music, a sort of tech-augmented super-hippie was born. To me, it just looked like a Day-Glo coat of paint on the same silliness, and now, decades later, when nobody knows what the heck a Zippie or the new edge is, I think my reaction was a sensible one.

I was even invited to be one of the speakers on the 1994 Zippy Pronoia Tour of the US, a cross-country rave and speaking tour. I politely declined. Thinking about my feelings and frustrations in dealing with the new age of my youth and the new edge of the Zippies, prompted me to write the following piece. As you will probably tell, I was feeling just a tad cranky when I wrote it. As with "Journey to Kooktopia," I come off sounding more incredulous than I usually feel. I'd been interacting with the Zippies on the *Wired* conference on The Well BBS and was feeling particularly annoyed with the whole business.

This essay first appeared in *Boing Boing* #13, our Goth issue. When my zine, *Going Gaga*, died, in the winter of 1991, "Gaga" migrated into *Boing Boing* and became a regular column there. This piece appeared as the Gaga column in that issue.

Anti-magician Penn Jillette loves to wag his red-nailed pinkie at the "new age" (which he insists on pronouncing so that it rhymes with "sewage"). As far as I'm concerned, the best thing about the so-called "new edge" ("newedge") is that it can be reduced to a similar effluent.

This is not a conclusion I've come to flippantly. I'm not rejecting the new age, and its edgier offspring, out of hand. I'm ashamed to admit it, but I was a crystal wielding member of the new age in the 1970s. In many ways, I joined its ranks out of desperation. I have a severe form of arthritis, and when western science failed to offer a cure, I turned to any and all forms of voodoo for healing. I wanted so desperately to find relief that I embraced each healing system in turn, reading all the books, going to the workshops, following the practices, and giving my money to practitioners. The priests and healers of each of these "disciplines" would always tell me the same thing: "We've had great success with arthritis. If you follow our program, in a few months, you'll experience dramatic results." And each time the same thing would happen. I'd follow the program almost to the letter. If it was, say, wheat grass therapy — the daily choking down and spraying up your ass of obscene quantities of liquefied wheat grass, I'd do it every torturous day for weeks. But maybe I'd miss a day or two along the way. When I'd report no change in my condition to the therapist, I'd be asked: "You followed the program to the letter?" I'd say "Yes! OK, I may have missed a day or two." That was the loophole needed. One day, one meal, one psychically-impure thought, and weeks or months of food torture was all for naught. The therapy could NEVER be called into question, it was always me. On the rare occasion that I claimed a perfect score in following the regimen, the failure would then be chalked up to karma. "You're just not ready to accept your healing, Gareth," I'd be told. Funny how they were always perfectly ready to accept my money.

From my experiences, after years in the large intestine of the new age, I offer a few observations:

CLOSED SYSTEMS ARE TOXIC

It's never the system at fault. The system is a closed loop, a narrow reality tunnel. Any feedback that might alter the belief system is rejected. Only the success stories get attention (so, in the above instance, they can tell the next mark "We've had great success with arthritis."). Once, I was reporting to a skeptical friend a whole series of psychic occurrences that I'd had. He said: "Yeah, but how many times do these premonitions and psychic hunches not pan out?" That insight doomed the closed system I had been attempting to construct. From then on, as soon I paid attention to each premonition, I realized that tons of them didn't come true. I wasn't even scoring 50%. Before, I just conveniently forgot the ones that didn't happen. I only kept what fit the model and ignored the rest.

THINKING: DON'T KNOCK IT 'TIL YOU TRY IT

New agers hate western science and logical thinking. Thinking is bad— the root of all evil. One scientist friend of mine went into therapy with his new agey girlfriend. He was completely chastised by the therapist and the girlfriend for "too much head, not enough heart." The girlfriend was instructed by the therapist to remind him whenever he was "in his head" by gently tapping his noggin'. Whenever he and I would get together, we'd start talking, and she'd immediately come over and tap him on his head. What infuriating bullshit! It's not thinking that's the problem, it's having a lazy, fat head. Your brain, like any other part of your body, needs exercise or it gets flabby. New agers who hate "thinking" are just saying they hate the limited collection of thoughts they have, and most of those probably have to do with painful memories, dark obsessions, and politically incorrect no-no thoughts.

NO SENSE OF HUMOR ISN'T FUNNY

New agers love to entertain the notion that they're opened-minded and zestfully ready for anything. That's the case as long as their closed system isn't jeopardized. Here's a perfect example: A friend of mine took a workshop on "Contacting Your Spirit Guide" (the unseen, benevolent forces that guide our lives). The culmination of the workshop was making contact with your spirit helper. At the time, my friend embraced all this new age jazz, but she also had an open mind and a wonderfully unhinged sense of humor. At the climax of the "contacting ritual," the participants, supposedly in trance, were supposed to see, standing before them, their spirit guides. She saw an image, all right...it was that lovable Barney Rubble from The Flintstones. She started laughing and the workshop leader became annoyed by the disruption. After the ritual, the participants shared their supermarket tabloid visions of angels, fairies, and benevolent alien beings. When my friend announced that Barney Rubble had revealed himself as her guide, the leader became incensed. She began making up reasons why ol' Barn could never be a "legitimate" spirit contact. "He's ... ah ... not real... he's a fictional character!" Excuse me, lady? Let me get this straight? Fairies, unicorns, elves, and angels are real, but a lovable, happy-go-lucky cartoon caveman, unreal? Look over the list, folks. Who would you rather have as your helpful astral sidekick?

UNITY IS BORING

Let's paint a picture of the dawning Age of Aquarius. Everyone would get along, there'd be no conflict. We'd all be vegetarians, spiritually attuned, and sensitive to everything and everyone around us. We'd "allow" others to be and do as they needed, to fulfill their karma (as long as their choices were politically and spiritually "correct"). We'd recycle, bike to work at the co-op, and constantly smile and make plenty of lingering eye contact. Critical thinking, science, and technology would be de-emphasized, and feelings, "following your heart," and the music of the spheres would be emphasized. Peace, love, tofu. Switching from the new age to the currently hipper new edge, not much changes. We get Terence McKenna instead of Ram Dass, the Orb instead of Enya, and we don't have to feel guilty about using computers. Four hour Dead shows are replaced by all-night raves. Other than that, it's pretty much the same agenda. Peace, love, and smart drugs. However you dress them, totalizing ideologies are always a snore.

LOGICAL INCONSISTENCIES

Your average new ager would probably giggle with delight at the idea of being held to logical consistency. He or she would give me that "Oh, you unenlightened little man" look. But it's fun to taunt new agers (and new edgers) about obvious holes in their reasoning. Someone once sent me a video of psychic readings from some large fellow in a flannel shirt named Lazarus. It was so goofy that our group house used to project it for laughs at parties. We called him Lavoris (like the mouthwash). I thought it was all a big joke until, one day, I was surrounded by new agers and started telling them about the tape. They began defending the guy, saying that many of his predictions come true, and that "he's helped a lot of people." I asked: "OK, so he claims he's channeling a medieval monk from Britain, right? Then why is he using concepts like "energy," "karma," and "chakras?" Their response was expected: "That's the channeler talking. He's translating Lazarus' ideas to relate to his contemporary audience." "OK... then why does he have a shitty Scottish accent? If it's the channeler talking, why isn't he using plain modern English? Or, if it's the spirit-monk talking, why isn't he using a perfect 12th century Scottish accent?" At this point, everyone grew uncomfortable. When I continued to raise doubts and insisted on calling him Lavoris, they got really mad. One guy even had to run outside to do Kundalini Yoga to repair himself from my damaging negative energy. I'm not kidding!

SAME OLD "NEWAGE"

And, if you think all this new age stuff is old news, a relic of the '70s and '80s, go to a rave or a Zippie gathering. It's the same stuff dressed up in synths and CPUs. Technology plays a bigger role, but that's about it. The underlying concepts are almost identical. Just look at this quote from Ambient Temple of Imagination, a techno record we received for review today: "Ambient Temple of Imagination will transform what we know today as 'religions' into true laboratories of consciousness wherein the Will will be able to expand and express its super-human cosmic potential and emanate LIFE-LIGHT-LOVE-LIBERTY beyond anything ever conceived in any previous civilization." Wow, all that from a rave CD? Let me guess, if I listen to it and it doesn't expand my super-human cosmic potential, it's because I'm still not ready to accept my transformation. Having hung out with the healed, the enlightened, and the glow-stick waving cyber-shamanic, this is most definitely the case.

Art: Shannon Wheeler

PLEASE CAPTAIN, NOT IN FRONT OF THE KLINGONS

In 1996, I got a call from a friend, Mikki Halpin, a fellow zinester who'd been an editor for L.A.'s legendary *Ben Is Dead*. She'd been handed a dream job and hoped to recruit me for it. The Internet provider Prodigy – whose walled gardens (along with CompuServe's and AOL's) were under fierce attack by teeming web hordes who didn't want to pay no stinkin' monthly subscription fees – was looking to upgrade its image. Mikki had been hired to edit *STIM*, a free, cutting-edge electronic zine on the web, one of the first of its kind. The hope was to keep the Prodigy brand relevant to a young, hip, and rapidly-expanding web audience. When I heard some of the people she'd recruited, or planned to (and how much I was going to get paid), I immediately signed on as a contributing editor. Joining me were the likes of Georgia Rucker (daughter of sci-fi legend Rudy Rucker), sci-fi author and fringe culture chronicler Richard Kadrey, Tiffany Lee Brown *(Mondo 2000, FringeWare Review)*, Mark Frauenfelder, David Pescovitz, John Marr *(Murder Can Be Fun)*, Lily Burana, Andrew Hultkrans *(Mondo 2000)*, and many others – it was a veritable who's who of fringe publishing superstars of the time.

And with the generous budget and editor-author dream team came an impressive degree of freedom. Prodigy was largely hands-off. We did what we wanted and followed our muses through cyberspace in whatever directions their screeching modem-toned siren songs led us. Besides the content, which loosely gathered around themes like "Money," "Truth," "Men/Women," "France," and in the case of the proceeding piece, "Star Trek," there was lots of cutting-edge creativity and technical innovation swirling around the project. Using an early "graphical chat program" called The Palace, *STIM* had an online group house you could beam into as an avatar of your choosing (or design). We held Happy Hour there every Friday afternoon and hosted art shows by such late 90s alterna-art darlings as Bill Barker of Schwa fame. We offered video chat way before that was common, using the CU-SeeMe software, and *Wired* multimedia artist Steven Speer used a new technology Prodigy had developed, called VirtualTelevision, to create a 360-degree viewable animated series called *The Stimples*.

Looking back on this experience, one of the things that's really surprising, and sad, is how much I took this opportunity, this wide bandwidth of awesomeness, for granted. Here was a job that paid good money, where I got to work with seriously talented people, exploring whatever we wanted. And it all just felt like another day at the office. During that time, in the explosive core-heat of the tech boom, it seemed like the world was full of such stellar opportunities – if it wasn't this one, it'd be another. I jumped from one pinch-me project to the next. I was making so much money (um....relatively speaking) that, at one point, I even forgot to invoice one publication for three months, at $2K a month. Six grand I almost forgot about because it suddenly didn't matter so much.

It's a shame that sometimes, in the words of the absurdist playwright Luigi Pirandello, "life, at the very moment we live it, is so full of itself, we can never actually taste it." This moment was most definitely full of itself and I took little time to fully savor these banquet years.

For our epic "Star Trek" issue, published in September 1996, we explored the stranger quadrants of the *Star Trek* universe and its fandom. We covered *Star Trek* zines, music, humor, android crushes, the commie answer to *Star Trek (Cosmos Patrol)*, tits on the bridge (crew breasts, both male and female), and hatred of the whole Trek franchise ([It's] "sticky with a condescending kind of McNugget humanism that makes me want to—at best—break things or—at worst—tear my own head off" —Richard Kadrey). My contribution to all of this sharp, quirky fun was to report on an underground form of homoerotic fanfiction known as slash.

It's the 24th century. A wide swath of the outer spiral arm of the Milky Way has been boldly explored by an interplanetary UN called the United Federation of Planets. The Federation has created a model organization built on military discipline, high-tech efficiency, and a cosmic cultural diversity program. Just check out the many alien races knocking back the synthahol in Ten-Forward; it certainly looks like an enlightened age of tolerance and cooperation. But, after spending some time in the Star Trek universe, a supernova-sized question springs to mind: where the hell are all the gays and lesbians? It's 400 years in the future, for chrissake! Surely they're not still debating gays in the military?

Star Trek: The Next Generation did flirt with gay and lesbian characters and situations: Dr. Crusher struggled, but failed, to maintain her love for a symbiotic entity that had to move from a male to a female host; it was rumored that Tasha Yar was written as a lesbian; and Gene Roddenberry, purportedly responding to pressure from some fans, was planning on bringing gay and lesbian characters into the 24th Century before he died in 1991. These almost imperceptible nods to gay characters, however, hardly impress fans who want to see same-sex relationships explored in more depth.

But, as any hardcore fan will tell you, the Trek universe doesn't end at the borders of the Paramount lot or the many merchandising franchises. Long ago, when female crew members were still in mini-skirts and go-go boots, fans began exploring the Star Trek universe on their own. Through conventions, live role-playing, fan fiction, and zines, Trekkers have veered off in many creative, obsessive, and delightfully bizarre directions. One of the most fascinating of these fan niches is called "slash."

Can you imagine a love affair between the swashbuckling Captain Kirk and that green-blooded nerd Mr. Spock? In the mid-Seventies, hardcore stories about such a relationship began circulating among some Trek fans who wanted to see the two men boldly go where no (heterosexual) man had gone before. Their stories, and the zines that published them, were called "Kirk/Spock" (pronounced Kirk-slash-Spock) or "K/S" fandom, later just shortened to "slash" (as in slash fiction, slash zines, and slash cons.) The slash zine scene has continued to thrive, over the years producing zines with names like "The Final Frontier," "Fever," "Cheap Thrills," and "Ten-Forward." The original medium of print slash has been joined by slash videos (Trek scenes creatively re-edited to bring out homoerotic messages), slash websites, newsgroups, and mailing lists.

The Vulcans have a saying: "Infinite diversity in infinite combination." Slash lives by that maxim. Since the introduction of the original K/S stories, many bold new homoerotic pairings have been charted. *Star Trek: The Next Generation, Deep Space Nine,* and *Voyager* have all been slashed: imagine Geordi and Data (is he *fully* functional?), Riker and Picard, Paris and Kim. Right now, one popular slash relationship is between DS9's dewy-eyed Dr. Julian Bashir and Garak, the Cardasian tailor (fill in your own in-seam jokes here).

Most people aren't shocked to discover that homoerotic fanfic exists, but many are surprised to discover that heterosexual women are its predominant producers and consumers. This was the case in the 1970s when slash first emerged, and it's still the case today. Why heterosexual women would devote themselves to the hobby of writing and endlessly discussing homoerotic fiction is a subject of much debate among feminist academics and the slash producers themselves. In *Technoculture* (University of Minnesota Press, 1991) Constance Penley, an English and Film professor at the University of Rochester, argues that slash provides its creators with a way to both examine women's relationship with science, technology, and the body, and to imagine a "re-tooling" of masculinity. Others claim slashers are simply filling a void left by unenlightened 20th century TV writers. As you'd expect, several of the slashers we talked to said they just do it for the fun and challenge of imagining "alien" sexual situations. (What *does* Spock's junk look like? What would sex be like between a male Cardasian and a human?) And, when you think about it, why shouldn't hetero women fantasize about boy/boy relationships—after all, girl/girl fantasies are extremely common among hetero men.

Slash writers often portray their characters as heterosexual men who, through a series of unusual circumstances, end up as lovers. To that end, many writers are fond of exploiting certain plot elements to construct such stories. The Trek episode "Mirror, Mirror" from the original series, with its parallel universe and a second Enterprise crew, proved to be fertile ground for a number of slash stories (e.g,. an evil Spock capturing and sexually torturing the goody two-shoes Captain Kirk). The friendship between Bashir and Garak on DS9 seems to have homoerotic overtones to many fans and has led to a proliferation of B/G stories. One writer/zine editor told us, "I have to feel there's real chemistry there, that something could happen between them. So my slash fandom began with B/G and has remained there."

One would think that the Internet would be a perfect place to take slash. It's a relatively inexpensive publishing medium that can reach an international audience. But the slash community is reluctant to embrace the Net. As one slasher told us via email: "The web is huge, and somewhat anonymous, and print-media-raised slash fans are something of an insular community. They like the feel of their community, and you can't maintain or have any control of that on the web." But *Star Trek* is not the only show in town when it comes to slashing—homoerotic tales are spun about *Babylon 5, Space: Above and Beyond, The Professionals, The Man from U.N.C.L.E.*, and the *X-Files*; many aren't wary of the net like the old ST slash scenesters. There are ST slash mailing lists and "locked" web sites, but they are carefully kept outside the view of the general net public. It seems unfortunate that if slash is a fictive way of working through issues surrounding technoculture, the future, science, the body, and gender (as some slash critics argue), that the slashers would still feel the need to do so behind closed doors and under a blanket of paranoia. It's not hard to understand that slash writers are secretive because they fear ridicule, but it's a shame that their fascinating take on popular TV and the DIY Trek universe they've built around it is held just out of the reach of most of us. I want my SlashTV!

THIS SHIT DOESN'T STINK,
(IT EXCEEDS THE ODOR THRESHOLD)

A round the time of *STIM's* "Truth" issue, in January, 1997, there'd been a lot of instances of "conceptual downsizing" being reported in the press, as Wayne Grytting, editor of the site *Newspeak*, dubbed it. So, doing a piece on Orwellian utterances seemed like a natural. Researching it, collecting some of the most outrageous examples I could tong into my specimen bag, I couldn't believe what I was finding. Calling grade school Fs and Ds "emerging grades" and failing "negative gain in test scores" just had to be a joke. But it wasn't. Nor was "outplaced," for getting fired. Or "servicing the target," for killing people in combat. Most of what I found, all proclaimed to be real, would be mistaken today for gags on *The Onion*. And we won't even bother delving into where all of this doublespeak has ended up, here in the mercurial "truthiness" of the early 21st century.

"The great enemy of clear language is insincerity." —George Orwell

I had a dream the other night in which Newt Gingrich proposed a national essay contest. Poor people, minorities, gays, and battered women were to write essays describing how their circumstances really didn't exist. The winners — those who wrote so compellingly that they could convince others of their circumstance that nothing more than perceptual adjustment was in order — would win a million dollars … and a free laptop!

Dreams are curious things. This one was obviously inspired by my assignment to "write something on doublespeak" and the news that the logorrheic Speaker of the House had responded to mounting charges that he'd falsified his statements to the House Ethics Committee by explaining that he regretted any "inaccuracies" in his reporting.

Language is as curious (and sometimes as capricious) as dreams. Newt calls them inaccuracies. The charitable might call them false statements; his adversaries would call them bald-faced lies. Post-modern English has turned to Silly Putty in the hands of politicians, their spin doctors, corporate PR flaks, the military, and other organizations and individuals who like to have bit-flipping fun with the facts — to make the negative positive, the violent peaceful, the wrong right, and perform other language sleight-of-hand.

In *The New Doublespeak* (HarperCollins), English professor and long-time editor of the *Quarterly Journal of Doublespeak*, William Lutz defines doublespeak as "language that avoids or shifts responsibility … that is at variance with its real or purported meaning … that conceals or prevents thought … Doublespeak is not a question of subjects and verbs agreeing, it is a matter of words and facts agreeing." Viewed through the distorting lens of doublespeak, an MX missile morphs into a "peace keeper," a bag of ice becomes a "thermal therapy kit," theft becomes "unauthorized withdrawal," sex becomes "penile insertive behavior," phone-sex operators become "discussion partners," crime becomes "a failure to comply with the law," making your employees work more for the same pay becomes "empowering the workforce," a bomb becomes a "vertically-inserted anti-personnel device," and AOL's new chief cybercop (a former CIA agent) is dubbed "Vice President of Integrity Assurance."

Even educators, those entrusted with teaching plain English, critical thinking, and communication skills to our children, are being seduced by doublespeak. Failing has been turned into "negative gain in test scores" or "sub-optimal performance." According to the *Quarterly Journal of Doublespeak*, in the Clark County school district of Las Vegas, Nevada, failing, passing, and making top grades have been replaced with "emerging" (Fs and Ds in oldspeak), "developing" (Cs), and "extending" (Bs and As). They're not even called grades anymore in some schools — they're now known as "student outcomes." Report cards currently sport such impenetrable evaluation categories as "Applies place value concepts to add/sub problems" and "utilizes problem-solving processes." One can only imagine what twisted new doublespeak will be created by students educated within the thorny thicket of such language obfuscation.

The scariest thing about doublespeak is that it appears to be on the rise. Increasingly sophisticated tools, such as focus groups wired to real-time analytic software, are being used to scrutinize the public's response to speeches and the media — in order to engineer more potent language (best serving the interests of the speakers, not necessarily those of the audience). Spin doctors can now examine, down to the specific word, the emotional responses generated by a speaker. Using this technology, they can build databases of positive and negative words and phrases and tweak future speeches accordingly.

It is necessary, for the healthy functioning of a democracy, to have free, open, and honest public discourse. In a world where plain English is being replaced by doublespeak and literal hot-button word engineering, such honest communication cannot take place. As William Lutz points out, the increasing corruption of our public language — the language we use to debate issues and decide public policy — is a corruption of democracy itself.

Believe it or not, all the of the doublespeak used in this article first appeared in real world contexts by people expecting to be taken seriously. Here's some more.

YOU WEREN'T FIRED, YOU WERE:

let go
downsized
unassigned
uninstalled
involuntarily separated from payroll
released of resources
given a career change opportunity
career transitioned

part of a normal payroll adjustment
a focused reduction
on no-pay status
transitioned
an ongoing effort to streamline operations
part of restructuring
outplaced
rightsized
workplace reengineered

IT WASN'T A LIE, IT WAS:

a strategic misrepresentation
the result of fictitious disorder syndrome
terminological inexactitude
reality augmentation
a misstatement
an inaccurate statement
incomplete information
being economical with the truth

IT'S NOT KILLING IN COMBAT, IT'S:

neutralizing
liquidating
collateral damage
servicing the target
decommissioning the aggressor
violence processing
a surgical strike
sanitizing the area
exceeding the threshold of physiological damage
substantive negative outcome

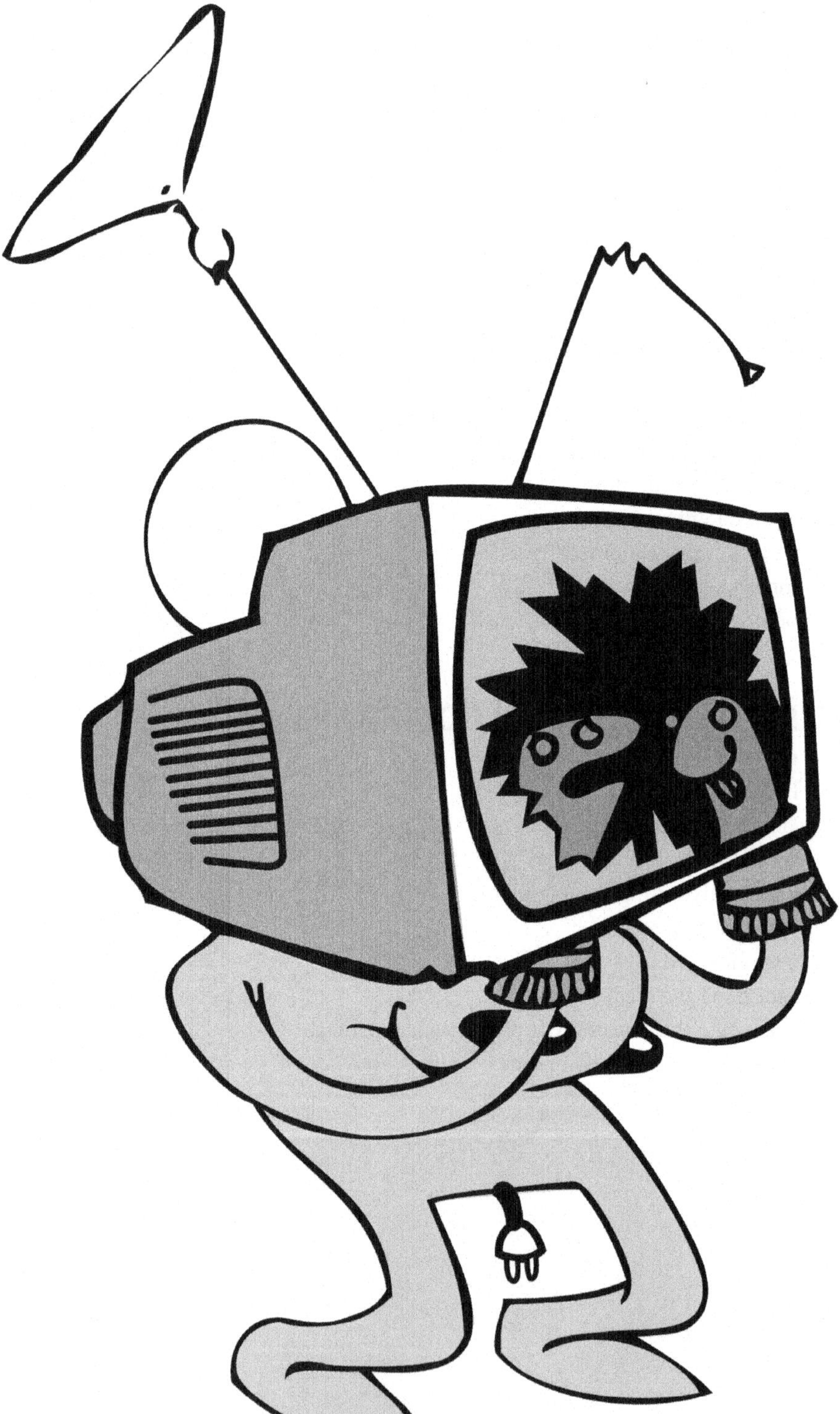

Art: Steven Raymond

NO-TECH
INTERACTIVE TV

When I lived in a group house, and afterwards, when my wife and I threw parties and had people over to our own home, we frequently couldn't resist monkeying around with the TV. Maybe, especially in the company of others, we assuaged our guilt at sucking at the same TV teat as the rest of America by at least talking smack to the set as we did so. At one point, we even got arty and stacked a bunch of TVs on top of one another – some sideways, upside down – all tuned to the same station – The Man Who Fell to Earth: The Home Game. Over the years, we developed a number of fun games we liked to play with the television. Sometimes, when my wife was out late, performing at a club, having nothing better to do, I'd start experimenting with the remote control to see what sort of Burroughsian nonsense I could get myself into.

This piece was written in 1996, appearing in *STIM's* first issue. I mention interactive TV in it, something that was getting plenty of ink and electrons at the time. The idea of ITV, circa 1996, basically involved cues that would pop up on your set for getting more information on an actor, or you could use your remote to buy the clothes an actress was wearing, or punch up players statistics during sporting events. That's a model of interactive media that never really went anywhere. Even today, on the internet, where TV is steadily migrating, there's little of this, beyond choosing your "commercial experience" before watching videos on *Hulu* or *YouTube*.

This piece can definitely be dated by the references to *MST3K*, *Star Trek: The Next Generation*, *The X-Files*, and *Barney the Dinosaur*. I have no memory at all of the talking faucet commercial I mention, but then, I never watched it with the sound on, so it could never fully cast its spell over me – which is perhaps the metamessage of this essay. The black magician really can't properly do his business if you're talking the whole time he's trying to enthrall you with his curse.

Why are you waiting for the Skinner Box version of interactivity (press bar, get treat) that cable companies have been threatening us with for years? You know it's gonna be a big snore, QVC brought to you by an ATM machine. At our house, we've been "gettin' interactive" with our TV signals for years. Here are some fun games you can play with your television.

SWITCHING SOUNDTRACKS

You can create an alternative soundtrack by turning off the TV's sound and playing something else on your stereo. Example: Find a fire and brimstone preacher on the radio and dial up Barney the Dinosaur on the tube. Hilarity ensues.

CHANNEL SPLICING

Using your remote control, find two channels (preferable next to each other or programmed into your remote's "flashback" feature) that have two story lines you want to splice together. This works best if you can find two conversations to "A/B" between. With some practice, you can actually create bizarre alternative dialog. Do William Burroughs proud!

EDITING ON THE FLY

Same as above, except here, you actually have have your entertainment system set up so that you're recording the audio/video mayhem you're splicing together. You may be surprised by what you capture. And you can further edit this material, and add a new soundtrack if you'd like, for more layered A/V fun!

MIME MODE

Sometimes, just turning the sound off can make TV infinitely more entertaining. The absurdity of commercials really comes through sans audio. (Try watching that commercial of the talking faucet in mime mode while keeping a straight face).

MST3K: THE HOME GAME

Why let that deadbeat space janitor guy and his two loud-mouthed junkbots have all the fun? Find a particularly vacuous program (rarely a problem), then you and your friends can add the witty commentary and snide asides. Recreating those embarrassingly-bad Mystery Science Theater 3000 skits during the commercial breaks is optional. One of the most entertaining nights of my life was spent playing MST3K: The Home Game after a party at our house. After most of the guests had left, we wrecked remains sat on the couch and turned on the TV to find some ridiculously bad movie on (I don't remember which). Our brains all racing along in that off-stimulated, post-peak, post-party mode, we riffed on the movie lines. Some of it was utterly brilliant and hysterical. We were giddy from laughing so much. It was as good as anything Joel, Crow, and Tom Servo ever came up with.

JAPANESE DUB

Turn the sound off on a foreign film and provide the narrative yourself. It's especially fun if you already know the film and can attempt to closely match the mouth movements.

SPURT!

Everybody knows how sexually titillating TV commercials can be. It's almost as if they've figured out a way to simulate the act of sex (through fast edits of flesh and moaning soundtracks) without any of the outright nasty. There's plenty of ejaculation, though! Once you tune into it, it's amazing how many images you'll see of bottles of liquids spewing their tops, bananas plunging into milk, water hoses bubbling into eager mouths, and hard candies splashing into fruit juice ... OK, you get the idea. We like to play a game at our house (after hours, of course), called SPURT! The object is to be the first person to yell SPURT! when you see spewing liquid on the screen. Keep score. Declare the winner a big-ass pervert.

RANT AND RAVE

TV makes us angry (and it should). It speaks down to us, hustles us, and takes advantage of our basest, most prurient interests. It steals our attention and sells it to the highest bidder. One small way you can counteract this mesmerism is to yell back at your set. Get pissed! Rant. Rave. No, nobody will hear you, but you'll be creatively venting your frustrations (always good therapy), and you'll be talking over the jive on the tube.

ELVIS VIEWING

A more aggressive form of Rant and Rave, Elvis Viewing involves firearms. Shoot the damn thing, just like the King did! If you don't feel like destroying your set completely (which would mean missing the next episode of the *X-Files*), you can use a toy gun that shoots suction cup projectiles. It's really fun to try and hit characters as they move across the screen. Of course, you'll have to get up to retrieve your "bullets," so make sure to keep a lot of them close-by. And don't be a gun hog; have several weapons on hand for guests.

FRAT HOUSE VIEWING

College students love to mix booze and TV (OK, college kids like to mix booze with anything). There are many variations to this game, but the basic form involves setting as a trigger some line of dialog or event on a TV show (say, "The Picard Manuever"—every time the shiny-domed captain tugs on his uniform) and drinking shots whenever that line/event occurs. To compete, each person can choose a different line/event that's likely to recur (every time Data cocks his head, every time the Enterprise changes course, etc.).

NAME MY NEUROSIS

Here, the object is to switch back and forth between daytime talk shows with the sound off. Try to guess first the theme of the show, and then, the reason each person is on the program (before that little identifying label pops up telling you: "Thinks wife dresses too sexy," "Revealing to boyfriend that she's a prostitute," "Used to be a man," etc). Try it. It's fun!

IN THE LABORATORY OF LANGUAGE

For the first twelve years of its existence, from 1993-2005, I was the editor of *Wired's* "Jargon Watch" column. The column was Kevin Kelly's idea, after seeing a piece I'd written in *Mondo 2000* about the recent publication of Steve Raymond's *The New Hacker's Dictionary*, a revision of the book that grew out of "The Jargon File." That iconic early hacker culture document collected slang and jargon from various tech cultures, at MIT, Stanford, Carnegie Mellon, and beyond. Kevin and I knew that the coming net population explosion of the 90s was going to create its own kind of culture. New cultures, especially tech-driven ones, tend to promiscuously coin language and we wanted to chronicle that. Together, we worked out the basic concept for the column (5-6 items per issue, entertaining and readable definitions covering all domains of the digital realm: business, politics, technology, science, culture, arts, and bring the funny). We decided to go easy on the lexicographical rigor. We didn't want to use single-use made up words, but we decided that, if a term was being used, at say, a single company or one online community, that was good enough. We weren't going to insist on three independent citations or other requirements that a serious language publication might require. We knew right off the bat that this was for entertainment purposes first and foremost. And we were excited by the napkin-sketched map of digital culture we suspected the language in this column might reveal.

During my tenure at *Wired*, and via my growing cachet as an "expert" on online jargon and slang, I ended up as a regular on MSNBC's *The Site*, TechTV's *Screen Saver* program, and was featured in many dailies, websites, books, and other media. As the editor of "Jargon Watch," I became a member of the American Dialect Society and my work frequently appeared in *American Speech*, ADS's academic journal. It was through all this that I was asked by Oxford University Press to be their Special Subject Consultant on computer and Internet terms for the 2001 *Oxford American Dictionary*. The year that the first edition of the OAD came out, I gave a copy (all 2023 door-stopping pages of it) to several family members for Christmas presents. I wrote "My latest book" on the card – obnoxious to be sure, but hey, how many people get to boast that they actually wrote part of the dictionary? Towards the end of my run, as the magazine was going through one of its seemingly endless redesigns and re-thinks, my editor told me that "Jargon Watch" was serving as their model for "front-of-the-book" column content the reader "had" to turn to as soon as they opened the magazine. I was proud of that.

The following is the introduction to *Jargon Watch: A Pocket Dictionary for the Jitterati*, the 1997 collection of my column published by the short-lived Hardwired Books. It is followed by some of my favorite terms from my 12-year tenure, the words that have become a lasting part of my everyday speech.

It's untamed and anarchistic, with no central authority and no stuffy committees to answer to. Noses are frequently turned up whenever it's mentioned in high-brow circles. Much of its lexicon is off-putting to outsiders and newcomers. It has a funky mix of global and local voices, covering a staggering breadth of interests and ideas. It can be poignant and inspirational or ridiculous, impenetrable, and rude. It's often riddled with hype and corporatespeak. A lot of it is infused with cleverness and great humor.

What is it? We could easily be describing the Internet, but we're talking slang. It is perhaps no accident though that the two have so much in common. While lexicographers argue over what it is, slang has found a suitable host within the world's high-speed communications networks, allowing it to leap over the traditional borders of close-knit interest groups and entrenched subcultures. Like a good joke, a newly expressed piece of viral slang can spread through interoffice email and over the Internet faster than a head cold in a kindergarten classroom. Good slang wants to be free.

DEFINING OUR TERMS

The word slang usually refers to informal, non-standard vocabulary coined by a social or special interest group (e.g. college students, skateboarders, drug dealers, NIN fans), whereas jargon is the special language of a technical profession (e.g. aviators, the military, computer hackers). Slang is often considered to be faddish, more short-lived than jargon.

The lexicon that is emerging from the digital cultures of the Internet has smudged the boundary between jargon and slang. The jargon of hackers and engineers (e.g. FAQ, RAM, and bandwidth) has invaded popular language. Subcultural argot and techspeak once migrated slowly from one group to another, because of the groups' relative insularity. Now, with the interconnectivity of the wired world, slang and jargon quickly travel from one group or locale to another as they find useful niches elsewhere. Accelerated cross-pollination occurs through newsgroups, email, bulletin boards, websites, and tech conventions. Jargon is also used as base material in net slang, evident in such terms as brandwidth, ROM brain, 404, and CaptiveX.

For the title of this book (and the *Wired* column that spawned it) we use the term jargon, although in truth, most of what it contains is technically slang. A precedent for this usage was set in hackerdom, whose tech-infused slang has long been referred to as "the jargon." That term, and the well-known "Jargon File" that has circulated among geeks since the mid-'70s (later collected and expanded in Eric Raymond's *Hacker's Dictionary*), was one of the inspirations behind *Wired's* "Jargon Watch" column. This book collects the terms published in that column from May 1993 to December 1996, with the addition of over 100 new entries.

Jargon and slang speak volumes about the people who use them. Like a form of data compression, they pack a tremendous amount of information—the values, ideas, anxieties, and humor of a subculture—into a single word or phrase. One can learn a lot about a subculture by decompressing its language. For instance, rummaging through the hacker lexicon you'll find a cluster of related terms (called a semantic field in linguistics) describing computer sales and marketing people (salesdroids, salescritters, salesthings, marketdroids, marketeers, marketing slime) and company management types in general (suits, droids, stupids). You'll also find an equally large number of terms related to new and casual computer users (lusers, lamers, wannabees, newbies, B1FFs, weenies, twinks, spods, tourists, read-only users). College slang, not surprisingly, is rife with words relating to drinking and drugging (blind, blitzed, trashed, toasted, greased, fried, blistered, ripped to the tits). Rock climber slang has many words related to cuts (flappers, gobbis), falling (to munge, to crater, peel), and fear (pucker factor, shaky legs). Corporatespeak offers us such manglish as calendaring (scheduling), audience development engine (website), advertainment (ads), and new consumer paradigm (market).

WHERE DO THESE TERMS COME FROM?

One of the most common questions we get in the "Jargon Watch" inbox is: "Do you all make this stuff up or what?" The answer is (mostly) no. We've collected these terms from online discussions and glossaries, websites, email submissions, trade shows and lectures, conversations with fellow geeks, magazines and newspapers, TV news shows, and computer programs. We also have a series of filters that scour the net for keywords such as jargon, slang, argot, lingo, colloquialism, and terminology. In a very few instances, we've coined terms within our own work and social groups after having a "there's gotta be a word for that!" discussion (e.g. egosurfing, idea hamster).

So, how common are these words in actual usage? Some have become very popular since appearing in the magazine (delurking, going postal, infobahn, Siliwood, Webmaster). Many terms come from a certain subcultural orbit and stay there, others are not necessarily practical for everyday usage but were entertaining or illustrative enough to publish anyway. The "Jargon Watch" column has always been more about entertainment than rigor and lexicographical correctness, more *Sniglets* than *Webster's*.

While collections like *The Hacker's Dictionary* take a more traditional linguistics approach, with etymologies, style notes, and historical anecdotes, "Jargon Watch" has mainly gone for entertainment and laughs. When someone submits a term, we're not overly concerned about its origins (although we prefer words that have established usage). If it strikes my fancy, I pass it down the editorial food chain.

If, after having gone through all the editor's hands, it hasn't been given the ax, I assume it's interesting and useful enough to get a shot in the magazine. I fancy myself a sort of slang impresario. If a term passes the editorial audition, I push it out onto the stage provided by the magazine. If it bombs, it gets the hook and its career is finished (or it ends up opening for a ventriloquist act in the Catskills). If it's a big success, it ends up making the rounds of email boxes, water coolers, and office cubicles, from Silicon Valley to Silicon Alley and beyond.

The words that made it into the column and this book are just a fraction of the terms submitted. Every week, dozens of terms pop into the "Jargon Watch" mailbox and get shuffled into three folders (A-list, B-list, and Jargon from Hell). Most of them end up in the latter two and never see ink. Over the years, I've acquired a perverse fascination with the hellish terms that have that so-bad-they're-good quality to them. Here, let me scare you with a few:

anticipointment
chronolibrium
e-gasm
gratuitml
infojaculation
inventrepreneur
javangelist
medtigious
nintendomaniaddictionitis
pageversationalist
pornetgraphy
webference

Can't you just picture the hapless jargonauts sitting in their Dilbertesque cubicles cutting and pasting the English language in a vain attempt to see their names in print? I weed these out of my mailbox each week, trying to keep my sanity intact while looking for those illusive gems that make it all worthwhile. The week in which I write this introduction has just offered up the awesome blamestorming (figuring out who to blame for a failed project), prarie dogging (office workers all poking their heads above their cubicles at once) and tract mansions (multi-million dollar homes built in tractlike developments).

MORE JARGON WATCHING

Most of us know more jargon and slang than we can recall when asked about it. As I circulate through parties, trade shows, and cyberspace, I always ask people about the jargon and slang that they use. Usually, they can't think of much off the top of their head, but will often email me afterwards. Frequently-used cant disappears into the fabric of our lives, and only professional and armchair linguists (and editors of jargon columns) are obsessed with teasing those threads back out. I hope this dictionary will inspire you to examine the in-group language that you use. And, hopefully, you'll type some into an email message and send it to us. We're especially looking for words related to all of the diverse niches of media, digital culture, business, and emerging sciences and technology. We'll also take a look at any neologisms related to life in the post-Gutenberg era. Please don't just sit around trying to invent terms to submit. If you think up a word you like, try it out on your friends and cubicle mates and see if it catches on. The good stuff quickly takes on a life of its own.

THE "JARGON WATCH" TERMS THAT STUCK WITH ME

For *Borg Like Me*, I thought it might be fun to look through the corpus of my 12 years of "Jargon Watch" columns and pick out the terms that have become a permanent part of my everyday vocabulary. Slang is ephemeral, it's the linguistic equivalent of throwing spaghetti up against a wall to see what sticks. So, what stuck? Here are my 23 choices.

Backgrounding:
The practice of not giving someone your full attention while multitasking. Occurs frequently during phone conversations when one party is reading email, facebooking, or surfing the Net. Dead giveaways: quiet typing, monotoned and equally-spaced "Uh-huh, uh-huh."

Bit Flip:
A 180-degree personality change. "Jim did a major bit flip and became a born-again Christian."

Bio-break:
Techie euphemism for using the toilet.

Blamestorming:
Sitting around in a group discussing why a deadline was missed, or why a project failed, and on whom the responsibility can be pinned.

Blow My Buffer:
Euphemism for spacing out or losing one's train of thought. Similarly, "blowing your buffer" occurs when the person you're speaking with won't let you get a word in edgewise or has just said something so astonishing that your train of thought gets derailed. "Damn, I just blew my buffer!"

Brain Fart:
A byproduct of a bloated mind producing information effortlessly. A burst of useful information. "I know you're busy on the Microsoft story, but could you give us a brain fart on the Mitnik bust?" Semantic drift from the older hacker slang which had a more negative connotations of a glitch in mental processing.

Egosurfing:
Using search engines or scanning articles and book indexes looking for mentions of your own name.

Frankenedit:
A gruesome job of editing a writer's work by a hurried editor. The resulting hacked up manuscript is usually returned with a note asking the writer to re-suture it together and breath life back into it (by the next morning).

Geekosphere:
The area surrounding one's computer where trinkets, personal mementos, toys, and "monitor pets" are displayed. A place where computer geeks show their "colors."

Going Cyrillic:
When a graphical display starts to glitch out, to fail and to display garbage. "This thing just went Cyrillic on me!"

Hand Salsa:
The slimy substance invariably left on game controllers after a round of high-stress gaming. "Sure you can play, if you don't mind the hand salsa."

Floodgaters:
Individuals who send email or text messages, and after receiving only a short, slightly favorable response, begin flooding you with multiple messages of little or no interest.

Interrupt-Driven:
Used to describe someone who moves through the workday responding to a series of interruptions rather than the work goals originally set.

PEBCAK:
Tech support/hacker shorthand for "Problem Exists Between Chair And Keyboard." A way of indicating that there's nothing wrong with the computer – it's the user who's clueless.

Percussive Maintenance:
The fine art of whacking the crap out of an electronic device to get it to work again.

Seagull Manager:
A superior who flies in, makes a lot of noise, shits all over everything and everyone, and then leaves.

Serendipity Search:
An Internet search in which you end up finding interesting and valuable things that have nothing to do with your original search. Searching willy-nilly. "I found this really cool site on Tiki collecting during an hour-long serendipity search."

Shoulder Surfing:
Looking over someone's shoulder to steal his or her credit or phone card number or computer password.

Vampire Time (VT):
A schedule in which one sleeps all day and then haunts the night life or works until dawn. Refers to writers, artists, slackers, club kids, and other bohemian types who rarely see the light of day.

Whack-a-Mole:
The "game" one has to play to quickly close interstitial ads and other pop-ups on some commercial sites. These pages will sometimes generate new windows every time you close one, creating a situation similar to the popular arcade game Whack-a-Mole.

Warnock's Dilemma:
The act of deciding whether the lack of response to a comment in an online discussion is because of its brilliance (i.e. there's nothing left to add) or because of its stupidity (it doesn't deserve comment). Named after Brian Warnock, who first described the condition on a Perl mailing list.

YMMV (Your Mileage May Vary):
A popular qualifier simple meaning: "the outcome may be different under different conditions." Often used in a humorous way: "This freeware program worked fine on my machine, but YMMV."

Yuppie Food Coupons:
The ubiquitous $20 bills spit out of ATMs. Often used when trying to split the bill after a meal: "Everyone owes $8, but all we have are yuppie food coupons."

Note: For more on "Jargon Watch" and some of the antics surrounding it, see "Cyburban Myths" in the Appendices.

"MEIN FÜHRER, I CAN WALK!"

Halloween. My favorite holiday. Growing up in a Catholic household, it seemed like one of the more transgressive things a youngster could "legally" be involved in. I was a huge fan of classic monster movies (I still am), and as a teen, I made many of the late 60s Aurora models: the Frankenstein monster, Wolfman, Dracula, and the Creature from the Black Lagoon. So I got excited every year when All Hallow's Eve crept closer and I knew that all of those classic films would be making their yearly rounds on late-night Richmond television. With the weather chilling outside, the aroma of burning leaves on the wind, and the The Great Pumpkin's looming arrival, it was extra exciting when my parents would go out for the evening and leave me at home to watch *Shock Theater,* hosted by The Bowman Body (Richmond's disheveled, stumble-drunk answer to such iconic horror hosts as Vampira, Elvira, and Seymour the Sinister).

For all the lead-up, the actual act of getting together a costume and going trick or treating was rarely what I'd hoped for. We had very little of what could be considered crafting supplies in our house. If you couldn't make it out of box cardboard and Elmer's glue, using a pair of dull office shears, you were shit out of luck. I can't remember ever feeling like I wore a costume I could be proud of. My dreams of Halloween were frequent and vivid, but the reality usually boiled down to amassing as much candy as possibly, engaging in at least one act of minor vandalism to feel suitably "tricky," and then hot-footing it home as fast as possible to catch whatever was left of *Shock Theater* that night.

So, when Paul Overton, editor of *DudeCraft.com*, approached me about a series he was putting together on people's childhood Halloween costume memories, I didn't have much to contribute. I've had much more Halloween dress-up fun as an adult, so I shared the following costume stories as my contribution to his feature.

An eerie aside: A truly bizarre thing happened one childhood Halloween night that spooked me good. My friends and I were heading back home after an epic candy haul. We could barely carry our buckets and sacks, they were groaning so loudly with sugar madness. Suddenly, someone in our posse of four or five kids (I no longer remember who) began screaming and flailing in bizarre spasms. We all laughed, thinking it was joke. But coming closer to him in the darkness, we could see that there actually was something moving in his shaggy heap of hair. A bat! Eventually it untangled itself and jetted off in a black smear. It was so hard for us to wrap our minds around what had just happened. An actual bat? On Halloween night? It seemed too strange to be real. And that made it genuinely scary. None of us had ever seen a bat for real. A few weeks later, we discovered where the bat had come from. A house on the other side of the lake from my house had a huge bat infestation in its attic. If the Halloween night bat encountered wasn't spooky enough, things got seriously Frankensteinian when angry villagers (OK, the neighbors) showed up at the bat-infested house with improvised rag and stick torches, smoked the bats out of the attic, and then burned them as they fell stunned to the ground. Over 90 bats were flambéed that night in a bizarre real-life horror movie memory that I will never forget.

My memories of Halloween as a child are fairly mundane, cookie-cut, a blur of cheap dime store plastic costumes, pillowcase candy sacks, and stutter-cut visuals recorded from inside of a sweaty mask with ill-cut eyeholes.

As an adult, I've tried to make up for these fright night fails by going all out whenever I can. I love the creativity of Halloween, the libidinal subtext of adult Halloween, and the pagan folk beliefs beneath it all, of veils between worlds suddenly becoming permeable, of spirits shambling into our world, the raising of the dead. And the raising of hell.

I have a reputation among friends of frequently dressing up in highly conceptual (read: incomprehensible) costumes. One year, the party theme was superheroes and I went as my own made-up caped crusader, called Mr. Wonderful. Think: Superman as rendered by Liberace. The party was at Twin Oaks, the commune I was living in, in a mechanics shop at the end of a really long driveway. I managed to convince a guy who was visiting, a limo driver, to drive me to the party in his Lincoln. I made flags with a Mr. Wonderful logo I designed on them that snapped away on the hood, as if heralding the arrival of a head of state.

Another year, I went as John Glenn, on his *third* trip to space. It was 1998, and at 77, Glenn had just taken off on his second trip, aboard the space shuttle. I was in a wheelchair at the time, before my hip replacement, so I needed to think of costumes that could incorporate the chair. I got a silver lamé flight suit at a costume shop, made mission badges for Glenn, Mercury, Discovery STS-95 (his shuttle mission), and Discover One (using images of the ship from *2001*). I wore a skull cap and made myself up in old man makeup. I looked like the wrinkled, dying Dave Bowman from *2001: A Space Odyssey*. I made up an elaborate back story about being 100 and on my third mission to space, to Jupiter's moon, Io. Mostly, the get-up was an excuse to get women to sit on my lap and get their pictures taken with me. Lots of them did and I perhaps enjoyed playing the role of a dirty old moon man just a little too much.

One of my all-time favorite, most successful, costumes was *Dr. Strangelove*. It was one of those truly serendipitous costume creations. I'd waited until the last minute, and by Halloween day, I still didn't have a costume, or even a decent idea for one. I finally hit on the idea of going as Strangelove. I needed to go in the wheelchair again, so the character was perfect. I also thought it'd be a relatively easy costume to put together. I had the 50s slim-cut suit, the glasses, the cigarette, the black leather glove, all I really needed was a blonde wig. My wife and I raced to the store to see if we could possibly pull this off.

The costume shop looked like it'd been hit by a rocket-propelled grenade. There was next-to-nothing left on the racks or shelves. No blonde wigs. We finally dislodged a sad blonde beard tangled around plastic swords and demon horns in a cardboard bargain bin. It'd have to do. We brought it home and she piled and pinned and trimmed, and I'll be damned if it didn't end up looking respectably like Peter Sellers' dramatic coif from the film. With the slim suit and skinny tie, the glasses, the one black leather glove on the dead hand, and the cigarette, I looked convincingly like Dr. Strangelove. I also shaved my beard for the occasion, for the first time in decades. I had found a few video clips from the film and even a sound file of Sellers delivering some of his classic lines (no small feat on a rather media-poor 1997 Internet). With these, I practiced my part.

At the party, a big DC artists' free-for-all in a downtown warehouse, I parked my chair at the edge of the dance floor. When a song came on that I really wanted to dance to, I'd start to shimmy and shake in my chair, like my crippled ex-Nazi was being uncontrollably reanimated on the shockwaves of rock n' roll. I would then feebly spazz myself upright and cry out, in a croaking German accent, "Mein Führer, I can walk!" Then I'd start dancing in front of my chair like my life depended on it. People laughed and seemed to get a kick out of it. I put this routine on rinse and repeat a few times over the course of the evening (legitimately needing to rest and recharge after every three or four songs). It was, of course, a goofy act, a way of incorporating a wheelchair into a costume, but there was a deeper personal ritual being played out.

In my late teens, as my arthritis worsened and took up full-time residence in my hips and spine, I'd headed down a very dark path emotionally. I had even seriously considered suicide for a time. One of the things that had yanked me back from that brink was discovering my passion for dancing. I love to dance more than just about anything and am actually pretty good at it, especially for someone without a spine (and if the '80s post-punk band Shriekback taught us anything, it's that the "spine is the bassline"). I discovered in dancing that the transcendent joy of it, that feeling of riding along and physically interpreting the sound waves of the music, is actually greater than any pain or limitation I experience while doing so. I can be in a lot of physical pain, and if an irresistibly danceable song comes on, it can feel as though I've been miraculously healed. I can instantly lose myself in the sensual, sonic gumbo of the music. For a few brief moments, I become a physically different person. I feel beautiful. And free. Healed. *Mein Führer, I can walk!*

One of the years that Pam, Blake, and I were living at Gesundheit Institute, the whole group went as The Addams Family. That's Patch Adams as Gomez. I'm Cousin It on the left. My whole-hair body is made from fur-like rug material. It was hot as Hades in there and I couldn't see out of the constantly shifting eye-holes, which perhaps brings us full circle to those arrested memories of my youth.

TEARS IN THE RAIN

I wrote this piece in 2012 for a series that *Boing Boing* was doing on "Mind Blowing Movies," films that had a profound and lasting impact on the invited essayists. Picking a film like Ridley Scott's iconic *Blade Runner* was risky, as I knew it would likely be high on BB readers' best lists and so much had already been written about it. It and William Gibson's *Neuromancer* series came to define the cyberpunk subculture of the late 80s and 90s.

My hope in writing it was that the sheer intensity with which I hold my memories around the film; their now almost haunted associations, would be enough to overcome anyone's squeamishness over me deciding to tackle it. As I started writing, the innvocation of these memories was so powerful, I felt almost overtaken by the process. The resulting essay seemed to similarly resonate with *Boing Boing* readers. The comments were, hands down, the most moving and positive for anything I've ever written. I sobbed as I was writing the piece. I cried harder when I read the comments. So many tears in the rain.

In 1982, my wife and I had just moved from a rural commune in Virginia to Washington, DC. We moved to the city so that she could pursue her music career (among other reasons). We were still country mice, easily awoken in the morning by street traffic, bothered by the air quality, and longing for the open skies of the country.

Every year my wife would go to Nantucket to perform at a restaurant called The Brotherhood of Thieves — a place that wouldn't look at all out of place in Treasure Island. It was dark, brick-walled, candle and lantern-lit, with big oak-slab tables and wooden ass-numbing chairs. In 1982, she was performing a duo act with well-known New England folkie Linda Worster, with whom she frequently played on the island.

Seeing them perform every night was a joy, but some nights I'd want to drift onto the streets of Nantucket, get swept up into the tide of pink and Nantucket-red golf clothes and flouncy summer dresses, and see where the night might wash me up.

On this night, a somewhat cold and cloudy one, I ended up under the marquee of Nantucket's Dreamland Theater, a giant, creaking, wooden ship of a building that smelled of mold, popcorn grease, and sunscreen.

Blade Runner, it read. I knew nothing about the film, but it was sci-fi and had Harrison Ford in it, so I figured it'd at least be the perfect way to kill a couple of hours before the ladies' last set. Little did I know that I was stepping into a portal and would emerge a different person, on a different life trajectory than the person who was stumbling down the shabby carpet in the dark, looking for a seat.

I can't really say what made such a fundamental impact on me. The dark noir mood of the film, certainly, and the questions it raises about the nature of life, memory, what constitutes humanity, and whether "androids dream of electric sheep..." What I didn't know I was looking at was a cyberpunk aesthetic that I would soon become completely immersed in, through the work of William Gibson, John Shirley, Bruce Sterling, and others — dystopian worlds, fifteen minutes into the future, where mega-corporations run the show, where personal and planetary technologies permeate society, and where the street finds its own uses for things.

I found the brutality of the film, the violence of the film's rogue replicants towards humans, and their "retirement" at the hands of police special agent Rick Deckard (Ford) shocking to my country hippie sensibilities. But all of those shocks only made the final scene of replicant Roy Batty's (played by Rutger Hauer) "natural" death all the more effective and moving. At the time, I thought it was the most beautiful thing I had ever seen and ate up Hauer's (allegedly ad libbed) Tannhaeuser Gate/tears in the rain soliloquy.

It was in that moment that the mood of the film throughly soaked into me. I felt as though I were in it. It ended and I unceremoniously swam back out into the boisterous, drunken nightlife of downtown Nantucket, which didn't feel at all like Nantucket anymore. Fittingly, it had started to drizzle and a fog had crept up Broad Street from Straight Wharf — *Blade Runner's* perpetual rain had descended upon Nantucket.

I made my way back to The Brotherhood. I stood outside the street-level windows right next to where Pammy and Linda performed and peered in. I don't know what song it was, but they were in the middle of some energetic, smilie-faced, folk number. As I stood in the chilly rain, now getting seriously wet, Pam sensed I was there and turned to me as she sang. Her face dropped as she saw the faraway look on mine. I forced a smile. She smiled, satisfied, and turned back into her music. But I was a universe away. I was peering into that antique-glass window from the future.

I didn't go into the restaurant that night, one of the rare occasions I didn't catch at least one set. I went upstairs to the Brotherhood's "Ent Room" (Entertainer's Room) where we stayed and I cried. I cried a lot. Again, I'm not really sure why. It is one of my few "molting moments" (as Cocteau called them) where I can't tell you what gears got turned, what wires in my nervous system got spliced. But I had changed. I cried for the loss of something. Humanity, perhaps. I knew, without knowing it, that post-humanity had just dawned on me. Long live the new flesh.

I would quickly travel from this moment into cyberpunk sci-fi, industrial/ electronic music, *bOING bOING, Mondo 2000, Wired,* and my own *Beyond Cyberpunk!* I cried for the death of that country hippie. And like Batty, in that moment, I could feel the full weight of my life, the amazing adventures I'd already been on, full of "things you people wouldn't believe," and somehow, I could sense wondrous adventures to come, And like Batty, I was sad to think that all of this, all of this accumulation of experience and knowledge, all of my memories, would vanish when I died.

Pammy is gone, eight years now, by her own hand. I think of that "scene" from our life together frequently, that frozen moment at the window. It has become a scene in *Blade Runner* itself. I can't think of one without the other. I hold these and other memories in a precious kind of stasis 'cause I know that "all those moments will be lost in time, like tears in rain."

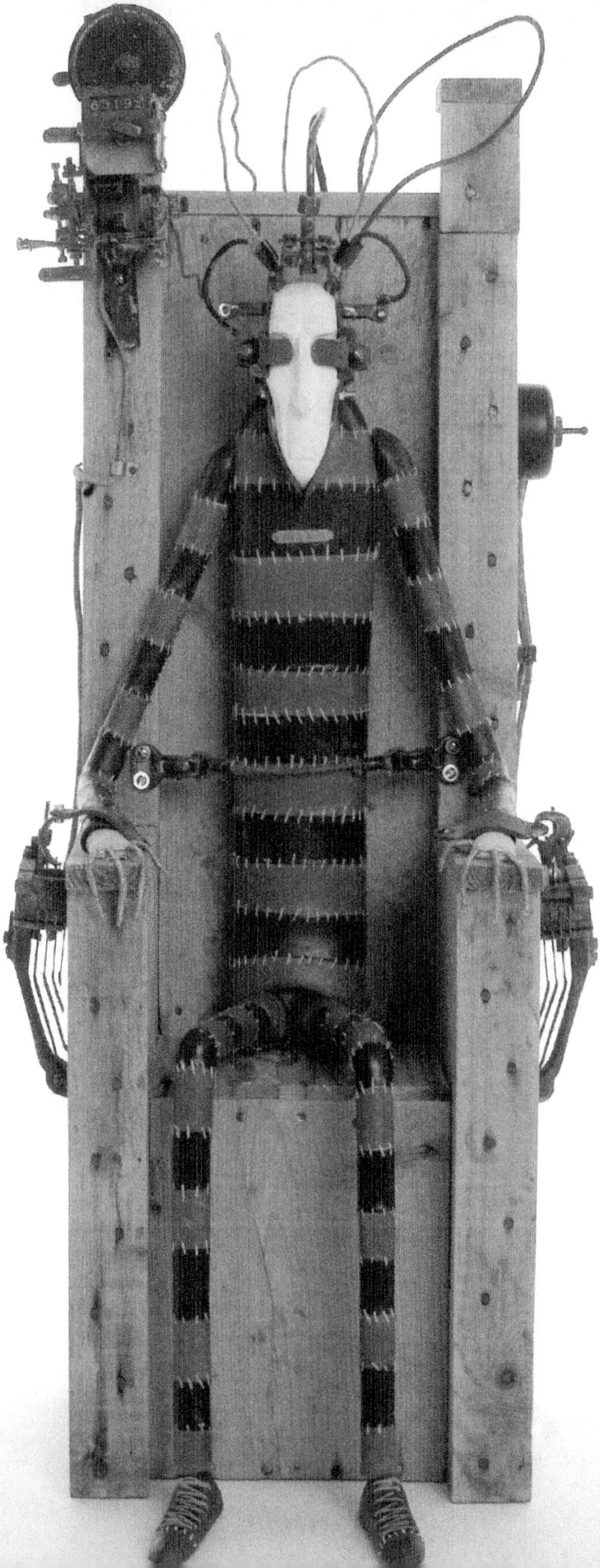

Sculpture: Stéphane Halleux

APOCALYPTIC BONE DANCING

From Psychic Terrorism to the Ecstacy
of the Post-Industrial Dance Floor

So much was happening in my life and the burgeoning cyber-culture in the early 90s. My zine *Going Gaga* was finding itself being praised in such places as the *Village Voice*, *Whole Earth Review*, and *Factsheet Five*, The Well BBS (pretty much the Gertrude Stein Parisian salon of early cyberculture) was busy incubating the future of the Net, *bOING bOING* was steadily evolving from a zine to a small commercial magazine, and *Wired* was promising to astound the world with the good news of the dawning digital revolution.

And then there was *Mondo 2000*.

I first discovered *Mondo,* in its previous incarnation as *Reality Hackers*, on the newsstand of a hip DC record store. (It had even had a different name before that, *High Frontiers*.) With content mixed into the same cocktail of psychedelics, music, art, high-tech, and high-weirdness that I'd been imbibing since Shea and Wilson's *Illuminatus! trilogy*, I quickly became a fan. When R.U. Sirius, the editor of the magazine (now under its new *Mondo 2000* moniker), showed up on the Well

BBS, my regular online haunt, we began exchanging email. I soon became a contributor, then a section editor.

High Frontiers had once been called a "party-on-paper." *Reality Hackers* and *Mondo 2000* very much carried that party forward although the paper got a lot slicker, more expensive, and the party's art budget grew larger. I never made it out to any of the actual, infamous parties at the Mondo House (aka the "Mondo Mansion") in the Berkeley Hills, but the weirdness that went down there was legendary and even managed to worm its way through the narrow 28.8k pipelines of early 90s cyberspace and into my Deco radio of a computer, the Mac SE, back here in Arlington, VA.

As with *STIM* and *bOING bOING*, it is only in retrospect that I've come to realize how ridiculously lucky I was to be part of the *Mondo* madness. There weren't that many people that got to be at the head of that particular parade. If *Wired* ended up heralding the mainstreaming of the digital revolution, *Mondo* did lots of the recon and fired some of the first significant salvos. Looking back, it's now hard to believe that I was one of the soldiers in that advance guard.

There are so many awesomely wacky *Mondo* anecdotes I could tell, but here's one of my favorites. *Mondo* was famous for writing about, and featuring advertisements for "smart drugs," a 90s fad of ingesting prodigious quantities of various chemicals, dietary supplements, and specially-formulated "nutraceuticals" purported to make you smarter, more creative, improve memory recall, etc. The staff was known to be users of these drugs, but in the muck and mire of daily magazine production, you'd sometimes wonder what good they were doing.

Mondo 2000 was the first publication where most of my day-to-day communications, article pitching, delivery of drafts, fielding edits, and begging for money were done almost exclusively through email. For one of my articles – I'm half-certain it was the one you're about to read – I sent R.U. a draft, on the day it was due, and never heard back. Three or four days later, I sent him an email and asked if he'd gotten it. Twenty-four hours or so later, he responded, with a no.

I re-sent the manuscript. And the same thing happened (waited several days, emailed, heard back several days later. Another no, he couldn't find it). I sent it again. Amazingly, the same exchange occurred a THIRD TIME. I finally called, exasperated. Probably being more frustrated than I should've been in addressing my editor (let alone the editor-in-chief), I couldn't help but blurt out: "How can you people be *so* fucking disorganized? How can you lose an emailed manuscript *three* times? I mean, Jesus, I thought you guys were on smart drugs!" Without skipping a beat, R.U. replied: "Yeah, but you didn't see what we were like *before* we started taking the smart drugs." Touché, my friend. Touché.

I hesitated putting the following article in the collection. There are a number of pieces that I wince at a little now, but thought they were important to include because of the waypoints they mark in my personal journey or because of the impact they had on readers at the time. This piece is principal among the latter.

Over the years, I've had so many people tell me that this article, this entire, rather iconic issue of *Mondo 2000* (issue #5, 1992), had been so important and inspiring to them. Several have referred to this piece as my "post-industrial manifesto," which is funny because it was never titled as such. In the issue, it was simply called "Post-In-dustrial Music" and was used to kick off a music-themed issue, which included my interview with Trent Reznor of Nine Inch Nails, an interview with arts and music collective Sound Traffic Control, New York experimental musicians Glenn Branca and Elliott Sharp in conversation with brilliant stand-up semiotician Mark Dery, a piece on The Residents, and a cover story about Dr. Fiorella Terenzi, a glamorous, big-haired Italian astrophysicist who'd figured out how to turn radiation from celestial objects into music.

This piece probably suffers from me reading too many breathless music writers (I'm looking at you, Simon Reynolds and Greil Marcus) and the tortured prose of the post-modernist academics of the time. But it *was* written in a sort of inspired reverie that I still think back on very fondly. I wrote it after a spectacular night out at a DC gothic-in-dustrial club. I wrote the entire piece in one intoxicated download the moment I got home. I thought I'd Dervish-danced my way to something deep and meaningful that night and I tried to capture it in words. In a moment of dance floor ecstasy, I'd felt something greater than myself, a movement of tectonic shifts happening in culture, a shift that *Mondo* (along with *bOING bOING*, *Gaga*, and early *Wired*) was reporting on and helping to effect. I stayed up well into the next day, sitting at my computer trying to capture some of this as it related to the increasingly-popular industrial music scene with which I'd become heavily involved.

My experience at *Mondo* was like the epiphany I felt that night, spiraling along the undulating edges of the mosh pit. The entire *Mondo* enterprise was a mad, drunken, inspired moment. We could palpably feel the gravity, the onrushing pressure-waves, of a dawning 21st century, a life that would be immersed in media, communication, data – full-on cyberspace. We felt an expectant lust for technologies to come and the new shape of a world they would invariably bring with them. As Kata Sutra, the "fractal anarchist" cartoon mascot for *Beyond Cyberpunk!* and *bOING bOING* liked to say: "The future? You're soaking in it!" We *weren't* soaking in it yet. Yet. But we'd dipped in a generous big toe and couldn't wait to baptize the rest of ourselves.

Immersive Media Note: To get the most out of this essay, listen to Front 242's "Gripped by Fear" after reading it.

"We're interested in information, we're not interested in music as such. And we believe that the whole battlefield, if there is one in the human situation, is about information." —Genesis P-Orridge (1982)

EXPRESSION THROUGH AGGRESSION

Early rock 'n' roll used pleasure as its main means of subversion. From punk rock onward, psycho-sonic terrorism has been the principal means of conveying the rattled collective id of the underground. In the arena of industrial music, this sonic assault has been offered as a massive wake-up call to legions of drones freebasing TV and Madison Avenue's trend du jour. "Wake up you idiot, you're a marketing unit," goes the message.

The sounds of "anti-Muzak" have echoed a great distance from the early garage electronics of Throbbing Gristle, SPK, and Cabaret Voltaire to the slick sounds of today's industrial dance music. The current style is so different from 70s and 80s roots industrial that "post-industrial" would probably be a better label. Little is left of the early conceptual purity, the impact of its shock tactics, or the desired depths of the cultural subversion. Today, "Industrial" has come to encompass everything from the ambient sounds of the Hafler Trio to the "uberthrash" of Ministry to the experimental rap of MC 900' Jesus and the activist ideologues at Consolidated. If there are any threads that connect these bands (sampling, a preoccupation with darkness and decline, and socio-cultural ostracism) they are overcome by the diversity of musical styles and raisons d'être. Sub-genre labels are offered as a way of sorting all this out. People talk of "industrial dance," "ambient-industrial," "industrial noise," and "industrial thrash," to name a few. Perhaps the most sensible general demarcation of post-industrial is between experimental (noise, ambient, sound collage) and the many flavors of industrial dance (industrial-thrash, industrial-rap, techno-industrial, attack house, etc.)

Today's legitimate industrial bands are lost in a sea of imitators and non-industrial music (some of it excellent in its own right) that's been strategically marketed under the industrial label. As the industrial dance genre has became popular, it's increasingly being reduced to a 2D image of terror and defiance. This has killed almost any hope of industrial music as being a mechanism for cultural confrontation and change. The economic history of rock 'n' roll has proven that commodity culture is masterful at maintaining the facade of rebellion while removing any of the vitriol that might prove truly poisonous to the status quo. Industrial music is just the latest victim. Image over action, style over substance. The pop culture industry wouldn't have it any other way.

"Noise is about fascination, the antithesis of meaning. If music is a language, communicating moods and feelings, then noise is like an eruption within the material out of which language is shaped." — Simon Reynolds *Blissed Out: The Raptures of Rock*

Noise has overtaken information in our age. Signal and noise have switched places. We live in the value-dark dimension, a black hole of imploded values and exploded worldviews. Early industrial music looked at this cultural wasteland, gathered up some of the junk and ejecta and decided to make music with it. In the process, it discovered new possibilities for "art noise," exploring the boundaries of music and anti-music, order and chaos, terror and bliss, beauty and bestiality. If the age of empire was dying, industrial music wanted to score the funeral march.

As industrial music has "advanced," so has the music technology that produces it. With the introduction of MIDI systems and samplers, the metal-on-metal rhythms of the junkyard have been replaced with the cut-and-paste sounds of the videodrome. The nightmarish hissings of smokestacks have been replaced by the sound-collaged marketspeak of the culture industry. The fascinations of industrial artists have also shifted emphasis from messages of control through subjugation and outward violence to the insidiousness of control through pleasure and the mesmerism of the videodrome.

And as with its forebears, all this is still shot through with noise, cut-up nonsense, and the cybernetic strategy of feeding the noise back into the system to hasten its decline. Today's experimental industrial artists—like their close cousins, the cyberpunks, the concrete poets, and the modern primitives—have the intuitive wisdom to know that post-verbalism and irrationalism are important territories to explore. The breakdown of an old language creates the opportunities for a new one. And the resonant echo of a primal scream shudders towards infinity.

POUNDING OUT THE ANALOG AGE

While the industrial scene has lost some of its underground cache' on the way to more commercial success and the urban dance floor, it would be unfair to write it off as culturally irrelevant. Front 242, Die Warzau, Clock DVA and Young Gods are all examples of bands that still bleed when you scratch their surface.

Even if the more radical messages of industrial are getting recuperated, victimized by overexposure and wider marketability, the music still offers transformative possibilities... at least on the dance floor!

Post-Industrial is white-hot funky dance music beaten out on synths, samples, and everyday white noise. "Softened" news and other fragments from the soundtracks of our lives provide the back beat, over which snarls a processed, demonic, from-a-sonic-distance voice of domination, control, and disaffection. Post-Industrial dance (true to its early Industrial roots) is built around the sounds our culture makes as it's coming unglued.

There is something totally sublime about thrashing to industrial music on a scuzzy urban dance floor, a tangle of punks, goths, nerds, Rastas, and other outcasts, all in the pit together. The DJ, high on a perch, surrounded by banks of electronic equipment, relentlessly hammers the audience with the latest from

Nine Inch Nails, KMFDM, Coil, Skinny Puppy, Front Line Assembly, and Nitzer Ebb. Lasers, also raised above the crowd, slice through the smoke that's venting up from dry ice machines below. People scream and howl, beating their arms against their bodies, pumping them into the air. From the balcony, you have to squint to see through the sympathetic pollution of smoke, light, and vaporizing body heat. The dancers writhe together, jerk and stomp, bashing into each other—true friendly fire.

I rather gingerly throw my tender, arthritic frame along the fringes of the fray along with the rest. I sacrifice "the meat" to a high purpose—sonic and psychic ecstasy. I'm exhausted, I'm in pain from hours of dancing. I'm frightened by the self-imposed danger. And I'm as high as I can remember.

The DJ punches up Front 242's "Gripped by Fear." I go bananas, press the pedal to the metal, and spin around in circles like some mad cyberpunk dervish.

"Recession/repression/regression"

The throb of the dance floor becomes a ritual of thermodynamics and surrender.

"Your tyranny I was part of is now cracking on ev'ry side..."

I feel like we're pounding the brutal analog age of sword and steel into the pages of history.

"...your own life is in danger, your empire is on fire."

Questions of sellout be damned—in this moment of pure and private ecstasy, the late-stage industrial program redeems itself. Life just doesn't get any better than this.

I awaken the next morning to a call from a friend. Rumors are flying that WaxTrax is negotiating a sale to Warner Brothers. Last night's paradigm-shaking bliss—and the future of industrial music—brought to you by a global mega-corporation?

"Th...th...tha...that's all folks!"

BEYOND CYBERPUNK!

...catio...
...circ...
...it, h...
...onfused...
...get eno...
...ho claim...
...an't wait f...
...arrive).

...rs the entire field...
...nce augmentation" (...
...ugs and cyberspace) with t...
flash and irreverence of a roc...
and roll mag. Each issues
creates a **"temporary autonom...**
zone" where people, events,

INTO THE FUTURE! THE MAKING OF BEYOND CYBERPUNK

S ome parts of the following originally appeared in my book *Jamming the Media* (Chronicle, 1997).

"What is the use of a book, thought Alice, without pictures or conversation?"
—Lewis Carroll, *Alice's Adventures in Wonderland*

When Apple Computer released its HyperCard program in 1987, the computer world scratched its read/write head, not quite sure what to make of it. The computer press struggled to explain ("It's a graphical database program," "It's an alternative to the Mac desktop," "It's a software construction kit."). Consumers were intrigued but largely clueless as to how to use the program. We were told it was easy to use, easy to program, and that it could magically link together text, images, and sounds into something called "hypermedia." In today's world of a ubiquitous, media-rich web, what HyperCard heralded seems painfully obvious, but at the time, it didn't click for most people. There was little frame of reference, the technology was years ahead of its time.

CLICK!

I got my first inkling of the potential for HyperCard/hypermedia in 1989 when a floppy disk arrived in the mail from my good friend Peter Sugarman, then living in rural Virginia. The disk had a chunky-bit, digitized picture of Peter, in a particularly pensive pose, on the laser-printed label. At the time, even a digitized photo on a disk label was kind of fancy. Booting up the HyperCard document (called a "stack" in the program's parlance), I discovered more pictures of Peter and his family and a map of Virginia that made goofy sounds. And a little animated guy skulked throughout. I found myself peering at some weird hybrid media, a cross between an interactive letter, a family photo album, and a whimsical stroll through an eccentric friend's mind. While it was obvious that Peter was basically digitally doodling, testing out the capabilities of this new medium, I found the potential of it very exciting.

At the time, I was running a monthly salon in the DC area, called Café Gaga. The purpose of these gatherings was to send a group of people, from different professions and viewpoints, on a fun journey deep into some theme or idea or to pursue some sort of quest. Some events were experiential, arty, others more cerebral. The credo of the group was "art, information, noise." Each event was supposed to have some component of art, information (data, science, the exposition of an idea), and of course, everything produces noise. When I saw Peter's HyperCard stack, I immediately thought of how this technology could be used to create little "salons" on disk. After several weeks of blathering to others about this, someone sent me a HyperCard stack in the mail called *Passing Notes*. It was exactly what I was talking about, a broadly-cast conversation that threaded its way through art, science, religion, and philosophy, all grappling with a single idea (in this case, the question: "Are we more than the science that explains us?"). The stack even had a link to an online bulletin board (BBS) so that you could add to the conversation and see what others thought about the stack and the question it posed. Again, this all sounds like ancient history as counted in computer years, but back in 1989, this was eye-opening stuff.

Peter and I began having regular phone conversations about hypermedia and how it might change the nature of storytelling, media delivery, information organization and navigation. I'd always been struck by cyberneticist Gregory Bateson's idea of forever being mindful to balance "rigor and imagination" in one's pursuit of knowledge. It seemed to Peter and me that hypermedia provided a perfect environment to pursue ideas deeply and rigorously, while building in fun, whimsy, and a sense of the unexpected—a kind of orchestrated chaos, a vibrant little media ecology in which people could derive their own meaning. We began kicking around ideas for a collaborative HyperCard project.

BUILDING A CYBERPUNK "DATA BUCKET"

While Peter and I were anxious to get our hands dirty with hypermedia, I'd discovered a rather exhaustive list of cyberpunk sci-fi novels on The Well BBS and thought it might be a perfect subject for our stack. I'd been reading as much of this sci-fi subgenre, about near-future worlds and high-tech low-lifes, as I could get my hands on, so it was a perfect fit. The idea was originally to create a "data bucket" into which we could toss all of the information on cyberpunk that we found while surfing the Net. But, like a lot of hypermedia projects, once we started seeding our little pocket universe, Beyond Cyberpunk!, as we soon dubbed it, quickly began teeming with lots of unexpected life. We quickly decided to go all out, to make it as exhaustive as possible, and release it as a commercial product. At the time (1990), the Internet was not yet in the media spotlight. So-called cyberculture (where these near-future speculative worlds met the bleeding edge of real-life technoculture and high technology) was in its heyday, but still known only on the cultural fringes. We could sense that all things "cyber" were about to bust into the mainstream and we wanted to chart the course cyberculture had taken, from its sci-fi and early hacker roots, through the Internet, and soon, we suspected, into everyday life.

The project quickly mushroomed. I began talking to Mark Frauenfelder of *bOING bOING* about it and he got very excited. My email inbox (a rather quiet and lonely place back in 1990) and fax machine began to light up at all hours with Mark sending book and film reviews and ideas for other things we might include. Peter and I would eventually joke about the fact that, in the beginning, we weren't even sure how serious we were about BCP until Mark jumped onboard, started taking it seriously, and we thought: "OK, I guess we're doing this for real – we have another contributor who assumes it is!" I also soon approached the brilliant Silicon Valley interface designer Jim Leftwich, whom I also met on the Well, and convinced him to sign on to our quickly expanding project, for no money.

As we began publicly discussing plans for the project on The Well and elsewhere, we started attracting some amazing contributors. Somehow, fearlessly approaching a well-known writer or luminary seemed so much easier on the long end of an email message. We sent mail to many of the founders of the cyberpunk genre and were actually shocked to get enthusiastic encouragement and contributions from Bruce Sterling, Rudy Rucker, Richard Kadrey, Mark Laidlaw, Paul DiFillipo, and Stephen Brown. We also received contributions from Robert Anton Wilson, RU Sirius, Hakim Bey, Joan Gordon, Steve Jackson, Steve Roberts (the "high-tech nomad"), and countless others.

The process of working on BCP creatively invigorated all of us. We'd work late into the night, each in our own home offices, Peter and I in two different Virginia locations, and Mark and Jim in two California locations. We'd trade content and stack demos via email and our faxes machines would grunt and squawk to attention at all hours, sputtering out some new icons sketches from Jim, some new page designs from Peter, cartoon ideas from Mark, or dialog or essay drafts from me.

Peter was the creative force behind the stack architecture and programming, and I was the producer of the content. With the untold number of hours it took to program BCP, Peter learned every eccentricity, fudge, and nuance of HyperTalk, the scripting language that HyperCard spoke, and he applied it all brilliantly. I still hear from people how in awe they were of the cleverness of his scripts and the way BCP was all put together. Before BCP, Peter and I had done a lot of talking and note-taking on what makes good digital interface design. We even thought at one point we might do a book, or at least an instructive HyperCard stack, on the subject. We applied these ideas (most of them Peter's) to BCP and it seemed to pay off. Another aspect of BCP that was very innovative for its time was the full use of sounds and animations in concert with the written content and pop-up texts, graphics, and whimsical stack "events." The stack was narrated throughout by Kata Sutra (voiced by my late wife, Pam Bricker). Every time you went to a new section, hit a glossary link, or triggered an error message, Kata would tell you where you were going, or would playfully chastise you for screwing up ("Achtung, Chucko!"). Again, Peter earns the credit for his brilliant use of sounds and events to create a sense that the stack was a giant, clanking, well-meaning, but goofy data-contraption, all held together with chewing gum and bailing wire and threatening to exhaust itself at any moment.

In fact, there were a couple of special "chaos events" that could be triggered and the stack *would* fall apart. On the Survival Research Labs card, for instance, if you hit a certain sequence of buttons, the stack would emit the ungodly sounds of a machine taking its last dying breaths. With metal clanking and springs a-sproinging, chunks of the stack would appear to fall off the screen, its wiry guts spilling everywhere in the process. To accomplish these F/X – rather impressive using only 1991 consumer computer technology – Jim laser-printed and glued the card onto foamcore, cut out the breaking-off bits, and animated the destruction photo-frame-by-frame with real wires and springs spewing forth from beneath the foamcore. It was all extraordinarily funky, but it worked, and people flipped when they saw it.

There was an exuberance and sense of humor about *Beyond Cyberpunk!*, along with a slightly askew and grubby street tech aesthetic, that made it seem old, alive, and greater than the sum of its parts. The subtitle for BCP was "A Do-It-Yourself Guide to the Future." We also sometimes called it "A Cut and Paste Cyberpunk Manifesto." The idea was to create this giant data bucket, loosely wire some of the contents together through hypermedia links, and then let the users create their own connections, drawing from that bucket the information and ideas that best suited them.

JACKING INTO THE MATRIX, PLEASE STAND BY...

So, what exactly was contained in *Beyond Cyberpunk!* and how did it work? The main program, which was released on November 14, 1991, was a 5.5mb HyperCard stack. It came as a compressed self-extracting archive on five 3.5" floppy disks. The black disks had embossed silver and black labels on them and came in a clear Lucite box with a silver and black booklet. You also got a 20-page *Kata Sutra in Beyond Cyberpunk!* mini-comic with art by Mark and text by Mark and myself.

Kata Sutra, a character Mark originally created for *bOING bOING*, was a punky, fiery-tempered "fractal anarchist" who lurked amongst the pages of the zine, usually thinking of elaborately outrageous reasons why readers had to subscribe. When she saw the fun the rest of us where having on BCP, Kata couldn't resist ingratiating herself into the stack's multimedia "cards." She brought with her a new character Mark created (and I helped write), an opportunistic data-retrieving AI with a K9 personality and a nose for mischief, known as codeHound. With their rather rough-shod, chaotic but endearing personalities (with tongues always drawn into their cheeks), Kata and codeHound were in many ways cartoon expressions of the four of us. Kata became the voice of BCP and haunted the stack via text pop-ups, audio statements, and Director animations (which had her zooming across the screen on a circuit-board-encrusted hover-disk designed by Jim Leftwich). All the statements and animations were programmed into the stack as random events or triggered by set sequences of user's actions.

Beyond Cyberpunk! was divided into four zones: Manifestos, Media, Street Tech, and Cyberculture. Each zone contained essays, reviews, artwork, animations, and sounds. There were over 600 "cards," over 300 articles, 122 different sound clips, 19 animations, and 35 text pop-ups. There was also a glossary with vocal pronunciations, and a 1000-word hyperlinked index.

Each zone in BCP had a series of essays followed by a resource section (books, magazines, zines, organizations, etc.) associated with the theme of that zone. Manifestos covered higher-ordered thinking around cyberpunk fiction and cyberculture and looked at things like the political ramifications of the genre and its relationship to the post-modern thought/critical theory of the time. Media was the heart of the stack and explored hundreds of books, movies, comics – mainline cyberpunk science fiction. Street Tech looked at real-world hacker culture, media hacking tools, and pirate media. And finally, Cyberculture looked at art, music, fashion, and modern primitivism.

In 1993, we released a one-disk follow-up called the *Beyond Cyberpunk! Update Stack* with the subtitle: "What happened to the future since the last time we talked?" This release provided us with an opportunity to assess where cyberpunk/cyberculture had gone since the release of BCP proper and it was the first time I'd had an opportunity to tell my side of the Billy Idol story (see "The Internet is Punk Rock!"). It also contained a bizarre and beautiful interactive art piece by Darick Chamberlin (author of the infamous cyberpunk novel, *Cigarette Boy*). Dubbed "The Blipvert Zone," it was a dynamically-assembled collage of art, text, sounds, and narration done in the same Burroughsian "mock machine epic" style as *Cigarette Boy*.

"IT'S THE FUTURE, NO?"

It's the the second annual CyberArts Festival in Pasadena, California, November 1991. Peter, Mark, myself, and several other contributors meet and shake hands literally in front of the program as it merrily gurgles and chugs through its cyber-industrial soundtrack. Mark and I, and Mark and Peter, are meeting face-to-face for the first time. We've spent months, hundreds of hours, working together in a virtual computer lab, and now we've gathered in Pasadena to dine on the fruits of our labors. *Beyond Cyberpunk!* has been chosen as a featured exhibit for the CyberArts Gallery. We're munching hunks of cheese and sipping wine while proudly showing off our rude and rowdy little digital baby to the world. We meet the *Mondo 2000* staff, and some of the future staff of *Wired* (who are showing off a preview of the magazine on a portable video player). We show BCP to Timothy Leary, Dwayne Goettel of Skinny Puppy, and other members of the cyberatti. Italian astrophysicist and musician Dr. Fiorella Terenzi bends down in her tight and squeaky leather mini-skirt to watch the stack on its tiny 9" Mac screen for awhile, then looks up in amazement: "It's the future, no?" That statement becomes an oft-repeated phrase for the rest of the weekend and beyond.

We're immediately struck by the sight of our low-budget, indie project alongside expensively produced, commercial multimedia programs. BCP looks humble and unassuming on its little black-and-white SE screen, but as soon as people start playing with it, they're drawn into its dense, engaging content, its irreverent humor, and its startling periodic "chaos events."

In the months that followed, the critical acclaim for *Beyond Cyberpunk!* was overwhelming. It received positive reviews in *MacWeek, MacWorld, TidBITS, Mondo 2000*, even the *New York Times* and *Newsweek. MacWeek* claimed that BCP "put the Mac back on its revolutionary track." It was also mentioned in a cyberpunk cover story that *Time* did. In November, 1993, University of Iowa professor and sci-fi scholar Brooks Landon published a lengthy essay on *Beyond Cyberpunk!* in *Science-Fiction Studies* (Vol. 20, No. 3), arguing that it was one of the most important documents in "the first generation of canonical hypertexts." Other tech journalists and writers who praised it included David Pogue, Adam Angst, Ric Ford, and cyberpunk founding father Rudy Rucker.

Famous fans of BCP included Robin Williams, Lily Tomlin and Jane Wagner, William Shatner, Billy Idol, and filmmaker John Badham. (Legend has it that, on the set of *Point of No Return*, Bridget Fonda was lusting after Badham's BCP Kata Sutra shirt so badly that he literally gave her the shirt off his back.) Years later, Peter, bound for a tech gig in Europe, sat next to Doug Rushkoff on a plane. Doug proclaimed: "It all began with BCP."

But despite all of the positive press and wild enthusiasm from early purchasers and some very influential people, BCP never found a wide audience. We invested thousands of hours and thousands of our own dollars into it. The critics loved it, but ultimately, BCP bombed at the box office.

The program itself wasn't the problem, it was the ugly specter of exposure and distribution that still plagues DIY projects today. We can only imagine how things might've been different if we'd hooked up with a software company, or even a small, aggressive distributor. But, as with many such labors-of-love, the real riches gained are not measured in dollars or units sold. We made tremendous connections and friendships that continue today. Creator of the web, Tim Berners-Lee, once defined the web as "a universe of interconnected hypermedia documents." Several years before the web would make its official debut, *Beyond Cyberpunk!* was like a web on an individual's desktop, with HyperCard as the browser.

Working on BCP was one of the happiest times of my life. The entire team gained valuable experience and exposure for our ideas. We ended up in major media venues and got work opportunities out of it. We built significant parts of our careers on the project. It was partially because of my knowledge of hypermedia through BCP that, in 1993, I was asked by Ventana Press to write *Mosaic Quick Tour: Accessing and Navigating the World Wide Web*, the first book about the web.

The strangest thing about this whole chapter of my life is the extent to which people are now ignorant of the link between HyperCard/hypermedia/*Beyond Cyberpunk!* and today's hyper-webbed world. I've had more than one person ask me: "Hey, you know that whole hypermedia thing that you were so into in the early 90s – whatever became of all that?"

Seriously? The future – YOU'RE SOAKING IN IT!

Sculptures by Stéphane Halleux; Photo Credit: Muriel Thies

IS THERE A CYBERPUNK MOVEMENT?

I joined The Well BBS, now dubbed "the world's oldest virtual community," in 1987, several years after it had lashed itself onto the flotilla of data domains that made up the late-80s internet. By 1992, in the early "cyberculture" heyday, when *Wired*, *Mondo 2000*, *bOING bOING*, and *Going Gaga* were going strong, I was already a veteran and host of a number of Well conferences, including co-host of the bOING bOING conference, and the Mondo conference for a time.

One of the more pervasive topics of discussions in a number of The Well conferences concerned cyberpunk, and exactly what it was. Everyone knew there were a number of sci-fi authors who'd been placed beneath that umbrella, William Gibson, Bruce Sterling, Rudy Rucker, John Shirley, Lou Shiner, Richard Kadrey, and others. But usage of the term had clearly leaked out into the real world and people weren't sure why or exactly what it meant beyond the confines of fiction. Mainly, people seemed keen to dismiss it as a meaningless marketing label slapped onto music, fashion, and art to push product.

So, one evening in mid-January of 1992, I felt inspired to try and summarize what I understood real-world cyberpunk to mean, at least to me, and used it to kick of a discussion about how others might answer the question: "Is there a cyberpunk movement?" I'd already written a similar piece for another Well conference, trying to define post-modernism (which had gotten a decent response), and I'd recently written a piece for Mondo on post-industrial music (see "Apocalyptic Bone Dancing"). So I felt emboldened enough to tackle cyberpunk and the question of whether it was really some kind of cultural movement or simply a fad.

Besides the surprising reach this piece ended up having (which is detailed in the next essay in this collection), it also represents one of the key principles found in my "Gareth's Tips on Sucks-Less Writing," "Sometimes, the Best Things You Write, You Write by Mistake." If I'd known how far this post was going to travel, I would have written something far different, more self-conscious and hard-won, and it possibly never would have had the impact that it did. I was simply writing a conference post (analogous to a blog or Facebook post today), over a cup of after-dinner coffee. I had no expectation of anyone outside of the Mondo conference ever reading it. It was shot from the hip with little thought about style, voice, or audience. I was just having a little chat. I certainly wouldn't call it one of the best things I've ever written, but it is certainly one of the things that's enjoyed the widest reach, and worked its way into the most unlikely niches.

From the conference header, it looks like the topic ended up getting 362 comments before it was finally closed.

```
mondo.old 383: Is there a Cyberpunk "Movement?"

#2 of 362: chaos agent (gareth) Fri 17 Jan '92 (10:43 PM)

I don't know if there is a "movement" and I don't know
what it is or is not to be called, but there certainly
is something a-foot and it's more than mere marketing.
```

IS THERE A CYBERPUNK MOVEMENT?

To write it all off as such is to throw the baby out with the bath water or not to see a baby in the first place. To me, a pattern of activity has emerged that contains many smaller domains connected into a larger whole. This larger something has been called cyberpunk, cyberculture, the "new edge," techno-culture, the silicon underground, and many other things. Much more important to me than what you call it is what it means.

Some things to point to would be:

• Cyberpunk literature proper and its popularity.

• Connected to that is the realization by many people that much of the worldview implicit or explicit in cyberpunk is real, here-and-now stuff:

a) the future has imploded onto the present. There was no nuclear Armageddon. There was too much real estate at stake. The new battlefield is people's minds.

b) Megacorporations are the new governments.

c) The US is a big bully with lackluster economic power.

d) The world is splintering into a trillion sub-cultures and designer cults with their own codes, languages, and lifestyles.

e) Computer-generated information domains are the new frontiers.

f) There IS better living through chemistry

g) Small groups or individual "console cowboys" can wield tremendous power over governments and corporations.

• The coalescence of a computer "culture," self-aware and expressing itself through electronic/computer music, art, virtual communities, and as hacker/street tech culture. People are not ashamed anymore about the central role that the computer has assumed in this culture. The computer is a cool tool, a companion, important human augmentation.

• We're becoming cyborgs. Our tech is getting smaller and smaller, closer to us. Soon it will disappear inside of us.

Some ideas and attitudes (many taken from the hacker ethos) that seem to be related:

• Information wants to be free.

• Access to computers and anything which may teach you something about how the world works should be unlimited and total.

• Always yield to the hands-on imperative.

• Mistrust authority.

• Promote decentralization.

• Do It Yourself.

• Fight the Power.

• Feed the noise back into the system.

• Surf the edges. ("You have to look at the edges to find out where the middle is going" —Stewart Brand.)

Being someone who is very enmeshed in much of the above, I can say that most of my experience with it has been very non-market oriented. When there are "cyberpunk" events in DC, the crowd is far from cyberchic. It's a gloriously diverse and motley crowd. And I would say that scrounge-tech is far more interesting to east coast wireheads. Improvisation, jerry-rigging, getting a great deal on gear are all held in high esteem. Of course, having the latest and greatest screaming box ain't so bad either, but I don't think it's a focus. I don't know… maybe it's a geographical difference, but I definitely don't think that consumerism is a big driving force with most of the cyber-techno-hacker-whatchamacall-ems that I know.

THE INTERNET IS PUNK ROCK!

As a writer, you crave impact. Some might say writers write because they have to, compulsively, relexivefly, and that's probably true for many of us vocational scriveners. We also write because we have a burning desire to truly reach people, to move them. Audaciously, we want our work to touch hearts, to change minds, make people think, make them laugh, cry, to make them see the world through our eyes. We want people to read our articles in magazines, buy our books, come to our readings, subscribe to our blog and social media feeds. What most of us who write for a living can only dream about is for another artist to be inspired enough by our work to want to incorporate it into their own.

This otherworldly episode in my life, from the early 1990s, is about when that latter dream came true for me. Like Cinderella being swept into that golden carriage, I found myself at a dizzying big-night royal ball – before soon ending finding myself back at my shabby cottage, with a pumpkin, some mice, and a missing shoe.

It's the kind of bizarre life moment that makes reality curdle around its edges. It had been a typical workday, and after a late morning and early afternoon of writing and doing administrative work on *Beyond Cyberpunk!* (mainly taking orders as they came in over the phone), I went to take a nap. When I got up, I wandered downstairs to find my wife, Pam, dusting. I stood at the landing and asked groggily: "Did I get any messages?" Not looking up, doing her level best to affect a posture of work-a-day detachment (when *did* we ever bother to dust, BTW?). She said: "Yeah. Just one. Billy Idol called." She played it so straight, it was priceless, like she was telling me the shop had called and our car was ready. I tried to process what I'd just heard. "Wait, what?" She lowered her dust rag. And then her cool. She began squealing, jumping up and down like a kid in a blow-up bouncy house. "Billy Idol called! He wants to use something you wrote in *Mondo* as lyrics on his next record! He's calling back in twenty minutes!"

Almost exactly twenty minutes later, the phone rang, and sure enough, the snarly-lipped one was on the other end. And yes, he really did want to use something I'd written on his next record.

This was actually the second time I'd talked to Billy that day. He'd called earlier in the morning to order a copy of *Beyond Cyberpunk!* Giving his credit card info and address, he'd used his birth name, William Broad, which I hadn't recognized. At the end of that first conversation, right before hanging up, he'd asked me my name. Turns out, he'd read what he called my "cyberpunk manifesto" in the new *Mondo 2000* collection, the *User's Guide to the New Edge,* and had been trying to track down its author. He wanted to use parts of it on his next record, a cyberpunk concept album called.... wait for it... *Cyberpunk.*

It was beyond surreal to be talking on the phone with him – Billy Idol! He told me that he had this idea of using my piece as the intro for the record. (My piece, called "Is There A Cyberpunk Movement?," had actually started life as a post on The Well BBS, later getting reprinted in the *Mondo* book.) He wanted to read it over music, like "Late Lament," the poem recited on the Moody Blues' *Nights in White Satin* album.

The next thing I know, I have Billy Idol—Billy Fucking Idol—on the other end of the phone dramatically reciting *my* words back to me, in glorious "Breathe deep the gathering gloom" fashion. His reading was surprisingly sincere and powerful, so potent and sincere that it even choked me up a bit. And, OK, I may have snickered some, too. Not dismissively, just because it was all so surreal that my brain had suddenly turned to cornmeal pudding.

I found Billy charming and instantly likable. He was funny, thoughtful, goofy, and self-deprecating. We talked about cyberpunk, virtual reality (which he was very taken by), *Mondo 2000* and *bOING bOING*, and the ongoing traditions of DIY. "I'm so fucking into the internet," he declared. "The internet is punk rock!" At the time, I found this a rather vacuous statement and didn't really understand what he meant. But as I came to know Billy more, and follow the whole trajectory of the recording, release, and touring of the record, I came to see what it meant to him, and why the discovery of the internet was so powerful and important to him. And I came to understand some of the sad truths about celebrity isolation. And what some celebrities will do to break free of it.

"Do you have an agent?," he finally asked. Miraculously, I did. I'd just gotten one, so I felt all fancy-pants in answering "Yes." "Good then, I'll have my manager contact your agent and they can work out the details," he said. He couldn't see my goofy grin. "I mean, that's what we pay them for, innit?," he added. I laughed, maybe too heartily, and said "Yes. Exactly."

Billy called back several days later to say that he'd received *Beyond Cyberpunk!* and was impressed with it. He wanted to know if we could do something like it to accompany his record, as a promotional piece and limited-edition collector's disk for hardcore fans. *Beyond Cyberpunk!* co-creator Peter Sugarman and I put together a proposal and a bid. Eventually, Billy decided to go with another early HyperCard innovator, Jaime Levy, who lived near Billy in LA. Around this same time Billy also met Mark and Carla at a *bOING bOING* event in Hollywood. Mark and Billy hit it off and Mark began doing work on the record, too. He did graphic design on the album and promotional materials, and helped get Billy set up on the internet.

The disk that Jaime created was very similar in look, feel, and sensibility to the buzz-worthy *Electric Hollywood* disks that she was producing at the time. Created in the Director program, the *Billy Idol Cyberpunk* disk was divided into quadrants offering the album's cyberpunk framing concept (my words, now slightly mutated by Billy), the lyrics to the rest of the record (with some hypertext), a biography written by Mark, and a resource section by me. There were also animated sequences of Idol images and some other hypermedia doodads. The disk was colorful, fun, and made good use of sound samples. Many of the images were grabs from the videos director Brett Leonard (*Lawnmower*

Man) had done for Billy's techno-dance cover of the Velvet's "Heroin" (here rendered into a bittersweet tale of virtual reality/simstim addiction).

Jaime's disk was released as part of the digital press kit for the album which included the first single "Shock to the System." The kit came in a "Digi-Pak" CD folder which had a plastic panel holding the floppy and one holding the CDS. A limited edition full album used the same Digi-Pak packaging with cover graphics by Mark.

At one point early on in the recording process, Mark was at Billy's home studio and Billy mentioned that he wanted to get on the Internet. Mark suggested he join The Well. The Well BBS, created by Stewart Brand, Larry Brilliant, and some of the other *Whole Earth Catalog* folks, was housed in a closet in the WEC offices in Sausalito, CA. At the time (1992), The Well, that closet, was the cybernetic brain pool you wanted to be swimming in. There were a few early enclaves at the time where some of the Internet's most influential and creative dreamers and schemers were hanging out. The Well was one of them, MindVox in New York was another. Nearly all of the editors of *bOING bOING, Mondo 2000, Wired, Whole Earth Catalog/Whole Earth Review* took up residence on The Well, along with writers, editors, and journalists from many other magazines and newspapers. We were all trading electrons with each other along with scientists, artists, musicians, activists, lots of Bay Area computer nerds and academics, and many first- and second-wave cyberpunk sci-fi authors. A lot of the digital culture and technology that we're now soaking in first pooled there, or at least filtered its way through The Well before it flowed on to nourish and fertilize the future.

Mark thought The Well would be a good place for Billy to make camp in cyberspace. Mark and I could help him negotiate the rather gnarly world of The Well's UNIX-based command-line conferencing interface, which was not at all for the faint of geek. So, Mark helped him set up with a PC and modem and Billy finally jacked into cyberspace.

Billy was thrilled to be on The Well, and was very open and playful there. He tried to laugh off the rather rude reception he got and the rampant suspicions his presence engendered amongst regulars. Right from the start he was accused of not actually being Billy Idol, of only being there for craven marketing reasons, and of being about to ruin The Well by his mere presence – drawing unwanted attention to this still rather gated virtual community. Billy asked what his user name should be. Someone, more as a joke than anything else, suggested "Lyl Libido" (an anagram for "Billy Idol"). Billy loved it, and ran with it. He used that as his Well handle from then on. He asked people for input about his music, suggestions of what to do next. One poster replied: "Never, ever record another Doors cover!" (Referring to his cover of "LA Woman"). "In fact, never record a cover of *anyone* else's song!" He graciously yukked that off along with other insults.

What was amazing is that Mark and I would defend him, telling people: "No, he's not here as part of some record company master plan. He's here because *we* brought him here. He wanted to be online and we brought him into the community that we know. That's the extent of it." But people, on both The Well and the alt.cyberpunk USENET group, continued on as if they hadn't heard us (or didn't believe us). It quickly became clear that people had a cardboard cutout image of Billy Idol (and what his motives surely must be) and they really weren't interested in anything that contradicted such an image. This was all very bizarre to experience, now from the POV of the celebrity himself. It forever changed my view of people in that position and how we and the media so harshly judge them and interpret their motives (seemingly always to default to the most nefarious ones) without knowing (or caring about) the truth.

As my brief association with Billy continued, I realized one aspect of what he'd meant in that initial phone call, about the internet being punk rock. In both dealing with this intractable image of himself in the public eye, and in him having to deal with the industry people around him, Billy was desperate to break through all of these levels of filtration, the barricades of protection and isolation (agents, managers, PR people, record executives, an entourage of yes-people) that the starmaker machinery insists on erecting around any successful artist.

Billy saw in desktop publishing, home music recording, the internet, and hypermedia, a way of being able to break free of all of these industry and fame barriers, to truly feel DIY again. He could talk directly to his fans, he could record his records at home, he could help design his own album art – he could regain a measure of control that every artist of his stature inevitably loses (and most, like Billy, probably long to reclaim).

On the advertisements that he and Mark created for the record, Billy even went so far as to print his Well email address. Again, this was met with suspicion and criticism, people seeing it as a rank marketing gimmick (and a further affront to The Well's gated virtual community). I saw it as something very different. A statement of desire to directly connect. A kind of bold declaration of his freedom.

I have many awesome and silly Billy Idol stories. Here are a few choice ones that I've often repeated:

- His answering machine message. It said, in a deep, ominous voice (I may not recall it exactly): "*This* Idol demands human sacrifice. [Deep, sinister laughter.] Beep."

- When Mark and I were first tutoring him on using The Well's conferencing system, Billy was not the sharpest student in the classroom. One night, he called me and needed to be reminded how to access his email. I ran over the basics. The next night, at almost the exact same time, he called back. He needed me to tell him how to access his email. "Billy, I just told you that last night." He chuckled and said (I always wish I could recreate his thick working class London accent when I tell this story in person): "I know. But last night, I'd just gotten in from the studio, I rolled myself a big doobie, and I've now forgotten everything you told me." We both had a good laugh. I went over everything again and hoped that he hadn't "rolled himself a big doobie" before calling me this second time.

- I ended up BEING Billy Idol for a day. In cyberspace, anyway. Billy was on tour and couldn't figure out how to get onto the internet from Europe (a daunting task for anybody but the most tech-savvy at the time). A Boston rock paper wanted to do a "cyber-interview" with him (which basically meant emailing questions and him answering them over that controversial email address he was spreading everywhere). Since he couldn't get online, he gave me his Well password. I logged on, downloaded and printed out the first round of questions, and then faxed them to him in Europe. The answers would come back to me, written long-hand by Billy on legal-pad paper. I would transcribe them into an email message, send them to the paper, and then wait for follow ups. It was highly entertaining getting to pose as him. We didn't tell the paper that they weren't talking directly to Billy and they were saying "Thank you, Billy" and similar conversational pleasantries, and I was responding as him. I may have even added a "Rock on!" or two, just because I could. In cyberspace, nobody can be sure that you aren't Billy Idol.

- After the Boston rock interview, I told Billy that, for security purposes, he probably should change his password. He had used a very insecure password to begin with, so it was a good excuse for him to create something safer. He said he would. I knew he wouldn't. A long time afterwards, maybe six months? A year? Two years? Well after he and I had fallen out of touch, I was sitting at my computer one day and thought: "Gawd, I wonder if Billy ever changed his Well password?" I couldn't resist. I tried logging into good ol' Lyl Libido's account. And there I was, staring at his inbox. I immediately logged off and had a good tsk-tsk head shaking.

When the album finally came out, it was widely panned. If Billy's heart and intentions were in the right place (and I never doubted that that), whatever muse he'd found within cyberpunk and DIY cyberculture didn't translate very effectively into the music. The record just didn't seem honest to me. My intro text, which he'd read so movingly over the phone that day, was recited in a heavily machine-processed voice burried beneath loud, oscillating synth wails. The words were barely audible. And he'd made a number of changes to my text, which I'd contractually agreed to allow, but I had no right of refusal and was not shown the additional lyrics beforehand. I couldn't cringe enough when I finally heard the track, especially as it ends on Billy's addition of "Welcome to the CyberCorporation, Cyberpunks." It's really hard when you have your name on something, for something as huge as a Billy Idol record, and that (altered) work ends up expressing something you would never, EVER say. I'm not even sure what that statement means!

But while the whole Billy Idol *Cyberpunk* episode is now widely regarded as the moment that 90s cyberpunk/cyberculture officially jumped the shark, time has proven at least a little kinder to the music, perhaps because of its nostalgic and kitsch qualities. A lot of Idol fans, who had initially dismissed the record, have come to embrace it. The album currently enjoys 4 out of 5 stars on Amazon. Even I get a kick out of listening to it once in awhile.

While the final product may be lacking, one of the things that no one can deny Billy is some of the forward-thinking innovations of this record. It may have ended up driving the final nail in the coffin of cyberpunk, but at the same time, it cracked open a doorway onto the digital media world we all live in and take for granted today.

The multimedia diskette that came with *Cyberpunk*, which I believe was the first of its kind, preceded all of the mixed-media discs and apps that followed and leads all the way up to the iTunes LP today. And Billy's embracing of home recording was not common at that time, especially for an artist of his stature using some of the consumer-grade equipment that he did. His involvement with the artwork for the record and creating it all on home computer equipment was also unheard of in mainstream music. And his promiscuous outreach and desire to engage with his fans, de rigueur in today's social media world, was a rarity. A few other musical artists were pioneering digital and interactive media in early 90s, namely like David Bowie, Thomas Dolby, and Todd Rundgren – Billy Idol deserves a prominent seat at that table.

If the "internet reads censorship as damage and routes around it," as EFF co-founder John Gilmore once so brilliantly put it, and the insulating barricades of fame create a kind of censorship, then the internet can route around that, too. In the early 1990s, at least for a brief, glorious moment, Billy Idol stepped out of his gilded cage and glimpsed our "cyber-future," at least a decade ahead of most everyone else.

DIY media makes up a huge portion of today's net content. Almost everyone creates content of some sort. It's also a place where celebrities directly and unflinchingly advertise themselves, their twitter handles and social media addresses, and post the most intimate "selfies."

On today's internet, any musician or anyone else with something to say has a soapbox on which to say it. The net has become one giant, global garage and most of us are in some form of a band, hoping to he heard, to be discovered. And *that's* what Billy Idol was trying to tell me on the phone back in 1992:

The internet is punk rock!

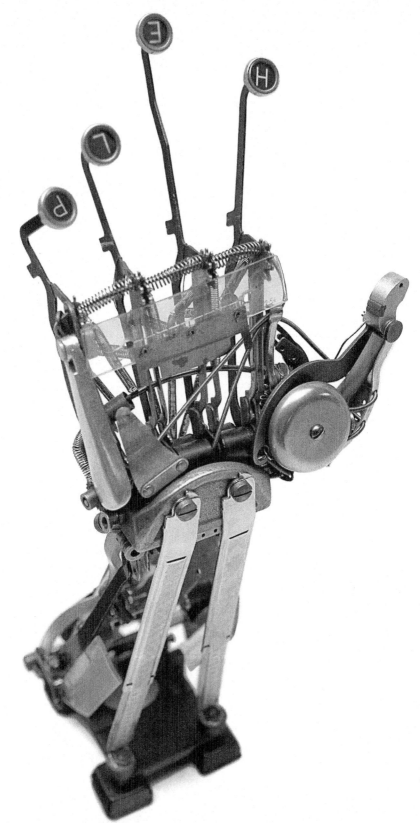

Sculpture: Jeremy Mayer; Photo manipluation: Blake Maloof

BORG LIKE ME

Since the age of thirteen, I've had a disease I still can't spell (and I'm determined to keep it that way). Google tells me it's "Ankylosing Spondylitis." It's basically spinal arthritis, but it effects all of the major joints in my body. It arrived alongside puberty and has been my "dark passenger" ever since. Atypical to this form of arthritis, it started in my toes and knees and then worked its way towards my spine, taking up residence in my hips in my early 20s. By my 30s, I was told I was "ready" for a right hip replacement. Degeneratively speaking, I might have been ready, but psychologically and emotionally, not so much. Fear of the procedure and possible complications made me put off the operation far longer than I should have. I ended up spending several years using what I took to calling my chair on wheels (rather than wheelchair). I wasn't confined to it, but had to take it with me wherever I went because I couldn't stand for more than 20 minutes. Frequently, I'd push around my own empty seat until I needed it. In early 2000, I could no longer cower from the inevitable. I still vividly remember that beautiful spring morning, driving to the hospital for the operation at the crack of dawn, watching my house fade away in the sideview mirror, wondering if I'd ever see it and my beloved family again. Needless to say, I made it back, and I was faster, better, rebuilt. They had the technology.

This piece was originally written for the February 2001 issue of *ArtByte*, a sadly short-lived New York digital arts and culture magazine, edited by Mark Dery at the time. The article was surprisingly well-received. I rarely get congratulatory phone calls when I publish articles. This one inspired a few. The best was from cyberpunk sci-fi pioneer Bruce Sterling. He was particularly tickled by the piece because he saw in it the beginnings of a trend: aging cyberpunks beginning to be borged for real. "Chairman Bruce" (as he was called in the cyberpunk twilight of the 20th century) loves irony, and as you'll see, this experience had no shortage of that.

It's fun to read this now and find references to *NYPD Blue*, the Sony AIBO, and a more innocent (pre-9/11) era when an artificial hip didn't set off airport metal detectors. Today, I have a full performance of security theater to look forward to whenever I travel, complete with invasive crotch groping. We live in strange times, a "cyber" future that even astute speculative fiction writers like Sterling could scarcely have imagined.

Like *Wired* after its sale to Conde Nast, I am now officially "post-hip." Last year, after decades of trying to shake off the pain of severe degenerative arthritis in my right hip (and nearly every other major joint in my body), I had a total hip replacement ("THR" in the trade). With months of Steve Austin/Six Million Dollar Man jokes under my belt, and after enduring such forehead-slapping questions as: "Will you set off metal detectors?" and "Is the Sony AIBO going to hump your bionic leg?," I was suitably hardened for anything the operating room might decide to throw at me.

Over half a million people have major joint replacements every year, but my visit with the bone saw had special poignancy. Since the early '90s, I've frequently written about neural prosthetics, plastic muscles, foreskin farming and other state-of-the-art cyborg technologies. I've also participated (online and in print) in nosebleed postmodern theorizing about our "cyborged" bodies and the growing border war between meat and machine. In the introduction to Beyond Cyberpunk!, the 1991 hypermedia book I co-created, I wrote: "Our tech is getting smaller and smaller and soon it will disappear inside of us." Somehow, I managed to overlook the fact that this "disappearance" was already a reality for many, and little did I know that I would soon be host to some incredible shrinking tech of my own.

I'm here to tell you that fantasizing and rhapsodizing about it are worlds away from having a hunk of metal and plastic literally hammered into your own body (and having a major part of you hacked away with power tools to make room for it).

As my wife and I made the final, nerve-wracking decision to go through with the surgery, I started to feel like one of those liberal D.A.s on NYPD Blue who's just discovered that the baby raper he helped exonerate has moved into his own apartment building. I was now going to become a real cyborg - not one of the metaphoric borgs academics have discussed to death, a softwired creature of computer interfacing, gender dysphoria, and postmodern mythology, but a hardwired one, a literal borg: part man, part machine - a biomechanical being. The very thought of it - the risks involved, the cold, hard fact of putting my hardware where my hip once was — scared the stuffing out of me.

Hip replacement surgery has become surprisingly safe and commonplace, but because arthritis has fused my sternum (constricting my chest), and thanks to the fistful of immuno-suppressant drugs I gobble down daily, I am at a higher risk for post-surgical pneumonia, a complication that could kill me. I am also predisposed to something called "heterotopic ossification," a horrifying side effect, where pieces of bone begin to form in the muscle around the implant, which can cause as much or more pain and limitation than the excised hip. Browsing books on hip surgery and doing online research on the subject only cranked up my fears to "11."

But then I got to fondle the hardware. During the initial visit with my orthopedic surgeon, he brought in an implant for me to play with. It was a gorgeous, awe-inspiring piece of modern machinery — almost Zen-like in its shining simplicity and austere precision. The cementless implant technology my doctor's clinic uses was co-developed by them and has been implanted into thousands of patients.

The description of it reads like something from a William Gibson novel. I now sport a Duroloc® 100 acetabular titanium cup with sintered titanium beads for in-bone growth adhesion. I have a bleeding-edge Marathon® polyethylene liner with irradiated cross-linked polymers for tighter bonding and longer wear rates. My Prodigy® brand stem has a 28mm cobalt-chrome head and a cobalt-chrome femoral component with sintered cobalt-chrome beading for bone in-growth fixation. Where 2001's HAL 9000 was fond of telling people that he was made at the H.A.L. plant in Urbana, Illinois, I can now boast that part of me was manufactured by DePuy Industries of Warsaw, Indiana.

Geeking out with the doctor, discussing the details of the hardware while absent-mindedly gliding the sensuously smooth cobalt-chrome ball around inside the polyethylene cup, I felt a growing reassurance. The doctor, a third-generation member of an orthopedic dynasty (with books on Amazon!, I comforted myself); the world-renowned clinic; the smart-looking hardware — it all started to hum like well-oiled machinery, machinery to which I found myself increasingly willing to submit. In the midst of my newfound courage and enthusiasm, I looked over at my wife and realized, by the green cast to her cheeks, that the she was more in need of smelling salts than tech specs.

As if to drive home the irony of my situation with all the subtlety of an operating room bone hammer, I had to endure several unpleasant procedures other patients usually get to skip. Because of my higher risk of mutated bone growth, I had to have my hip irradiated the morning of the surgery. There I was, at 8am (closer to my bedtime than my morning), strapped to a slab, having my thigh sketched on with markers by a team of X-ray techs. Then, the slab started moving upward and I was raised into a room-sized X-ray machine in a scene unsettlingly reminiscent of *Bride of Frankenstein*. Once inside this giant, Soviet-looking contraption, I was asked to remain stock-still, while the machine creaked and twisted around me. Along the rim, in an obviously feeble attempt to entertain the children unfortunate enough have to endure this frightening device, marched a parade of little worn cartoon stickers of *The Jetsons*, featuring everyone's favorite mechanical domestic, Rosie. The semiological significance of this gave me something to bite down on as the flesh around my femur received a full-on assault of gamma radiation.

I also had to brave the terrifying experience of being intubated while I was still awake. Most patients can have their head tilted back to establish an airway while they're doped beyond memory. Because of my fused-forward neck, I had to be semi-awake while they shoved tubes into my throat and my body tried to heave them up. I have the most bizarre alien abduction-like memories of masked and hooded technicians frantically struggling to overcome my gag reflexes. They also wanted me to be awake in the recovery room before they removed the air tube. This felt a little bit like drowning, which mercifully, lasted for only a few seconds.

In Donna Haraway's landmark 1985 essay "A Cyborg Manifesto," she suggested that severely handicapped people often have the most heightened understanding of their relationship with technological augmentation. Being handicapped, I can vouch for the truth of Haraway's statement - in spades. Recovering in the hospital, I discovered a huge cyborged population she had apparently overlooked: the elderly. The average age of a joint replacement patient is 63. At 42, I was the ward's resident whippersnapper. Sitting in our wheelchairs, our patient-controlled morphine pumps clicking away, our catheters sluicing liquid into alarmingly-full urine bags (they don't empty those things nearly enough), I was stunned to hear all of my fellow implantees' war stories. Most everyone on the ward was on a second, third, or fourth replacement. One patient was on her sixth implant (two shoulders, two hips, and two knees). She's eighty and has made plans to live past a hundred, so she takes all of the risk, pain, and rehabilitation in stride. For her, it's a worthwhile investment to buy a few more decades of life. My hospital roommate, in his 70s, had basically stopped off for a knee replacement before he and his wife took a trip around the world. Both of them had been plagued with recent health problems (quadruple bypass surgery, ovarian cancer, arthritis). "I'm just here for a little tune-up before we hit the road," he joked.

The procedure was not fun, the hospital stay was filled with frustrations I won't enumerate here, and the six-week recovery period was one of the biggest challenges of my life. But make no mistake about it, this is miraculous technology that it is radically changing my life. A giant throbbing knot of pain is gone from my body. I was reduced to a walker when I went into the hospital, now I don't even bother with a cane. I have more energy and enthusiasm than Richard Simmons at a fat farm dance class. I had a major joint replaced and was out of the hospital faster than it takes to get over a head cold. Good thing too because there's likely more joint hacking in my future. My left hip is also circling the drain and will probably come out in the next few years. My knees are nearly shot and my shoulders are fused so I can't raise my arms above my head. Each one of these replacement procedures will augment me and amputate me at the same time (to borrow a theme from Marshall McLuhan). And what of upgrades and repairs? I may have to go back for some of those, too.

I woke up this morning with a painful limp, in my new leg. This is not supposed to happen and it made me flush with fear. It's probably nothing, muscles and tissue still trying to recover from the surgical trauma, but what if it's more? What if it's heterotopic ossification, my leg mutating into some Cronenbergian horror with bone growing where it's not supposed to? What if it's an infection in the wound site (it's possible that something as common as the flu or a teeth cleaning can lead to site infection, and in worse cases, removal of the implant). These fears, these suspicions of an alien presence in my body, will be with me for the rest of my life, and will only be compounded by each new biological-to-mechanical parts swap.

What I've learned from all this is that the subjective process of becoming a cyborg, in the hardwired sense, greatly suppresses one's appetite for high-minded theorizing about it. Where "wounds are openings to possibilities," as the French technocultural critic Jean Baudrillard once suggested, they are equally openings to infection. There's nothing like having a stinging, aching, seven-inch scar running down your thigh and a large foreign object lodged inside of it, slugging it out with your body's defense mechanisms, to make you appreciate the complicated trade-offs and mixed emotions involved in real-life bio-mechanical bonding. It is as much a world of wound management, site infection, tissue mutation, implant extraction and rejection, and reams of HMO paperwork, as it is a world of life-restoring body repair and trendy cyberpunk mythology. All rhapsodic cyborg theorists should book a date with a bone saw (or at least heed the words of those of us who have) to remind themselves that, in our cyborgian future-present, and in the end: it's all about the meat, stupid.

—Gareth Branwyn

UPDATE
(posted to my website in 2004):

Over the years, I've gotten numerous emails, some from complete strangers, asking about my current "condition," and how my second hip replacement went. I really appreciate the interest and concern. I love you, too. I thought I'd go ahead and update people on how it's been going.

I got this total hip replacement in the spring of 2000. Even months after the surgery, my remaining hip (or my "bio hip" as I started calling it) was still in lots of pain, as was my back, neck, and other joints. Gradually, as the artificial hip started to make itself at home, the pain in my bio hip and back went away. I guess it was a compensatory sort of thing. I was putting all sorts of exceptional stresses and strains on other muscles and joints to compensate for the bum hip, and after it was replaced, gradually, those pains faded away. I'd also started on a new drug therapy a year or so before the surgery, and the combination of the two has been nothing short of miraculous. I now have no pain to speak of in any part of my body except for my neck (and my right wrist, but that's more likely a writer's injury than an arthritic's).

I'm actually in the best shape I've been in decades. The increased physicality has allowed me to lose a lot of weight, build muscle, and leap tall buildings in a single bound. I don't use a cane anymore, or any other gimp tech. I can even fit into clothes I wore when I was in my 20s [Cue pictures of me in the mirror marveling at myself in 80s parachute pants — wait, scratch that. I think the Hammer pants are best left to the moths in the attic.]

So, in answer to your questions: I'm doing amazingly well, and at this point, I don't need the second hip replacement, or any other replacement. I'd take a new neck if they had one handy, but medical technology is not there yet.

BTW: I actually *did* get some of that creepy heterotopic ossification I mentioned in the piece, but thankfully, it's an extremely small patch and it has never bothered me.

If anyone reading this has a bad hip and is contemplating a replacement, I say: GO FOR IT!!!! In the article, I really focused on the negative aspects of the process, 1) because the fear and discomfort of the whole experience were still fresh, and 2), the point of the piece was to contrast my years of cheerleading cyborg technologies as a cyberculture writer with the very real and direct impact of tying on a backless hospital gown and facing the upgrades myself. Four years later, with the perspective of distance and living with the successful results, I'm here to tell you, it could have been two or three times more painful, challenging, and intense, and it still would've been worth it.

ASIDE: Do Cyborgs Dream of Bionic Upgrades? Yes they do! I get a bi-monthly newsletter, appropriately called *The Joint Journal,* from my orthopedic clinic. In it, they're always showing off the latest hardware and discussing new research findings and less invasive surgical procedures. Like ogling the latest Macs, I find myself wistfully thinking: "Damn, I wish *I* had one of those new Biomet M2a metal-on-metal jobbies! You lucky bastards, implanting metal in the 21st century!"

MAKERS VS. THE BLOB

From 2006 to the spring of 2013, I worked at *MAKE* magazine, first as a contributor, then as editor-in-chief of the *MAKE* website, and finally, as their Editorial Director. *MAKE* is the flagship publication of the "maker movement," the modern do-it-yourself movement that's a confluence of the *Whole Earth Catalog* ethos of the 60s and 70s, hacker culture of the 70s, 80s, and 90s, Bay Area/Silicon Valley tech culture, punk DIY, Burning Man, and various other expressions of the DIY impulse.

If *MAKE* is the house organ for this movement, then its in-person show and tell is the Maker Faire, which was first launched in 2006, in San Mateo, CA. Maker Faire is now held annually in San Mateo as well as New York City, and at mid-sized events in cites like Detroit, Kansas City, Rome, and Tokyo. And there are smaller, locally-grown Mini Maker Faires being held in cities and towns throughout the world. A Maker Faire is a hard-to-describe mash-up of county fair, science fair, craft show, inventor's convention, Comic-Con, and Burning Man (minus the drugs and rampant nudity). Mark Frauenfelder once said he thought the hackerspace movement (of face-to-face hacker/maker "clubs" springing up all over the world) was due to the computer geeks of the 90s migrating from software to hardware hacking. When you're making software, an email connection is all you need to share your work with others. But when you perform some cool hardware hack, you need to physically share it with others, and this involves getting together in person. So, out of this desire, hackerspaces, Dorkbots (an international organization that brings artists and engineers together), and other face-to-face maker organizations have sprung up. And the annual mega-meetups for these groups and individuals are the Maker Faires.

My son Blake's and my first Maker Faire was the second Bay Area event, in 2007. I've been to most every Bay Area and New York Faire since (and the two MAKE-run Austin Faires). The first day of that first fair, walking up to the fairgrounds, watching trucks unload supplies, tents being hastily erected, carts whizzing by carrying crewmembers intently jabbering away into walkie talkies, I joked: "Ah, the carney life, son. We're in the circus now." Little did I know how right I was. Being involved in putting on ten such events was an exhilarating and exhausting experience. I've never worked harder in my life or felt more inspired by the work that I did. I'm in awe of the core team who puts on these events, year after year. I also acquired a newfound appreciation for those who travel around and mount carnivals, circuses, and other large-scale and complicated events. It's a ridiculous amount of work and logistical juggling.

The heart of the following piece was written after that first Maker Faire Bay Area. It first appeared on my old hardware review website, Street Tech. I was not a regular contractor at *MAKE* yet, but they liked the piece so much, they reprinted it on the *MAKE* blog and as the Welcome editorial in the magazine (Volume 11).

This essay has two sections, an expanded version of the original piece, followed by a series of anecdotes about Maker Faire that will hopefully help convey some of the uniqueness of these amazing events.

Everything at a Maker Faire is cranked to 11. The size of the event, the breadth of creativity in evidence, the excitement of fairgoers, the diversity of the people who show up. And this high amperage is experienced by fairgoers and presenters alike. Common refrains heard around a Maker Faire go something like: "This is so awesome." "I've finally found my people!," "There's too much amazing stuff, I'll never take it all in!," "This thing needs to be a whole week," "If I'd only had something like this when I was a kid."

The first year I worked at a Maker Faire (Bay Area, 2007), my son Blake and I ran a workshop based on an article I'd written for *MAKE* about "Mousey the Junkbot," an analog computer mouse I'd turned into a light-seeking robot. The first day, we did open-ended workshops, selling Mousey parts bundles and helping people build them at workstations we'd set up. The end of that day was probably the most tired I've ever been in my life. The second day, seeing the error in our ways, we ran three one-hour workshops, which was far more humane. That gave us some time to wander around and actually see some of the fair.

In running the workshops, it was so inspiring to see people who'd never attempted anything like it in their lives taking the plunge. My favorite was a woman who saw the mousebots, really liked them, and said: "You know, this is *so* outside of my comfort zone, but I'm going to do it anyway. I think I need to challenge myself more." She bought a parts bundle, chose an old recycled computer mouse from the giant box of them we'd collected, sat down, and set to work. There were lots of kids with their parents, moms and dads alike, whole families working intently together. It was very touching.

One of the things that really strikes me about Maker Faire is the impressive diversity of attendees (think: Burning Man bohemians and steampunk cosplayers meet Harry and Harrieta Homeowner after church). The *MAKE* ethos really does appeal to an extremely broad range of people. The staggering diversity and creativity were also evident in the vehicles that freely circulated throughout the fairgrounds. After the end of the first day of the 2007 Faire, when the announcement came over the loud speakers that the fair was closing, Blake and I hobbled toward the benches in the center of the fairgrounds and sat there vacantly — aching, exhausted, stunned into a vacant kind of silence. Nearly unable to move, we watched as a parade of bizarre vehicles began to float by in front of us on their way towards the gate.

It was the most insane, and insanely great, fleet of conveyances I've ever seen: all manner of odd craft, from electric bikes and cars, to pedaled recumbent bicycles, homemade Segways, a solar-powered motorcycle, and a guy riding a motorized unicycle while holding a regular unicycle in front of him as a second wheel. And then there was the chariot pulled by a Roman centurion robot, and a covered wagon pulled by two robotic horses. It was so surreal, so ethereal, it felt like a dream, if your dreams were designed by Salvador Dali and engineered by Rube Goldberg.

I was recounting this moment with Mark Frauenfelder at dinner that first night and expressing it as a dramatic contrast to the continued, cancerous growth of the American monoculture, as it spreads across the planet like the chocolate pudding blob from the classic 1950s sci-fi horror film of the same name. There are few regional differences anymore, little local color. The cyberneticist Gregory Bateson is famous for saying "information is difference," and "information is difference that makes a difference." That's what's so scary about our planet-invading monoculture. No difference? No information. It's writhing, undifferentiated pudding from sea to shining sea, and increasingly, beyond our shores. The blob now travels by boat, by plane, and one day, it will likely stow away on spaceships as we begin colonizing the solar system. McNuggets on the moon. Walmart on Mars. The Sun, brought to you by GE.

The beauty of the Maker Faire is that it's about exhibiting and celebrating crazy expressions of difference. It's utterly anti-blob. At that first fair, so many people came up to me, looked at my Mousey project, and were giddy, almost drunk, with excitement, not only for the cleverness behind this project, but over all of the monocultural boxes they saw being transcended at booth after booth throughout the fairgrounds. "There are so many innovative ideas here!" they'd enthuse. Some of them almost looked like blissed-out cult converts, giant smiles on their faces, their eyes pinwheeling as their brains try to make sense of so much novelty, innovation, and outright creative craziness.

After my first experience, here's how I described a Maker Faire to friends back home:

Imagine that you're suddenly looking at one of the coolest thing you've ever seen in your life. You are gobsmacked by how original, creative, and just plain amazing this thing is. You digest it long enough to feel satisfied and then you move over to the next booth. And you're suddenly looking at something equally as mind-blowing as the first. You take a deep breath, try to rein in your growing excitement, lest you start blowing out brain circuits, and you move your attention to the booth next door to the second one. And darned if its wares aren't as inspired and noteworthy as the first two. And on and on it goes for hundreds of makers showing off their creations at the show.

When I first started working at Maker Faires, every year, I would pick the most poignant moment I had experienced at the event, which I began calling my "Maker Faire Epiphany." That moment at my first fair, sitting on the benches watching the alt.vehicles parade by, was the first such moment (which in turn inspired the above "Makers vs. the Blob" piece). Below are three more memorable moments from the two Maker Faire Austin events that we did, in 2007 and 2008. For a couple of years, I'd recount one of that year's epiphany at the staff dinner on the last night of the Faire. And I'd do a post on the *MAKE* blog asking editors and attendees to share their own priceless moments. Here are three of mine.

YOUR BRAIN: IF YOU CAN'T OPEN IT, YOU DON'T OWN IT

I was in the Maker Shed store at the second Maker Faire Austin, off in a corner, preparing for a workshop. I was working at a bench. Although this was in a busy retail pop-up shop, with lots of merchandise, the area I was in was clearly a less-trafficked work area, with high workbenches and tools and projects strewn everywhere. A young teen girl came sidling along the benches. She had a uniqueness about her, a gravitas, that was instantly recognized and impressive. She scanned the benches with that superficial retail gaze that people affect when they're perusing tables of merchandise. But there was no merchandise. She'd wandered away from the store, but still had that air of shopping. She starting picking things up, messing with them, which piqued my attention.

She finally made her way over to my bench and started poking through my personal belongings. I tensed. I had a cardboard box of tools and workshop supplies. She peered over the edge into it, saw something, and exclaimed "Ah-hah!" She pulled out a little white metal candy tin from the box. The tin was a product that we'd just started selling in the Maker Shed. On the lid was printed: "If You Can't Open It, You Don't Own It," a sort of open source motto/ maker manifesto expressing the demand for tech products that you can easily open, understand, and fix yourself. With a slightly nervous hesitation (as if she expected it to bite her), she quickly opened the tin and peered inside.

"Can I help you with something?," I finally asked, in that slightly put-upon tone that retailers assume when they're annoyed by your in-store behavior. "Oh...," she said, as if shaken out of some deep thought, "your box said 'If you can't open it, you don't own it,' so I was just seeing if I could open it."

It took me a second to wrap my head around what she had just said. I started laughing. I couldn't really argue with her logic. "Well then, I guess you own it!" I pushed her hand holding the tin toward her (it was new and empty). "Cool!," she enthused, and stuffed it into her messenger bag. She pulled out the map of the fairgrounds, brandishing it in my face, and said: "OK, If you were a 14 year old girl, where would you go next?" Again, slightly thrown by her rather unique skew on the world, I said: "Combat robots in the Arena? That's where I'd go." "Oh my god, like Battlebots?," she shrieked, "I LOVE those!" She thoughtlessly punched the map back down into her bag and blasted off into the crowd in a smear of motion and youthful enthusiasm.

I wish I had gotten that girl's name so I could remember her. Something tells me she's going to end up doing something really interesting with her life.

MEGAPHONES FOR FAIRIES, MONSTERS IN DUST, AND 21ST CENTURY BABY BLOCKS

It was the 2007 Maker Faire Austin. Again, I was tired, after being in the Maker Shed and demo area all day. This time, I was doing demonstrations of some projects from the magazine, including Mousey the Junkbot again. I was on my break, the first moment I'd had since the fair opened to actually have a look around. I stumbled into the show barn, the dusty dirt-floored, open-sided building where Texas farmers show off their prize livestock during conventional fairs.

I was so lost in my head, still getting my bearings, that I couldn't even focus on what was going on around me. The next thing I knew, I was standing in front of two large, wheeled sculptures. One of them looked like a giant megaphone, the other like the horn of an old gramophone, but huge. They were gorgeously constructed. As I drew closer, I saw that the megaphone-shaped piece had tiny little crank handles along the surface of its 14' metal cone-shaped horn. I began cranking one if them and could hear a faint tinkling as I turned it. A person walking by the bell end stopped and bent their head down. Another person had drawn up to the other side and begun twisted another of the tiny cranks. The fairgoer with his head in the bell was beaming from ear to ear. Now that several more people had manned the cranks, I moved to the end and bent my head into the bell. The little cranks along the edges were from 24 mechanical music boxes. The horn of the sculpture combined and magnified their sound and fed it out of the bell. Sticking your head into that bell was like sticking your head into the land of Fairy. I cannot describe to you the little chill of enchantment I felt in that moment. Then I moved onto the second giant gramophone horn. It was 8' long and bent in such a way that four thick metal strings had been strung along its top. Plucking them created a deep vibrant sound that was almost the opposite of the other piece. Reading the display card, I discovered that these two interactive sculptures were called Cranky and Plucky, and were the creation of Austin-based artist Dominique Vyborny.

Dizzy with delight over what I'd just experienced, I wandered deeper into the barn. Having all of those people milling around in a large roofed space with a dirt floor raises a lot of dust. I saw a blue Toyota parked inside the barn covered in dust, something that seemed completely likely in such a situation. But drawing closer, I saw a man hunched over the dirty side windows. As he pulled away, I saw that he'd been creating these gorgeous portrait of classic movie monsters, by brushing the dirt off the windows. He was making art in dust! Talking to him, I learned that his name was Scott Wade. Living on a dirt road, he'd originally begun drawing on his dusty car with his finger for fun, but after his strange little art hobby grew, he began using brushes and putting oil on the windows to create a better base for the dirt. The results he calls Dirty Car Art. The car I was looking at was covered on all four sides by the likes of the Phantom of the Opera, Dracula, Frankenstein, and the Wolfman.

Dirty Car Art. Something about it struck me as awesomely, sublimely ridiculous. And I felt proud that we had provided a venue for this bizarre form of self-expression, and a home for Cranky and Plucky, too.

Next I wandered to the first row of booths in the crafter's area. There I met a charming husband and wife team, Andrew Waser and Michele Lanan. They'd started a mom and pop business called Xylocopa Design. Combining old world woodworking and new laser cutting technology with their love of science and all things nerdy, they'd developed a line of wooden toys and jewelry. The product that caught my eye and tickled me to no end was their steampunky Mad Scientist Alphabet Blocks. Laser-etched onto the surfaces of maple blocks were intricate scenes depicting things like "C" is for the caffeine molecule, "F" is for freeze ray, "R" is for robot, and "Z" is for zombie. I had to have a set! I still have them — they're stacked on a shelf in my library, proudly flying the colors of my own mad scientist freak flag. BTW, the name Xylocopa is taken from the scientific name for the carpenter bee, one of nature's original woodworkers.

BUTTERFLY BIKES ON THE HORIZON

The image used to open this piece is by alt.culture blogger/photographer extraordinaire Scott Beale. It is a photo of one of the "butterfly bikes" built by the Austin Bike Zoo, and it captures part of the scene of another grand and magical Maker Faire moment. It was powerful enough that it ended up inspiring another presentation that I gave at Dorkbot DC, after the 2007 Austin Faire.

It was the Friday evening before the start of the event. After a long and very hard day of fair prep, all of the makers and crewmembers were in the chow line anxious for some much-lauded Texas barbecue. We had already drafted big plastic cups of locally-brewed beer, and being as tired and hungry as I was, it didn't take me long to acquire a bright and pleasant little buzz. I was talking to Dave and Cheryl Hrynkiw from Solarbotics. They were telling me the origin story of their little Canadian robot parts company, one of the first such ecommerce sites on the web. (They were maker pros before anybody even knew what that meant.) As we talked, I marveled at the fact that this was only one such story. Around me stood dozens more. This was still early on in the burgeoning maker movement, but I was starting to get many inspiring glimpses of its potentially significant impact on small business and tech innovation.

The fall Texas twilight was lovely, with a softness that quickly soothing away the day's labors. As Dave, Cheryl, and I, and a number of other makers talked in line, I started scanning the fairgrounds, thinking about the day's work, and what was about to descend upon us over the next two days. The area of the grounds that the concessions and dining were in was some of the lowest in elevation. On the other side of the grounds, between the big enclosed arena (think: rodeos and monster trucks) and the open-sided show barn, there ran a ridge. As the bottom edge of the western sky grew dramatically orange, with that last glorious gasp of light before darkness falls, I just happened to be scanning that area of the grounds. From the show barn emerged two giant butterflies and a white swan. They were kinetic sculpture bicycles being peddled along the pathway between the two buildings. The butterflies had multicolored cloth wings that flapped gracefully as the drivers pedaled. They also had lights along their edges that twinkled magically in the rapidly fading twilight. The vehicles moved across the middle ground of the ridge with a beautiful blue-to-orange sky and an emerging half-moon beyond them. The bikes were all being peddled by women wearing clothing that wouldn't have been out of place in a fairytale. I hadn't encountered these bikes since I'd been on the grounds, so I was seeing them for the first time, as if they had just glided in from some other realm.

The effect, especially in the context of my exhaustion, the warm beer buzz, the seductive smells of the barbecue, and catching up with old friends — it all made for a transcendently lovely little moment.

I was struck by these vehicles and the obvious question of: "Who would spend the time, money, and effort to build such a thing? And why?" They existed for no other reason than to charm people, to inspire them with a little vision of magic and whimsy. And then I thought how lovely the contrast was between the conversations we were having in line, about maker small business, about the technological innovations that might come out of the maker movement, while on the other side of the grounds, the other side of the maker impulse was parading by: Play, doing it because you can, doing it for the art, doing it for fun. Doing it because it is most defiantly anti-Blob.

And out of the yin and yang dynamo generate between those two poles, the engine of a movement is being powered.

vol. 06

Make:
technology on your time

Throw
Me!
page 116

Credit: MAKE/makezine.com

ROBOTS!

Build this pair of electronic **insects** and more

» Rodent-
Powered
Nightlight

» Floating
Tower
Sculpture

» Bug Sucker

54   76

88   100

O'REILLY   makezine.com

A VCR WAS HARMED IN THE MAKING OF THIS ARTICLE

This essay was written especially for this collection.

I was thoroughly screwed.

I'd been assigned an article for *MAKE* about how to build BEAM robots, little solar-powered critters inspired by biology and made out of junk. I'd made many BEAMbots before, but usually from kits or parts bundles, or by carefully following someone else's instructions. For this assignment, I was going to have to completely design and build one of the two solar-powered vehicles. Called a solaroller, the basic circuit and concept had been done many times before, but there was no set design for it, so it was up to me to figure out a workable chassis and drive system (one that others could easily replicate). I'd seen many other robots in this class of BEAMbots before and thought "how hard could it be?"

Thinking it easy, I went ahead and wrote up the rest of the how-to (all of the steps for the 2nd BEAMbot, a kind of solar-powered spinning top called a Trimet, and all of the steps for constructing the common solaroller circuit). Being the devout procrastinator that I am, I waited until two days before the piece was due to begin working on the solaroller's mechanics. I figured I had two full days to build a simple vehicle no bigger than a pack of cigarettes – plenty of time!

The first morning I got up, gathered my tools and supplies, and set to work. My first attempt was a little drag racer made out of soldered paper clips. It seemed like an obvious idea (I'd seen a number of them online), but I couldn't get it to work. It just wasn't structurally sound enough to handle the stresses of the drive train. I was trying to use the little rubber drive belt from a cassette player to transfer the motion from the motor (also from a cassette player) to the drive wheel. The alignment had to be perfect – and it wasn't.

I moved onto a body cut from plastic stock. I couldn't get that to work either. I tried epoxy-gluing all of the parts together so that I didn't have to fashion tiny hardware brackets. No joy. Same problem with the alignment of the drive components. A solaroller needs to have incredible smooth rolling action. The solar cell and the energy it generates to power the motor (stored in a high-capacity capacitor) doesn't really offer that much juice to turn the motor, so you want to squeeze out every bit of it that you can. Everything needs to be strong, perfectly aligned, and the wheels need to be level with the ground. It all turned out to be a lot trickier than I'd assumed.

I was thoroughly screwed.

I went to bed that first night with nothing to show for a full day's effort. My dining table looked like it belonged in the Unibomber's cabin, littered as it was with electronic components, bits of epoxied cardboard and plastic, little fussy paper clip assemblies, and wires, nuts, bolts, and batteries everywhere. One day down, one to go.

The next day was as maddening as the first. I spent a large portion of the morning searching for other solarollers online, hoping that I could swipe one of their designs. By lunchtime, I was no closer to a solution. I knew of a design approach that used one of the large tape rollers from a VCR as the main wheel, but I didn't have a spare VCR, in fact, the VCR we did have was only a few month's old. It was a cheapie (we didn't watch VHS tapes much anymore), but I obviously couldn't use it. You make BEAMbots from junk, you don't junk new consumer electronics in search of BEAM parts. I made another pot of coffee and redoubled my efforts.

The day ticked away on the living room clock as I tried design after failed design. Time was running out and I wasn't getting anywhere. I'd reached that dreaded point in a project where it all seemed cursed, where every move seems designed to frustrate your efforts. It was now closing in on dinner time and desperation with it. The piece was due the next day! My editor had already asked several times how everything was going and I'd said "Great." How could I now tell him that, in fact, one half of the article, one whole project, was not working, and was not going to be delivered?

That new VCR had been taunting me all day. I couldn't stop thinking about the fact that one of the critical components I needed, one that would likely make my project a success, was just a few feet away, calling to me from its shelf on our living room entertainment center.

Suddenly, a sort of bottled-up rage exploded in me. Without thinking more about it, I attacked our defenseless VCR, angrily yanking it from the shelf, sending a device-switching box tumbling back into the spaghetti tangle of wires behind the media center. I unplugged all of the connections from the back of the VCR and rushed it over to the dining table like a gunshot victim to an EMT gurney. I had the case off in seconds and found myself furiously field-stripping the machine. I was thrilled to find the precious part I'd been lusting after, the large tape roller. As I suspected, it looked perfect for my purposes.

The next few hours were as enjoyable and inspired as the last two days had felt frustrating and cursed. Once that part was in-hand, everything fell into place. The big, very stable and smooth-rolling tape wheel married perfectly with the pancake motor from the cassette player. The tape wheel from the cassette machine easily epoxied onto the other side of the motor case. A large nylon control wheel I had from an old servo motor fit snuggly onto the motor gear and was the right size to create a large drive wheel. This wheel was the exact width of a rubber band, allowing me to glue one around it to serve as a tire. I was even able to use part of a paper clip assembly from the day before as a rack to mount the electronics and the solar panel. Within a few hours, I had a working solaroller!

The sense of accomplishment I felt was indescribable. I had come so close to giving up several times, just telling my editor that we'd have to cut the piece in half and have it only cover the Trimet. And that's if they even wanted such a different piece than the one I'd pitched. The article that I'd proposed was about how this one simple electronic circuit and solar cell could be used to power different types of BEAM devices.

But I didn't have to worry about any of that now – I had a working and very cool looking solaroller. As I went to bed that night, I knew that, because of the East Coast/West Coast time difference (I'm east coast, the *MAKE* offices are in California), I could get up early the next day, finish the how-to instructions for the chassis, and still be able to deliver the piece on time. I drifted off that night into a very satisfied slumber.

The piece was very well-received, but the real icing on the cake came a month or so later when my contributor's copy of the magazine arrived in the mail. I pulled the issue from the envelope and was shocked and delighted to discover that my two BEAMbots had made the cover!

Staring at my two little bots below the *MAKE* masthead, I recalled those two very frustrating days. Holding the issue in my hand, I couldn't think of a better way of driving home the idea of never giving up — and always being willing to improvise in the clutch.

Years later, when I joined the staff at *MAKE*, I had a giant poster of that cover (*MAKE* Volume 06) printed out to always remind me of the lessons it represents, to never give up and not be afraid to cannibalize perfectly good hardware in search of the parts you need. They just might end up as a robot on the cover of a magazine.

SEEK YE THE HILARITAS!

I originally wrote this for the blogging stint I did on *Boing Boing* in early 2009. One of the great things about blogging is its immediacy. The day I posted it, I was having an exchange with a woman online who is so brilliant, funny, and flirty. A favorite new word, hilaritas, which I'd recently been introduced to, came to mind as a way of defining the feeling I was getting while playing sexy brain tennis with her. I immediately wrote the piece (about the word, not the flirty exchange) and posted it over my morning coffee. Of course, when you're writing for a high-profile blog like *Boing Boing*, millions will read your words, so you can't get too seduced by the immediacy of being inspired by something and firing off a post. I've picked more than enough egg out of my goatee for such missfired content.

BTW: *Boing Boing's* Mark Frauenfelder embodies an impressive amount of hilaritas. I also have a sneaking suspension that Mark may actually not be human, but rather, a cartoon character of his own creation. But that theory is beside our point and best left for another time.

I've written about hilaritas elsewhere, but thought I'd bring it up here for the benefit of *Boing Boing* readers who may not be familiar with the concept. I was introduced to the term via the work of Robert Anton Wilson. The more common *hilarity* springs from the same root. Hilaritas was a Roman goddess of rejoicing and good humor. She appeared on Roman coins from the time of Hadrian until the late 3rd century AD. On coins, she's usually depicted holding a long branch of palm in one hand and a cornucopia in the other. Children often dance at her feet. The greenery represents joy and celebration, the cornucopia, abundance, the children, playfulness and life.

Hilaritas was a Roman public virtue, something that people were supposed to strive to exhibit and inspire in others. Wilson was very keen on this word as he thought it perfectly expressed a rare and precious quality of being that revealed a unique personality. He defined hilaritas as "profoundly good natured" and made clear that, for him, it was more than just being happy or having a good sense of humor. I've also seen it defined as "being of pleasant spirits." St. Augustine defined it as "a mixture of intellectual excitement and sheer aesthetic pleasure at a notable display of wit."

I was first introduced to the word in one of Robert Anton Wilson's books (I don't remember which one), applied to Timothy Leary. RAW also uses it, and applies it again to Leary, on the CD interview series I've already mentioned, *Robert Anton Wilson Explains Everything*. In that interview, he says he got the term from Ezra Pounds' *Cantos*, and that Pound got it from an obscure Greek philosopher named Gemithus Plethon. Here's the passage from Cantos 98:

CANTOS 98
A soul, said Plotinus, the body inside it.
"By Hilaritas," said Gemisto, "by hilaritas: gods;
and by speed in communication.
Anselm cut some of the cackle, and relapsed for the
sake of tranquility.

Allegedly Pound loved the idea that Roman gods possessed this quality of mirth, with its roots in the "sublime joy of wonder and intellectual love." He also likened it to a form of "mental velocity" (which nicely dovetails the

Augustine definition). At one point in the *Cantos*, Pound likens it to the grace and playfulness of "minds leaping like dolphins." That's a lovely, poetic way of defining it.

In all of these slightly different definitions, there's a kind of cosmic "It factor." People possessed of hilaritas are people you're drawn to because they have something indefinable that you want, a kind of bright and playful knowing about the world. They seem to be having just a bit more fun on the slip'n slide ride of the Tao then the rest of us. Bugs Bunny has hilaritas. Hotei. Albert Einstein. The Dalai Lama. Mark Frauenfelder. And, of course, our dearly-departed Bob Wilson seemed to fully embody this quality, especially in the latter part of his life.

It's ultimately hard to define, but (as they say with pornography) you know it when you see it. Or in this case, feel it — the dance of happy, leaping minds and playful spirits. And sexy games of brain tennis.

SHOW US YOUR SAINTS

One of the more interesting, exciting things about posting content online is that you have little idea how well a post is actually going to do. Sometimes, when you think you have great content that's going to get a strong response, it gets a weak one. Other times, you might even be tempted to not post something because you're unsure of its merit, and it ends up firing the net's cyber-neural pathways to an extent that shocks you. I never could have predicted that the following piece, which I posted during my 2009 guest blogging stint on *Boing Boing*, would have struck the nerve that it did.

The concept of having people in your life that you venerate to almost a religious extent, whose lives and ideas you regularly hold out to inspire you – this seemed rather obvious to me. It was apparently something of an odd idea to many people, but after they thought about it for awhile, *BB* readers had lots of fun listing their own "saints." I think, in their enthusiasm, the criteria I was using (see below) got lost and people just started listed people they liked a lot, their intellectual and artistic heroes. One commenter tried to differentiate by referring to these as "lights" rather than saints. I have listed at the end of this piece a selection of saints as contributed by BB readers. Many of these would quality as "lights" for me. A couple, like John Lennon and Brian Eno, come close to my pantheon of saints.

I also caught a raft of shit for not having any women on my list. Again, I think the point might've been missed. I only had five people on my list, the five thinkers and doers who've fundamentally shaped my thinking, my world view. No public female figure has even come close to that for me. There are many lights (Patti Smith, Kate Bush, Dorothy Parker, Mary Shelley), but no saints.

I was raised Catholic (thanks, I'm better now). I also spent my teen years studying meditation, yoga, and eastern philosophies. So maybe as a result of this upbringing, I tend to think in terms of gurus, (spiritual) teachers, saints, heroes, muses, angels and daemons — no longer in a theological sense, but I still find these concepts useful in the poetic sense.

When I was kid, I loved all of the trappings of the Catholic saints: the icons, the scapular medals, the miracle stories, the statues, the reliquaries, the veneration. I'm a pagan at heart, and when you think about it, this is all nothing more than high paganism, ceremonial magick. I loved the idea that there are different saints that help, guide, and protect us under different circumstances. And I loved that they represent different virtues and qualities you could meditate on, invoke, and try to emulate, as you lit candles and prayed to their icons and rubbed their relics.

Recently, I've come to the realization that I still engage in various forms of this practice. I have amassed teachers — writers, philosophers, artists, musicians, and scientists — whose work has had profound influence over me. They've become hugely symbolic in my life and have come to represent different aspects of myself that I wish to improve upon and magnify. I keep them close to me, mainly in the collection of books (and other media) in my library that I browse and meditate on whenever I'm in need of a little guidance or inspiration.

Below is my list of "saints." Do you have such a pantheon? These are more than just your heroes. These are the people that you think have taught you the most, that you near-venerate in your love and respect for them, and whom you feel have helped form the bedrock of your beliefs and worldview.

MY "SAINTS"
(and what they represent to me)

William Blake – I venerate this late 18th/early 19th century artist, poet, and proto-psychologist above all others. He's the closest thing I could ever have to a guru. Blake's entire mission in life was to use his art and ideas to wake us all up from the somnambulism he believed the State, organized religion, even our own sensoria, were hell-bent on inducing in us. I use him as my constant reminder to stay "spiritually" awake and creative, to keep my imagination as supple and expansive as possible, and to always "fight the power" (the rote mental habits, institutions, and belief systems that seek to shackle me – what he referred to as "mind-forg'd manacles").

Gregory Bateson — One of the fathers of cybernetics, Bateson was something of a saint to the *Whole Earth Catalog* folks and *Whole Earth* was a huge influence on me in my youth. It was through Bateson's work that I was introduced to Blake. Bateson reminds me to always focus on relationships over objects and to look for the patterns that connect ("What is the pattern which connects the orchid to the primrose and the dolphin to the whale and all four of them to me?"). And Bateson taught me to tie all of my ideas and beliefs with slipknots.

Robert Anton Wilson — Besides William Blake, no one has had a greater impact on me than Robert Anton Wilson. I've had unwavering interest in him — he's kept me laughing, thinking, and questioning my B.S. (belief system) —for close to 40 years. That elevates him to sainthood in my book. Wilson embodied the virtue of hilaritas (see "Seek Ye the Hilaritas!"). He taught me to be "open to anything, but skeptical of everything." And he reminds me to always embrace the absurd, or as he used to put it "Above all, keep the lasagna flying."

Buckminster Fuller — Fuller's mission in life was to see how much a single "human intelligence unit" could create, learn, and experience — what one person could do to make the world a better place — in a lifetime. I try to live my life as much in this spirit as possible. Amazingly, he embarked on this experiment, on the other side of an aborted suicide attempt, in his mid-30s. Everything we know about Buckminster Fuller happened after that. I also venerate Bucky's optimism and his faith in human ingenuity and the transformative powers of science and technology.

Aleister Crowley – I hate "The Beast" as much as I love him. He represents my faith in the powers of thelema (will) and agape (love) and the notion of syncretism (the amalgamation of different beliefs and practices, always using whatever works). I try to live by his motto of "The method of science, the aim of religion." Say what you want against him (and there's plenty), but his influence on modern, at least bohemian, culture and alternative religions is undeniable (and I believe that influence to be ultimately more positive than negative). He was such a significant influence on me in my youth that it would be disingenuous not to include him here. And every band of apostles requires a Judas.

(Sadly, there are no women on my list. I could easily come up with women I greatly admire, lots of them artists and musicians, but no one who's risen to the level I'm talking about here.)

So, who are YOUR saints? What lessons, virtues, ideas, or qualities do they embody for you?

BOING BOING READERS: SHOW ME YOUR SAINTS!

Frank Zappa
Robert Anson Heinlein
Isaac Asimov
Carl Sagan
Richard Feynman
Emperor Norton I
Charles Darwin
Albert Einstein
Isaac Newton
Richard Dawkins
Christopher Hitchens
Joe Strummer
Tom Waits
Douglas Adams
George Orwell
Jim Henson
Edward Gorey
Neil Gaiman
Violet Paget ("Vernon Lee")
JRR Tolkien
Hayao Miyazaki

H.P. Lovecraft
Lord Dunsany
Arthur C. Clarke
Stanley Kubrick
Gabriel Garcia Marquez
Alan Watts
Joseph Campbell
Lao-Tzu
George Carlin
Kate Bush
Jimi Hendrix
Sam Harris
Daniel Dennett
Dorothy Parker
H.L. Mencken
Kurt Vonnegut
Michael Gira
Pablo Picasso
Sigmund Freud
Marcel Duchamp
Marshall McLuhan

Siddartha Gautama
Padmasambhava (who brought
tantra to Tibet)
Francis of Assissi
The Baal Shem Tov
Abigail Adams
Jane Austen
Margaret Chase Smith
(first Senator to publicly
speak out against McCarthy)
Rosa Parks
Nikolai Tesla
Kurt Godel
Bruce Lee
Ursula K. LeGuin
Haruki Murakami
Gibby Haynes
Lux Interior
David Attenborough
William S. Burroughs
Caravaggio
Theodore Geisel (Dr. Seuss)
Henry Thoreau
H.R. Giger
Salvador Dali
Carl Jung
John Lennon
Hunter S. Thompson
Margaret Atwood
E.L. Doctorow
James Joyce
Jiddu Krishnamurti
Shakespeare
David Lynch
Steve Reich
Jean Cocteau
Emma Goldman
bell hooks
Nina Simone
Beth Gibbons
Aretha Franklin
Billy Holiday

Rosalind Franklin
Ada Lovelace
C.S. Lewis.
Chaim Potok
Oscar Wilde
William Wordsworth
Ayn Rand
Anne Lamott
Steve Martin
Woody Allen
Virginia Woolf
Amelia Earhart
Mohandas K. Ghandi
Mark Twain
Malcolm X
Amadeus Mozart
Captain Beefheart (Don Van Vliet)
The Dali Lama
Stephen Hawking
Patti Smith
Maya Deren
Audrey Hepburn
John Coltrane
Jerry Garcia
Kurt Vonnegut
Mark Rothko
Akira Kurosawa
Mary Parker Follett
Ian MacKaye
Ranier Maria Rilke
Robert Pirsig
Ray and Charles Eames
Joan D'Arc
Fred Rogers
Guy Debord
Herman Hesse
Edgar Allan Poe
Michelangelo
David Bowie
John Stewart Mill
Benjamin Franklin
Brion Gysin

Harry Smith	Joseph Cornell
Jack Kirby	Thomas Merton
Stan Lee	Daniel Johnston
Toni Morrison	Christopher Alexander
Andy Warhol	Charles Schulz
Alan Turing	Gary Gygax
John Von Neuman	Stewart Brand
Martin Luther King, Jr.	Bob Dylan
Thomas Paine	Elizabeth Frasier
Brian Eno	Joni Mitchell
Karl Marx	Stephen Jay Gould
Andre Breton	Octavia Butler
Crazy Horse	Johannes Gutenberg
Albert Hoffman	Manfred Clynes
Terrence McKenna	Doug Engelbart
Ram Das	Syd Mead
Friedrich Nietzsche	Frank Herbert
Robert Crumb	
Allen Ginsberg	
Robert Fripp	
Yoko Ono	
Alan Moore	
k.d. lang	
Bruce Springsteen	
Jean Genet	
Walt Whitman	
Jean Arthur Rimbaud	
Jorge Luis Borges	
Giordano Bruno	
Neil Gaiman	
Grace Jones	
Walt Disney	
Queen Elizabeth I	
Archimedes	
Johannes Kepler	
Nicolaus Copernicus	
Sir Richard F. Burton	
J.G. Ballard	
Emily Dickinson	
Jesus Christ	
Andrei Tarkovsky	
Martin Scorsese	

THE WHITE GODDESS

I had an event in my life, an unexpected epiphany, that has become a watermark to my happiness. Of course, celebrations of big milestones, things like my marriage, the birth of my son, are seismic, life-altering events. But this was categorically different. Those were engineered moments of happiness, 21-gun odes to joy; the sorts of experiences that sketch the bold outlines of a life. This was a quiet, gracious moment in which I felt like I had peered under creation's skirt and had caught a glimpse of the underlying beauty of things. Over the years, this experience has acquired almost sacred dimensions. It has even become part of my own mytho-poetic lexicon, what I now refer to as a "white goddess moment."

This very personal, never-before-published piece is my working attempt at defining what this term means to me.

It was soon after my wife, son, and I had moved into our new home. Buying a house, packing up and moving to it and fully *into* it—spreading the collected contents of our lives onto its shelves, into its empty corners, onto its walls—was something none of us had ever experienced. We'd certainly moved, first from a hippie commune in the country (where my wife and I had met) to a group house in the city. Then the whole group had moved to a new house together, and then, from the group we'd moved into our first rental – just our little nuclear family. But this journey had been bigger, and far more perilous. We'd *bought* this place. It was ours. And as trite as it sounds, it really does feel categorically different when you own it (even if that ownership is an illusion cast by the bank).

A few months after we'd moved in, DC had one of its rare serious storms. I don't remember how much, but I remember it being that level of snowfall where the house is completely encased in it, with drifts piled up against outside walls and doors, where the roof becomes heavy and exaggerated with thick slabs of white crystals. But, despite the intimidating weather, we felt cozy inside. Safe. We'd even lit a fire in our "new" gas-powered fireplace, which was anything but new and was a perilous, fire-breathing bitch to light. You had to get your head down below the level of the fiery gas-ball that VOOMED! out dramatically after minutes of it bleeding explosive gases into the room while you tried to light it. We only fired it up four or five times and then got too spooked to try again. Lighting it felt like trying to defuse a bomb. But we didn't know all that at the time – we still had that new homeowner smell — and so, a natural gas fire of ceramic faux-log glowed in all of its Rockwellian charm in our new living room.

The contentment I felt in those days was indescribable. That basic, honest feeling of hearth and home, mother and child. I loved my wife. I loved my son. I loved my work. And now, I had a home I was falling in love with, too; a home that was currently being surrounded by an uninvited superorganism of a bazillion snowflakes. But the warmth inside that house felt like it could heroically melt and destroy any alien invaders.

Late in the evening, before bed, I took my nightly shower. I made the shower extra hot to help soothe the stiffness in my body. After a long day of working, fixing, and unpacking, the hot water felt outrageous on my tired frame. As I stood there in the shower, stretching and groaning like a savanna cat in the sunshine, I looked at the frosted-glass bathroom window. I could make out little drifts of snow against the windowsill and snowflakes hitting and vaporizing against the warmed, milky glass. I wondered if the window could actually open. Probably painted shut, I thought. On a whim, I decided to find out. I unlocked it and pushed hard against the frame. Nothing. Stuck. I banged against the bottom and along the edges to free up where it might be glued tight with paint. I tried again. With some earnest pushing, it finally squeaked to life and cracked opened. Cold air and snowflakes blasted inside and mixed with the steam.

Along with the cold, something else streamed in and overtook me. Silence. It was as deathly-silent in our backyard as it was frozen. A nearly-full, waxing moon made the Earth glow. Everything had been rendered bright-white, smoothed to ambiguousness, and blanketed with a kind of silence so perfect, so pervasive, it had as much dramatic presence as any conceivable sound.

I raised the window as high as it would go and stuck the entire top half of my nakedness outside. The feeling was strange and delectable. My body didn't know what to make of a bottom half that was baking in seriously hot water and a top half that was rapidly venting its heat into a freezing moonlit night. I could see steam pouring off of my skin in dramatic swirls. Icicles rapidly formed on my beard. The feeling was glorious and enchanting, I became giddy and might as well have had Tinker Bell fairies fluttering around me.

When I finally settled into this strange situation, it was the silence that stunned me, a stillness that rapidly quieted my insides. The experience of that deep quiet made me instantly flash back to another time I'd experienced a profound silence in a similar snow-muffled world.

When Blake was maybe three, there had been a similar storm. Pam, myself, and our housemates, Patch and Linda, had dressed our two boys, Blake and Lars, in snowsuits late at night (naughty parents!). We'd all traipsed out into a new snow with not a soul awake, not a flake disturbed. The feeling of softly crunching our way into this magical landscape, with two bewildered little boys, waddling wide-eyed and awkwardly in their puffed-up snowsuits, is something I will never forget. We all struggled to stifle laughter and giggled conversation, lest we disturb the sleeping world around us. At the time, that experience became its own high-happiness watermark. I felt like I had witnessed unspeakable beauty that night, and such familial contentment in experiencing something so "non-ordinary" with my child and our extended family.

Years later, I was reminded that the poet Robert Graves, in his book *The White Goddess*, ascribes the image of the white goddess, the moon goddess, to such profound and fundamental moments that humble with their inspired beauty.

He believed these "goddess moments" to be the underlying subject of all poetry (at least what he called "muse poetry," which he thought was the inspired kind). In his poetic mythos (boiled out from many pagan religions), she is the white goddess because she is the seductive, reflected white light of the moon, and that feeling you get in inspired situations is you catching a glimpse of her otherworldly beauty, the beauty and mystery that underlie all created things. Such inspiration lives in any experience of poetry (in any form) when "the hair stands on end, the eyes water, the throat is constricted, the skin crawls, and a shiver runs down the spine," as Graves put it.

When I re-read of Graves' white goddess, I immediately remembered that night in the shower, and the earlier adventure with the kids in the snow. I started calling these "white goddess moments," anytime I'm brought to my knees by an experience, especially if "apparently unpeopled and eventless," where the "elements bespeak her unseen presence" and I feel like I've had a poetically authentic moment. I'm happy to say I feel my life has been blessed by many such moments, but none have yet rivaled the time I leaked into my snow-covered backyard from my bathroom window.

And if truth be told, in thinking back on this, my highest "white goddess" moment, I realize that the watermark is not that moment in and of itself. It has such significance to me because my relationship with my wife, with our family, probably hit its high watermark that night. That window had never been opened before and it has not been opened since. It's become something of my metaphorical "window onto Eden" (as William Blake called it), my window onto paradise.

It may sound silly to want to mark such a peak moment with a ritual gesture – shouldn't such a moment be its own celebration? But I have a plan for how I want to ritually acknowledge such a future high watermark of joy and contentment in my life, should I be fortunate enough to reach one. I will wait until there's a full moon, maybe it will again be winter, with new-fallen snow on the ground. In the dead of a gloriously black and still night, I will climb back into my shower and I will open my paint-sticky window onto Eden. I will then unfold my nakedness out, up, and into the stars, and there I will once again kiss The Blessed Lady…

The White Goddess.

BREAD OF THE SNOWPOCALYPSE

I've always been attracted to the ancient roots, the homely honesty, of bread. When I first moved to Twin Oaks Community, I lived in a satellite group, called Tupelo. The first Tupelo house was on an old farm that adjoined the main T.O. property. For the farmhouse, we purchased a gorgeous antique cast iron wood-burning stove that I lobbied obnoxiously hard for. I really wanted it to be our sole stove, but less ridiculous heads prevailed. It was purchased under the condition that it was to be set up on the back porch and used as our secondary stove. Few others in the group ever bothered with it. I cooked my weekly meals and baked goods on it. Given my pushing so hard for it, I tried to love it. But it was, in practice, a royal pain to operate; it felt like you were basically trying to cook dinner on the surface of the sun. It had two temperature settings: stone cold and Hades hot. I eventually tamed that old iron devil and made some pretty righteous apple pies and breads within its hell-fire. But truth be told, when I finally moved to the main community and "graduated" to a professional-kitchen gas stove and a giant Hobart mixer, I was thrilled. After I left the farm and moved to Arlington, I did very little baking. After the snow-bread episode described here,

I went on another baking jag for awhile, but have since fallen off the bread wagon again.

There is something fundamentally human about baking bread. It feels inextricably woven into the fabric of human history, to civilization, to the land, and to human communion. There's also something undeniably sensual about the process of making it, the life of the yeast, the soft, silky feel of the dough, the smell of it baking, and those first warm bites. This all might sound corny to some, but then, I bet you're not a bread baker.

This piece originally appeared on the *MAKE* blog, in February, 2010, during that year's record-breaking snowstorm. It was also used as one of the "Snowpocalypse" stories for a BLUEBRAIN video/music performance for the end-of-summer "White Party" at DC's The Phillips Collection art museum, in August of that same year.

It's been a very "exciting" few days here in the icy wilds of Northern Virginia. The DC area has been ground zero for the storm of the century, with back-to-back blizzards making this the snowiest winter on record for the Mid-Atlantic region.

The landscape around my house is, well… snowpocalyptic — giant drifts overcome fences, a totally collapsed, roofed trellis litters my neighbor's backyard, and a relentless wind whips up powder into white-out conditions. I have to admit, it's actually turned scary. Wednesday morning, I had to muscle and kick my way through banks of snow pressing up against both my front and back storm doors to pry them open. I haven't been near a grocery store since the first drubbing, but friends who have say it's like something out of a zombie film, with aisles of empty shelves and bug-eyed humans running around grabbing anything edible they can gather up in their arms.

If this keeps up, I might end up one of the shambling horde myself, moaning for food. I'm running low on supplies. I ran out of bread a few days ago (which took french toast, tuna sandwiches, and peanut butter and jelly off of the menu).

Last night, I'm sitting here thinking: Wait, I might be able to bake bread. I doubt I have all the ingredients, but I'll check.

The available supplies in my cupboard were sad. I found one sack of flour that was impressively rancid, but then, miraculously I found another, in an airtight bag. It smelled okay (even though it was at least a year old). I then pried up some yeast packets stuck to an unidentifiable goo on the door of my fridge. According to the info stamped on the packets, they were three years old. I wondered how many yeastie beasties were still viable in there. And then there were the crystallized hunks of honey in a forlorn-looking plastic bear with his nose punched in.

From the cookbooks on the counter, I dug out my old *Tassajara Bread Book*. Back in my communal youth, I knew the recipes in this book like daily-recited mantras and did some sweet-ass baking for a hundred hungry hippies. I was convinced the resulting bread would likely be a dense, brick-like disaster, but I had nothing to lose except time (and I had that stocked in abundance). I combined the flour, the yeast, and warm water, the honey (after I'd dissolved it over heat), and some oil. A bunch of kneading, rising, punching, and more rising later, and I had high hopes for the two respectable-looking loaves I was popping into the oven. As they baked, and I blogged—the wind whistling around and under my sun-porch home office—the smell of the bread was indescribable. Maybe it was driven by an unusual sense of need, stuck here in my cottage on ice, or the fact that I hadn't baked bread in close to a decade (outside of a bread machine — which is really a robot baking it for you), but these loaves smelled like all good things kneaded into one. If there's truth in wine, there's bosomy comfort in baking bread.

Amazingly, what I eventually pulled from the oven didn't look half bad. And let me tell you, they tasted even better. I speak in the past tense 'cause way too much of the first loaf is already nourishing my wind-whipped soul. I froze the second loaf.

Now I'm antsy to make something else with the limited provisions I have left. Tonight, looking through *Tassajara*, I realized I have everything I need to make cinnamon rolls. That'll be tomorrow night's cabin-fevered entertainment. So, grab a shovel, slip on your snowshoes, hop onto the snowmobile, and head on over for sweet rolls! PLEASE? It's getting really lonely here and the wind is creaking the snow-laden roof of my house in new and entirely unsettling ways.

The Marriage of Heaven and Hell (Copy I, 1827), an early example of Blake's invented technique of illuminated printing and something of a proto-zine/chapbook, with different writing styles, voices, postures, rants, and aphorisms.

WILLIAM BLAKE: PATRON SAINT OF MAKERS

William Blake. William Blake. William Blake. My family and friends (and social media friends, fans, and followers) are painfully aware of my seemingly inexhaustible prattling about William Blake. You don't have to hang around me for long before you'll hear a dropped Blake quote here, a verse of poetry there, or me quickly drawing some Blakean analogy for whatever we're discussing.

The sad thing (for me) is that a lot of this falls on tin ears. Anything by or about Blake seems to have the uncanny ability of taxing the attention spans of all but a stalwart few. I can almost count the seconds before I see eyes glaze over and begin to dart side-to-side in a panic, hands creeping toward smartphones itching to be checked for the latest likes and alerts. Over the years, I've come to think of understanding Blake and his art as probably analogous to learning a new language. You can't just "speak" Blake overnight (or understand him being spoken). This is, of course, the case with any artist, thinker, or crazy person who's created his or her own complex cosmology, as Blake did. So when people hear me frequently referencing Blake, I imagine what they hear is, say, Latin or German (or the adults in

Charlie Brown cartoons). They think "Oh God, he's speaking that foreign language again that I don't understand or really care about. HELP!" And away go their attention spans – "Hey, look, new kitty cat memes on Facebook! LOL!"

A relatively new friend recently asked me how I got interested in Blake. As I recount in this piece, it was actually through the work of anthropologist and co-founder of the science of cybernetics, Gregory Bateson. In reading Bateson, and listening to his lectures, he frequently mentioned and quoted Blake and seemed to imply that there was some real resonance between his work and Blake's. I couldn't imagine how this might be the case. How could there be significant commonality between an athiest scientist, naturalist, and pioneer of cybernetics, and a strange, maladjusted, mystical Christian artist from the turn of the 19th century who hallucinated angels and whose poetry we were forced to memorize in high school? So, I went to Blake looking for what connected him to Gregory Bateson and the things that were significant to me about Bateson's work. Since one of Bateson's memorable maxims was to look for the "patterns that connect" ("...the orchid to the primrose and the dolphin to the whale and all four of them to me") this seemed like a worthy quest. That quest has now consumed the better part of my adult life and my interest in Blake has long ago overtaken my interest in Bateson. And yes, now I completely understand what connects the two of them and their seemingly disparate ideas together. But I'll leave you to go on that quest yourself—connecting them to each other, and them to me, and me to you.

This piece originally appeared in *MAKE* Volume 17, the Lost Knowledge issue (aka the steampunk issue), which I guest edited. I thought it entirely appropriate to put the work of William Blake within the context of the crazed, creative re-imaginings of Victorian science, technology, and culture represented by the steampunk maker scene of 2009.

For the past 25 years, nearly every day, I've interacted with "the mad English poet" (as some contemporary detractors dubbed him) William Blake in some fashion. I poke my nose into one of the dozens of books I've collected, or I whisper (or shout to the rafters) a poem, or I chew on some gristly hunk of his ridiculously complex mytho-poetic cosmology.

For someone with the attention span of a four-year-old, having anything captivate me to such an extent is downright alarming. Equally strange is the fact that, I'm a writer. I live to communicate my ideas and experiences to others, yet I've never published a word about Blake until now.

Why am I so fascinated by this apocalyptic, outsider artist (in his day, anyway) whose work still defies full comprehension? What keeps me coming back?

In this article, I'll explain a little of Blake's invented printing method and make a case for why I think he's a perfect candidate for Patron Saint of Makers.

WILLIAM BLAKE, 18TH-CENTURY ZINE PUBLISHER

I was introduced to William Blake in British Lit class in high school, but ironically, it was during the desktop publishing revolution of the mid-1980s that I started to understand what he was really all about.

I came to the real Blake by way of cybernetics pioneer Gregory Bateson. Bateson was fascinated by how Blake famously "mixed up" modes of perception in his work; Blake claimed he possessed something called "fourfold vision" and that he could see things on different levels of awareness simultaneously.

Bateson had studied schizophrenia for the Veterans Administration and discovered that, similarly, schizophrenics confuse and conflate, for instance, the literal and the metaphorical; they don't organize thoughts, communication, and perceptions into logical categories the same way that non-schizophrenics do.

Blake also seemed to leak at the margins separating these logical types of communication and awareness. Of course, one can argue that all artists do this, but it's the extremes of the leakage in Blake's work, the sheer quantity, and the complexity of it (and its surprising coherence, if you stick around long enough to sort it out) that makes Blake so compelling. Bateson was also intrigued by how functional Blake was while living in his world of perceptual and categorical mashups.

As I began to delve deeper into Blake, one day I had something of an epiphany. I'd gotten a lovely two-volume set of his most popular works: Songs of Innocence and Songs of Experience, two of his masterpieces of "illuminated printing," a technique of free-form engraving, painting, and printing he'd invented.

Up until his discovery, illustration engraving and book printing were two separate disciplines, with the engravings etched, printed, and later, tipped into the books as plates. By combining these two arts on the page, Blake's technique freed him to write text, compose pages, design typography, and paint illustrations, right on the copper printing plates.

I was reading about all of this while working on an art and technology zine I was publishing, called *Going Gaga*, using an Apple Mac SE running PageMaker layout software. I was doing a lot of the writing, designing, even some of the illustrations, right in PageMaker, and printing out my zine on the Canon copier sitting next to my Mac. I realized that Blake had experienced the power of a different, but surprisingly analogous, set of media tools and had felt a similar sense of explosive creative freedom, more than 200 years earlier. William Blake had been a proto-zine publisher! William Blake was a multimedia artist![1]

"ON ENGLAND'S PLEASANT PASTURES SEEN"

William Blake was born on Nov. 28, 1757, in Soho, London, in a modest apartment above his father's hosiery shop. His parents were devoutly religious, but they were Dissenters (and at least his mother was probably a Moravian), nonconformists who opposed the established Church of England and its hierarchy. From an early age, Blake proclaimed religious visions, that he could see angels and other nonphysical entities. His father tried to beat such nonsense out of him.

Aside from punishment for seeing apparitions, Blake's early childhood was rather peaceful, even bucolic, as he wandered through fields on the outskirts of London, swam in farm ponds, haunted printmakers' shops, read the classics and the Bible, and studied as much art as he could get his hands on.

The rest of his life found him living through some of the most tumultuous times imaginable, including the American and French revolutions, great scientific and naturalistic discoveries, the dawning of the Industrial Revolution, and all the intellectual ferment and cultural activity excited by such seismic shifts.

It's no wonder that Blake's subject matter was so epic, so apocalyptic — all fire, upheaval, and psychic magma on the one hand, and Eden-like dreamscapes on the other. He saw tremendous potential in humanity and in the power of big ideas — and he dreamed of all of it coming to flower in his beloved Albion.[2] But he also saw the horrors of war, poverty, and class division, of state and religious intolerance, and the shortcomings of science and reason when divorced from imagination and wonder.

Blake showed artistic promise at a very young age and was enrolled in drawing school at age 10. At 14, his father, ever the pragmatic tradesman, wanted his son to know a durable trade, so he signed him up as an engraver's apprentice, where he labored for seven long years. It was as an engraver that Blake developed a lifelong love for Gothic art and architecture and for the nobility of the engraver's and printmaker's arts (though he resented being forever identified solely by those trades).

In 1779, at 21, Blake was accepted into the recently formed Royal Academy of Arts. He quickly found himself at odds with the teachings of the school and its first president, Sir Joshua Reynolds. Reynolds would become a lifelong artistic foil for Blake, a two-dimensional symbol of everything he found wrong about establishment art and art that generalizes, abstracts, and handily categorizes; art that no longer "rouses the faculties to act."

BLAKE DREAMS A NEW METHOD OF PRINTING

In 1788, Blake claimed he'd been visited in a dream by his dead beloved brother Robert (who'd recently died of consumption) and shown a revolutionary new printing technique.

Unlike traditional engraving, where the image outline is scratched into a plate prepared with an acid-resistant waxy "ground" and then the lines are exposed to acid, Blake's technique worked in reverse. The area to be printed was painted over with the acid-resist ground and then the plate was exposed to acid, eating away everything that was not the image.

After etching, he would touch up the image and clean the copper plates with his engraver's tools before printing the pages on a rolling press and then (usually) coloring the printed pages with watercolors.

For Blake, "illuminated printing" was the artistic breakthrough of a lifetime, "a method of combining the Painter and the Poet."

Anyone who's looked closely at traditional engraving tools and techniques can appreciate how painstaking, labor-intensive, and constraining the process is (a square inch of engraving can take hours). Now, imagine a method of engraving that combines text and artwork, where creation happens right on the plate, where it is literally brushed and drawn on, using traditional artist's tools.

Imagine how excited Blake must have been by such a discovery. Unlike traditional engraving, which was largely a copyist medium, a means of reproduction, Blake's new illuminated printing was a means of original production where you could compose your ideas, paint them, right onto the printing plate.

To get a better idea of how illuminated printing worked, in 1979, Blake scholar Joseph Viscomi had a series of photos taken by Todd Weinstein in his New York studio. They were part of Viscomi's attempt at preparing, executing, and printing a relief-etched facsimile of plate 10 of *The Marriage of Heaven and Hell* (1790). Blake wrote little about his technique, so his process is not exactly known. Few of his plates survive. Tragically, they were mainly sold for scrap metal after his death. Scholars such as Viscomi have managed to reverse-engineer the process and they think it went something like the sequence that Viscomi and Weinstein captured.

[Author's Note: MAKE was given special permission to reprint the images from this etching experiment for my piece in the magazine. You can see these lovely and vivid color images on the magazine's companion website at makezine.com/go/blake.]

FROM THE FIRE OF LOS' FORGE: PREPARING THE METAL

In Blake's poetic mythology, our inner poet/creative genius is named Los (likely "Sol," or sun, spelled backwards). Los is a blacksmith, and given the preparations required to create the plates that Blake regularly worked on, it's not hard to see how he would have made the connection between this preparation and the roots of his creations, both literally and figuratively. Copper sheets had to be hammered out and cut into smaller plates—planed, washed, polished.

RAISING UP HIS VOICE: PAINTING THE TEXT AND ART

Once the plate was prepared, Blake painted the text and artwork onto the copper surface with quills and brushes, using an "impervious fluid" that would resist the acid to which the plate would be subjected. For this, he used "stop-out," an asphalt-based varnish found in traditional engraving, used to cover already-etched lines to prevent them from being further "bitten" into during successive etchant baths.

Because the designs would be transferred onto paper in an engraver's press, the art and text all had to be painted in reverse. While Blake was already used to reverse composition in engraving, he raised free-form mirror writing and mirror painting to an art form in itself. (For a man who believed it was a mission for each of us in life to do everything in our power to keep our minds awake, our imaginations expansive, and to look at things from multiple points of view, conceiving and visualizing everything backward must have been a great "mind hack" in support of this worldview!)

"MELTING THE METALS INTO LIVING FLUIDS:" ETCHING

With the image painted onto the copper with impervious liquid, Blake would then create a dike around the outside edges of the plate with walls of soft wax. This allowed him to pour a bath of "aqua fortis" (nitric acid) onto its surface. As the corrosive acid bit into the exposed metal, Blake would hover over the plates like some Shakespearean witch, using a bird feather to keep the acid agitated and to stir away bubbles as they formed.

The process, with its noxious fumes, was not pleasant. Some have even suggested that the liver failure that finally took Blake's life may have been the result of "copper intoxication." It's no wonder that he called this an "infernal process," and that in his satirical masterpiece, *The Marriage of Heaven and Hell*, he located his printshop in hell.

With his penchant for leaking margins between modes of perception, Blake proclaimed that what he was really doing in his artistic process was "melting apparent surfaces away, and displaying the infinite which was hid."

After the etching was complete, he would remove the acid and the wax dike, rinse off the ink with turpentine, and polish the plate before inking.

"WITHOUT CONTRARIES IS NO PROGRESSION:" INKING

Ink was applied to the etched copper plate with a flat-bottomed linen dabber wetted with engraver's ink. The ink was made of a powdered pigment mixed with burnt linseed or walnut oil. For multicolored prints, Blake would use smaller dabbers or brushes to apply spot colors to desired areas of the plates.

"IN WHICH KNOWLEDGE IS TRANSMITTED FROM GENERATION TO GENERATION:" PRINTING THE PLATES

Blake's wife, Catherine, was his assistant in hell's printing house and she was especially adept at printing and hand-coloring the printed pages. They used an engraver's press (with the plate and paper on a bed that passes between two heavy rollers when the press is cranked). Blake would ink and deliver the plates to the bed and Catherine would place the paper, blankets, and backing sheets.

Given the metalwork, caustic chemicals, oily inks, and other "infernal" aspects of the process handled by William, and the pristine and expensive white paper delivered by the lovely Catherine, it's no wonder that he saw their extreme roles as a symbolic expression of the dynamic, two-toned, yin/yang life process, his "marriage of heaven and hell."

"EXUBERANCE IS BEAUTY:" HAND-COLORING THE PRINTS

For his illuminated books, Blake and Catherine would hand-color the printed pages with watercolors to complete an edition. Some editions, and individual copies, were painted very simply, others more elaborately.

Over the years, Blake also changed, sometimes dramatically, the ways he colored the manuscripts. This could depend on his mood, or whether he desired to bring out some aspect of the work in a specific copy he was creating. This has allowed connoisseurs of Blake's work to enjoy, interpret, and heatedly debate multiple versions of the same work from countless perspectives, something that surely would have thrilled Blake.

CREATE! THE END IS NEAR!

During his lifetime, Blake was uncompromising in his work and what he wanted to say with it. His art is so dramatic, so muscular and apocalyptic, because he felt an overwhelming sense of urgency. One can almost picture him as a crazy person on a street corner, wearing a sandwich board, waving around dirty fistfuls of doomsday pamphlets.

But instead of proclaiming "Repent, sinners! The end is near!" Blake's message was more like: "Wake up! There's an artist, a genius, asleep inside of you! Don't let the world lull you to sleep. Create! Wake up! Be the artist you were born to be!"

And that message, steadfastly encoded like a fractal, endlessly reiterating itself at every level of his work, is what makes William Blake a worthy saint of makers, of all active creators.

Blake called his illuminated prints "windows into Eden." They were designed to function something like stained glass windows, so you can see through them to something on the other side. What he hoped you'd catch a glimpse of there was your own creativity, your own "poetic genius," the "Los" within you. Blake didn't want to create work for you to passively consume; he wanted to create work that would inspire you to make something yourself!

Blake's early biographer, Alexander Gilchrist, said: "Never before surely was a man so literally the author of his own book." Blake was self-taught in every discipline but engraving; during his lifetime, he was a painter, poet, essayist, author, inventor, philosopher, engraver, printer, calligrapher, graphic designer, bookbinder, singer, songwriter, and metalsmith (to name but a few).

One of Blake's best-known quotations is, "I must create my own system or be enslaved by another man's." And there is no more of an ultimate "maker" statement than that.

Special thanks:

Information about Blake's printing technique used in this article comes from the article "Illuminated Printing" by Joseph Viscomi, available at the William Blake Archive (*blakearchive.org*). Many thanks to Professor Viscomi for providing the images used in the MAKE piece (which can be seen here: *makezine.com/go/blake*)

Endnotes:

1. Some scholars have even argued that Blake was a hypermedia artist. *Songs of Innocence and Songs of Experience* are not only two poetic cycles connected to one another, with a poem relating to youth and innocence, and a complementary one to age and experience, but they also contain additional images and textual passages that thread together in ways similar to linked content in a modern hypermedia document.

2. Albion is the ancient name for Britain. In Blake's mythology, it also represented the "cosmic man," the being who splinters through space-time, falls from grace, and yearns for unity in a new Jerusalem. Oh, and BTW, Jerusalem is also the female aspect/consort of Albion. Blake, you dirty boy!

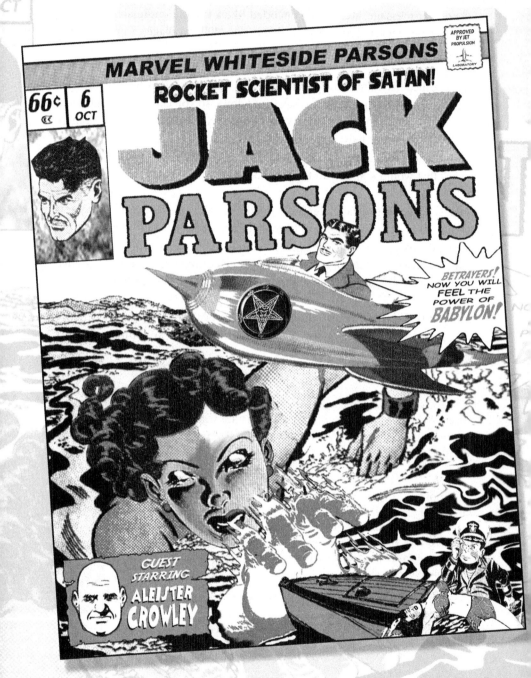

DARKSIDE ROCKETEER

Jack Parsons, the space pioneer history would rather forget.

Jack Parsons fascinates me. I knew little about him before the late 90s, when I read a piece in *21C* magazine, Richard Metzger's "John W. Parsons Anti-Christ Superstar." What blipped him even more brightly on my radar was George Pendle's excellent 2006 biography *Strange Angel: The Otherworldly Life of John Whiteside Parsons* (and also John Carter's *Sex and Rockets: The Occult World of Jack Parsons*). Since then, I've read everything I can find on Parsons, have started a modest collection of books, magazines, art, media, and memorabilia associated with him, and have even spent the last five years writing a novel which uses his life as a springboard for my story.

There are many reasons why Parsons holds such a fascination, including numerous parallels in our lives. We both grew up immersed in rocketry, sci-fi, and the occult, we're both over-the-top romantics, he suffered from dyslexia, and so do I, and neither of us went to college (something of an embarrassment to both of us). We both also attempted to summon the Devil when we were teens. He claims to have succeeded and the experience spooked him for many years to come. I just got really hoarse from Cookie Monster-like barking of my infernal summons, like some wannabe vocalist in a black metal band. I was also heavily involved in Wicca as a teen, a movement that post-dates Parsons, but only because he died before his plans to launch a new pagan religion, called The Witchcraft, were ever realized. If he'd lived, and The Witchcraft had been established as planned, Parsons might now be known as the father of modern witchcraft, instead of Gerald Gardner, who basically birthed the Wicca movement with the 1954 publication of *Witchcraft Today.* (Parsons died in 1952.)

When this piece was published in *MAKE*, I got a congratulatory call from *MAKE* founder and publisher, Dale Dougherty. He didn't know anything about Parsons beforehand and loved the fact that Parsons had done so much, gone so far as an amateur scientist, with no formal training, no money, just a lot of fearlessness and an unwillingness to give up. During that conversation, Dale said something that made lights go off in my head: "I bet he would've loved Burning Man!" Dale had no idea how right-on that statement was. He knew nothing of Parsons' passion for art, his Libertarian writings, his penchant for drugs, his deep love of the desert, and his dedicated bohemian lifestyle.

I got off the phone with Dale and began sketching out a talk and slideshow, based on the following article and other details from Parsons' life. I call it *Jack Parsons: The Original Burning Man* and have now presented it several times to very positive reviews. (BTW: There's a sick joke in my title, given how Parsons sadly met his end. How? Read on.)

When I was 12 years old, I was vice president of the Chester, Virginia Rocketry Society. This was no great political feat, as we had all of four members, but the point is, I lived and breathed rocketry. Almost literally. The smell of spent motor casings can still trigger Proustian memories. One whiff and I'm back in Virginia farm fields, 12-volt car batteries sparking Estes rocket motors to life, as we loft our latest affronts to aerodynamics and gravity into blue October skies. I read everything I could get my hands on about rocketry and space. I knew all sorts of relevant facts, figures, and key historical personalities. And yet, I never bumped into anything about one of the men chiefly responsible for solid rocket motor technology. His name was John Whiteside Parsons, but he went by Jack.

Apparently I'm not alone in my ignorance. I took a straw poll of friends and colleagues, and only a few had ever heard of Jack Parsons. Fewer still knew anything more than "Didn't he have something to do with JPL?"

Anyone who knew anything seemed to get it from a recent biography, George Pendle's *Strange Angel: The Otherworldly Life of Rocket Scientist John Whiteside Parsons*, which is also how my ignorance of this space pioneer was finally lifted. Turns out it's the "strange" part of the man's life that has probably fouled his scientific legacy.

Marvel Whiteside Parsons, later mercifully renamed John (and then nicknamed Jack), was born Oct. 2, 1914, in Los Angeles. His parents had recently moved to California to pursue their dreams. When the marriage went south, Jack and his mother moved north, into his well-to-do grandparents' Italian-style villa in Pasadena. Jack enjoyed a charmed childhood, with all of the trappings of wealth. Busch Gardens was behind his house, and close by was the Arroyo Seco, a natural playground of rock canyons and chaparral-covered slopes, a fantasyland right out of the Old West. As Pendle points out in *Strange Angel*, growing up in these sheltered environs, it's no surprise that Jack's imagination developed unconstrained by reality. This freedom to dream was only magnified when, at 12, Parsons discovered Hugo Gernsback's *Amazing Stories* magazine, and through its pulp sci-fi pages, an intense desire to reach the stars.

GAGA OVER ROCKETS

As a kid, Parsons began trying to build his own rockets, first deconstructing black powder fireworks and packing his own motors. When he reached junior high and found that others didn't share his bookish or geeky interests, things looked grim, until he met Edward Forman, an older student who would become Jack's lifelong friend and fellow rocket pioneer.

Ed Forman was not of Jack's social class. He came from a Missouri farm family who'd recently moved to California. The family ended up homeless for a time, living in the Arroyo Seco, until they found a place. The two boys discovered they shared many things. Both suffered from dyslexia, both read science fiction, and both were gaga over rockets. Soon they embarked on a two-man space race, egging each other on with bigger and bolder rockets.

As the boys grew from teens into young men, they continued to raise the stakes on their rocketry experiments. Parsons went to college for a time, while Forman went to work as a machinist. To try and save enough money to continue college, Parsons got a job working at an explosives factory. Here he discovered an uncanny affinity for chemistry, developing an encyclopedic knowledge of chemicals and chemical theory. Parsons and Forman combined their growing expertise to push the envelope even further.

But they soon discovered that, to go any further, they'd need to test the thrusts generated by different fuel mixtures. They didn't have the equipment or the math skills. It was this need for new collaborators that brought them, in 1935, to the doorstep of the California Institute of Technology. There they met Frank Malina, a graduate student also keen on space.

With the chemist Parsons, the machinist Forman, and the mathematician Malina, and the resources of Caltech at hand, they were poised for something big. But storming the beachheads of heaven didn't come easily.

While they managed to get the attention and enthusiastic blessings of world-renowned aerodynamicist Theodore von Kármán, director of Caltech's Guggenheim Aeronautical Laboratory (GALCIT) — no small victory for two young men without degrees — there was no funding. Supported solely by after-hours Caltech resources, junkyard finds, and their own money, they began years of intense, often harrowing, testing of various solid and liquid fuel mixtures.

RUN FOR THEIR LIVES!

The group, dubbed the GALCIT Rocket Research Group, undertook its first serious test, of a gaseous oxygen and methanol motor, on Oct. 31, 1936. Fittingly, they set up the test in the Arroyo Seco. The first test didn't go so well (picture the cartoonish image of rocketeers running for their lives while being "chased" by a flailing hose of ignited oxygen). But they learned a few things. A photo was taken that day, of the group relaxing before the fireworks. This frozen moment is now considered the "nativity scene" for the Jet Propulsion Laboratory (JPL), which these men would soon found.

The team would continue testing throughout 1936 and into '37. Given their raucous tests in the Arroyo Seco, and what von Kármán referred to as the "unnerving explosions of Parsons' rockets" resonating through the campus, the group was given a nicknamed of the Suicide Squad. Then, in 1938, Uncle Sam paid a visit to von Kármán.

The Army Air Corps had taken an interest in GALCIT's rockets. Specifically, they were interested in using rocket motors to assist heavy bombers taking off from island runways in the Pacific. The Suicide Squad had a job, and a budget, first $1,000, then $10,000. Back they went to Arroyo Seco, this time leasing land from the City of Pasadena (the plot where JPL stands today). Where the group had previously focused on liquid fuels, they now began to seek suitable solid-fuel concoctions that were up to their task. Parsons, the brilliant chemist, set to work.

By 1941, rocket history was about to be made. No one had yet figured out how to achieve a controlled, directed burn of a solid-fuel rocket, one long enough and powerful enough to do something like helping lift an airplane. How could you pack fuel into a motor casing seamlessly enough to form a gas-tight seal so that combustion wouldn't occur through fissures or between the fuel and the casing?

Parsons tried many materials, eventually coming up with something he called GALCIT 27 (the 27th formulation), nicknamed "the Goop." As Pendle jokes in *Strange Angel*, the ingredients read like the contents of a schoolboy's desk: amide black powder, cornstarch, ammonium nitrate, and stationery glue, with blotting paper used as the bond between the fuel and the 1'-long steel casing. The Goop was packed into the casing in 1" increments to maximize material density. Static tests showed they could get a controlled burn of 28lbs of thrust for 12 seconds. It was time to strap their motors onto a plane to see what would happen.

On Aug. 6, 1941, the Squad showed up at March Air Force Base with a truckload of motors that Parsons had struggled to keep from exploding in the back as they bounded down bumpy dirt roads. Static tests with rockets bolted to a single-engine Ercoupe airplane worked perfectly, but an in-flight test ended in one of the motors exploding. When the group reconvened two days later, both ground and air tests ended in explosions.

Finally, Parsons figured out that as the motors "cured," fissures formed, and the fuel pulled away from the case, allowing combustion to race through the fuel, expanding, turning motors into bombs.

The motors would need to be freshly packed. His breakthrough came just in time. The scheduled rocket-powered takeoff was on Aug. 12. With military brass, Caltech students, and others looking on, the tests were a roaring success. A normal 580' takeoff in 13.1 seconds was reduced to 300' in 7.5 seconds. America's first rocket program, the Jet-Assisted Take-Off (or JATO), was underway.

FADING FROM HISTORY

This moment in aerospace history was also encoded in a photo. It also perhaps represents the moment Jack Parsons begins fading from history. The image, found in history books and on the website of Aerojet Corporation (the aerospace firm the Squad also founded), shows the team standing around a plane wing, von Kármán in the center, feigning equations for the camera. Parsons is there, but for some reason, he's been cropped from the shot. Only the tip of his nose is visible (in some versions of the shot). It's unclear whether this was intentional or not, but it is emblematic of the historical cropping to come.

Parsons would go on to make other critical advances in rocketry, the most important of which was castable, case-bonded solid fuels, first using asphalt (as both binder and fuel) and potassium perchlorate (as oxidizer). This technology is still in use today, in the space shuttle's solid rocket boosters (SRBs). The science of rocketry owes a great debt to Marvel John "Jack" Whiteside Parsons. So why the cold shoulder?

When Parsons wasn't trying to reach the stars in a rocket ship, he was charting a far different course, using the ancient "technologies" of occult magicians. Parsons was a follower of the notorious British occultist Aleister Crowley, aka "The Beast." Parsons was even seen by Crowley for a time as his protégé, the person who'd birth Crowley's new religion, Thelema, in the United States. To this end, Parsons ran the Agape Lodge, a Pasadena commune of sorts, known for its wild parties, dark occult rites, drug use, and bed-swapping couples.

As the successes of the Suicide Squad's rockets mounted, and JPL and Aerojet rapidly expanded — and as rocket science in general grew in respectability — Parsons' private life became an increasing liability. He was sidelined, bought out. And things only seemed to crash and burn from there. Parsons' close friend and fellow magician, L. Ron Hubbard (yes, *that* L. Ron Hubbard) allegedly ran off to Florida with Parsons' girlfriend and money from his shares of Aerojet to start a yacht sales business. Parsons was disowned by his "magical father," Crowley, who died shortly after. He worked in the film industry doing pyrotechnics and dreamed of starting his own explosives company in Mexico. He was likely packing for a trip there when, in June 1952, an explosion in his home lab killed him.

Given Parson's chemistry knowledge and his decades of handling volatiles, some suspected foul play, or suicide, or otherworldy forces. But as Pendle told me, "The simplest solution tends to be the best — and the simplest solution is that a can of fulminate of mercury slipped out of his hand during an experiment. Parsons had worked for so long and with such success with chemicals that he no longer saw them as being particularly hazardous."

Parsons embodied the heart and soul of independent science. One of the reasons von Kármán invited young Jack and Ed into the hallowed halls of Caltech was that he saw in them the type of untarnished dreamers that make novel discoveries. Unfortunately, it was that same dogged determination, that same deep desire to stretch human horizons, that led Parsons down a darker, more serpentine path in his inner life.

But have history's authors intentionally sought to sideline Jack Parsons? In the internet age, his marginalization is due partly to the sensational side of his life: a net search finds the few fragments about his rocketry wortk buried amongst the occult, the Hollywood Babylon, and the Scientological. Yet even official histories of rocketry, the space program, and World War II aviation barely mention him.

Aerojet, the company he co-founded, doesn't mention him at all; the picture on their history web page is the famous cropped one. JPL's site also has few references. Pendle claims that when JPL's archivist, the late Dr. John Bluth, tried to gather material on the Suicide Squad, he discovered that most of their papers, drawings, and notes had been used as insulation, to plug up holes in leaky building walls.

Pendle neatly sums up why Parsons frequently is found swept under the rug of history:

"Rocketry underwent fundamental change within Parsons' lifetime, transformed from sci-fi fantasy to an integral part of the military-industrial complex (where it remained until recent private space endeavors). A lightness of spirit was lost in this transition; a certain sense of humor and individualistic attitude, which Parsons and the Suicide Squad encapsulated, all but disappeared. The space race, despite being built on the ultimate boy's fantasy of exploring outer space, came to be treated as a curiously nationalistic form of science. And nothing could undermine JPL's seriousness more (nor weaken its ability to attract investment) than to declare that its founder was a sci-fi-inspired occultist communist who had never been to university."

Perhaps it is those private space endeavors, and the resurging interest in the DIY ethos in general, that will rekindle interest in Jack Parsons, so that the next generation of rocket geeks will easily recognize his name alongside those of Goddard, Oberth, von Braun, Tsiolkovsky, Musk, and Rutan.

###

JACK PARSONS' ADVENTURES IN INNER SPACE

The life of Jack Parsons was colorful, to say the least. He lived equally in a world of science and science fiction, ancient magic and modernism. He recited hymns to the great god Pan before his rocket tests and liked to perform his magical rituals underneath the high-intensity power lines of the Mojave Desert.

Artist Howard Hallis captures the crazier dimensions of Jack's world in this faux comic cover (see opening illustration). It depicts an alleged scene from Parsons' life. Scientology founder L. Ron Hubbard is said to have run off to Florida with Parsons' girlfriend and his life savings, money Parsons got after being bought out of Aerojet to save them from the embarrassment of his sex, drugs, and rock 'n' roll (OK, romantic classical) lifestyle.

When Parsons showed up, Hubbard tried to flee a Florida marina in his yacht. As the apocryphal story goes, Parsons evoked the Martian demon Bartzabel from his hotel room balcony. A freak squall suddenly blasted across Hubbard's boat, ripping off the sail and forcing him back to shore. Parsons was waiting for them when they made port.

That's Hubbard in the boat with Betty Northrup, Parsons' ex-girlfriend (um ... who was also his sister-in-law), and that's the fiery hand of the sacred whore of "Babalon" attacking the boat.

Photo: Larry Burrows, 1950; Time & Life Pictures/Getty Images

THE ACCIDENTAL PIONEER

How a neurophysiologist's experiments in brain behavior created the first autonomous robots

Anyone who knows me knows that I have a "thing" for robots. Some people have spirit animals, totems. R2-D2 is my spirit animal. Because I wrote a how-to book on robots (2003's *Absolute Beginner's Guide to Building Robots*), everybody thinks I'm an expert on the subject. I have a confession – I don't know nearly as much about robots as you think I do. Here's how this happened: Throughout the 90s, I'd reported a lot on the field of robotics for magazines like *Wired, Yahoo! Internet Life*, and *Esquire*. Eventually, I got a call from Que Publishing, asking if I could write a how-to book on robots, I jumped at the chance – 'cause I needed the money, not because I really knew what I was talking about. I'd done some dabbling in hobby robotics over the years, but that was about it. The same thing had happened in the early 90s, my *Mosaic Quick Tour,* the very first book written about the Web. A (now-defunct) publisher, Ventana, who was familiar with my work at *Wired* and *bOING bOING,* called and asked if I could write a book on the World Wide Web... in 30 days! "Sure!," I enthused, "No problem," again because I needed the money. I got off the phone and said to my wife: "I'm not even sure I know what the World Wide Web is." But I wrote both books and they did quite well. A few months after the robot book came out, within the same day, I got email from a 13-year-old grade school student who'd entered one of the projects from the book into the school science fair, and won, and a cybernetics professor from the UK informing me that he was using it as a textbook in his classes and begging me to write a companion *Absolute Beginner's Guide to Artificial Intelligence.* A writer lives for days like that. While I might not have been sufficiently knowledgeable about robots and the web before these projects, what I think I'm good at is learning on demand and clearly documenting what I'm learning. As Kata Sutra, *Beyond Cyberpunk's* cartoon mascot, likes to say: "You can go anywhere and do anything if you look important and carry a clipboard." I carry a mean clipboard.

In doing research for the *Absolute Beginner's Guide to Building Robots,* I learned about the fascinating life and work of Dr. W. Grey Walter. His work has had a profound impact on various schools of "bottom-up" robot development, such as behavior-based robotics, BEAM, and the work of MIT's Rodney Brooks.

This piece originally ran in *MAKE,* Volume 19. It was one in a series of "Maker Saints" that I profiled for the magazine. Two of my other "saints," William Blake and Jack Parsons, are also included in this collection.

The photo shows a hipster with a goatee smoking a cigarette, watching his pet robots navigate his mod living room. A video created at the same time shows the man and his wife laughing and playing with their two bots, Elmer and Elsie, as the two curious robo-critters interact with each other and navigate around obstacles, one of them driving into a little recharging station on the floor.

What year do you think this is? 2009? 2001? Sometime in the 90s? Certainly no earlier than the 1980s. Not even close. Try 1949!

The location is Bristol, England. The man is Dr. W. Grey Walter, a neurophysiologist, and his wife, Vivian, also a scientist (who helped him build the robots). They both work at the Burden Neurological Institute (BNI). As part of his research into brain cell behavior, he's created these simple, autonomous robots from analog electronic parts. While the influence of these experiments on brain research is debatable, Grey Walter's robot experiments would lay the groundwork for one of the more successful fields of robotics (though that ground would remain fallow for decades).

PIONEER OF THE EEG

William Gray Walter was born in Kansas City, MO in 1910. He was brought up in England where he attended Westminster School, and then King's College, Cambridge. In 1939, he got a job at the Burden Neurological Institute in Bristol, England. He would continue to work there until a car accident in 1970 effectively ended his career (though he continued to be employed by BNI until 1975).

While Walter is best known for his robot experiments in the 40s and 50s, his most significant work was in the burgeoning field of electroencephalography (EEG). He founded the EEG Society, co-founded the International Federation of EEG Societies, and the EEG Journal. He made a number of significant discoveries in the field, including finding the location of the strongest alpha wave particles within the occipital lobe, using triangulation, the use of delta waves to locate the tumors and lesions that cause epilepsy, and he developed the first brain topography neuroimaging machine using electroencephalography. Later in his career, Walters would discover the contingent negative variation (CNV) effect, whereby a negative spike of electrical activity is registered in the brain a half a second before a person even becomes consciously aware of wanting to make a movement. Walter's experiments with stroboscopic light were also an influence on Brion Gysin's Dreamachine (a precursor to devices such as Mitch Altman's Brain Machine, which was featured in *MAKE*, Volume 10).

DESIGNING BRAINBOTS

It was in the course of his work with EEG, and his growing interest in the burgeoning post-WWII science of cybernetics, that Walter became interested in experiments that could explored the control mechanisms of the brain. During the war, Walter had worked on scanning radar and guided missiles (technologies that led to much of the germinal thinking that would become the field of cybernetics) and he became intrigued with the idea of creating a mechanical animal that could scan an environment and be goal-seeking. He thought he could use these creatures to model simple neurons in the brain and to study how these neurons interact. Walter wondered if, instead of it being sheer numbers of neurons that lead to complex brain functions, it was the richness of how these neurons interconnect that led to this emergent complexity. If he created the simplest machines, with two-neuron-brains (using two vacuum tubes), endowed with a few senses (sight and touch), would he see some unforeseen complexity in behavior emerge, especially if he had multiple machines interacting?

SPECULATING MACHINES

Walter began work on his first robot sometime in 1948. The prototype was dubbed Elmer, followed by a more reliable, fuller-featured version, Elsie (the two names are derived from ELectroMEchnanical Robots, Light Sensitive with Internal and External stability). The robots were called Tortoises because of the shell-like bump-sensitive bodies that covered them. As a new "species" of artificial animal, Grey named them *Machina Speculatrix*, a type of machine that "speculates," explores.

Built from a lot of post-war military surplus, each electromechanical tortoise was three-wheeled, with one front drive-wheel and two unpowered back wheels. Each side of the bot carried a vacuum tube "neuron" and a relay and the main active sensor was a photoelectric cell housed on a rotating spindle in the front of the robot, above (and connected to) the drive wheel. An ingeniously designed touch-switch at the top of a second mast towards the back made the entire shell touch sensitive. Any pressure against the shell would close the circuit and trigger an avoidance sequence. A linear wormdrive motor, located along the main spine of the bot, engaged a gear that spun the main drive spindle so that the photocell could scan for light. Once a light source was detected, the linear gear would disengaged and the drive wheel would be fixed in the direction of the light. Power to the robot was provided by a 3-cell lead-acid accumulator.

By using the switching power of two relays, and the amplifying (and oscillating) power of the two vacuum tubes, a series of routines, or "patterns," could be orchestrated within the circuit. Walter also referred to these as "behaviors:"

Pattern E: Speculation, or exploring. Moving around in a room without a strong light source to follow

Pattern P: Phototropism. Moving toward a light source

Pattern N: Negative phototropism. Moving away from a strong light source

Pattern O: Obstacle avoidance

One other important aspect of the design was what Walter called "internal stability" (as the robot pair's name indicated). We might call this autonomy today, the ability of the robots to "feed" (charge) themselves. A "hutch" was built with a charging mechanism and a bright light source inside. As the battery began to die on the tortoise, the gain on the tube amps would be decreased, making it harder to engage behavior N (normally, the brightness of the light would trigger pattern N) and the bot would be attracted to and drive towards the light in the back of the hutch. Once the battery was fully charged, pattern N would be excited again, the tortoise would react to the ultra-bright light, and back out of the hutch.

In the last two years of the 1940s, and into the early 50s, Walter did studies with Elmer and Elsie, and then with six other tortoises built by a technician at BNI, W.J. "Bunny" Warren. In 1950, Walter published his findings in an article in *Scientific American*, entitled "An imitation of life." This was followed by a second article in *Scientific American*, "A machine that learns," in 1951, and by Walter's book, *The Living Brain*, in 1953. In these papers and book, Walter claimed that he'd witnessed many surprises in the behaviors he'd studied in his interacting tortoises. He claimed to have seen actions he was not afraid to call "goal-seeking" (starting out in the dark and making way toward a light source), "recognition of self" (bots "performing" in front of a mirror), "discernment" (making distinctions between effective and ineffective behavior), "free will" (exhibiting unpredictable behavior and making choices). He believed he'd seen what we might call "emergent behavior" in a cybernetic system today. He both saw things in the behavior of the robots that he did not design into them and unanticipated behaviors emerge from the interactions of the robots.

EVER THE SHOWMAN

Most of the articles about Grey Walter's experiments, and the information about him available online (much of it inaccurate), take him at his word and don't question his findings or the effectiveness of his robot designs. Professor Owen Holland, from the Computer Sciences department of Essex University, was involved in building two replicas of the tortoises (with the help of Bunny Warren) and has carefully studied Walter's findings, photos of the tortoise experiments, and such artifacts as the BBC newsreel footage mentioned in my opener (which you can see for yourself here: bit.ly/yS6IqB). Holland points out many inconsistencies in the conclusions and the surviving evidence of the experiments (such as the time exposure photographs of Elmer and Elsie, taken in late 49 or 50) and obvious fudges and edits to the BBC footage to, for instance, imply that Elsie has made her own way into the charging hutch. There is no surviving evidence (or even written claim) that the charging hutch ever actually worked. And, while the tortoises were rather simple in design, with minimal components, they were still complicated enough, and their surplus parts meant that technical glitches were frequent. But even with some questionable conclusions, the documented accomplishments of these experiments are still impressive and the basic observations are borne out by more modern simple, behavior-based based *Machina Speculatrix*, such as BEAM robots, popular among robot hobbyists. As Owen Holland points out in his 2003 paper to the Royal Society, "Exploration and high adventure: The legacy of Grey Walter," Walter was very much a showman, who enjoyed the attention he got from his robots. This futuristic, high-tech human-interest story appealed to a Britain looking to shake off the ravages of a brutal war. And Walter was more than happy to appear in newspaper articles, on radio, and in newsreels, showing off his robots, and what one of his colleagues called his "immense talent for persuasive oratory," to which Holland adds "which may have occasionally carried him beyond the facts."

THE LEGACY OF W. GREY WALTER

In following the trajectory of robotic development, you would think a major course could be confidently plotted through Grey Walter and his pioneering work, but you would be wrong. It wouldn't be until people like Rodney Brooks at MIT started experimenting with "behavior-based robotics" in the 1980s, and Mark Tilden developed BEAM robots soon after that, that people started to take another serious look at Grey Walter's work. It's the ever-present robot dichotomy, represented by R2-D2 and C-3PO. We became so enamored with the idea of creating top-down, highly-intelligent humanoid robots that we lost sight of the less-sexy bottom-up, utilitarian robots. Look at a teardown of the first Roomba, and you will be shocked by how few parts there were inside. It was basically an electric broom, some bump-sensors, and recharging circuit (not that different from Elsie). It's amazing to think, if others had picked up on Walter's technology in the 1950s, and seen it as a legitimate path toward robotic development, we easily could have had something like the Roomba by the mid-50s. And if that were the case, imagine where behavior-based robotics would be today. It's also significant to realize that two of the most successful commercial robotics companies today (and there aren't that many), iRobot and WowWee (with their Robosapien line of robotic toys, designed by Mark Tilden), are both built on behavior-based approaches, an approach that Grey Walter would enthusiastically recognize as his own.

Notes:

Many thanks to Professor Owen Holland for providing me with two of his papers, "Exploration and high adventure: The legacy of Grey Walter" and "Grey Walter: The pioneer of real artificial life." Much of the information in this article was derived from those papers.

There are two surviving tortoises of the six that Bunny Warren made. One is in the Smithsonian, on display in the American History Museum, and the other is in the Science Museum in London. The one at the Smithsonian is damaged and has a few parts missing.

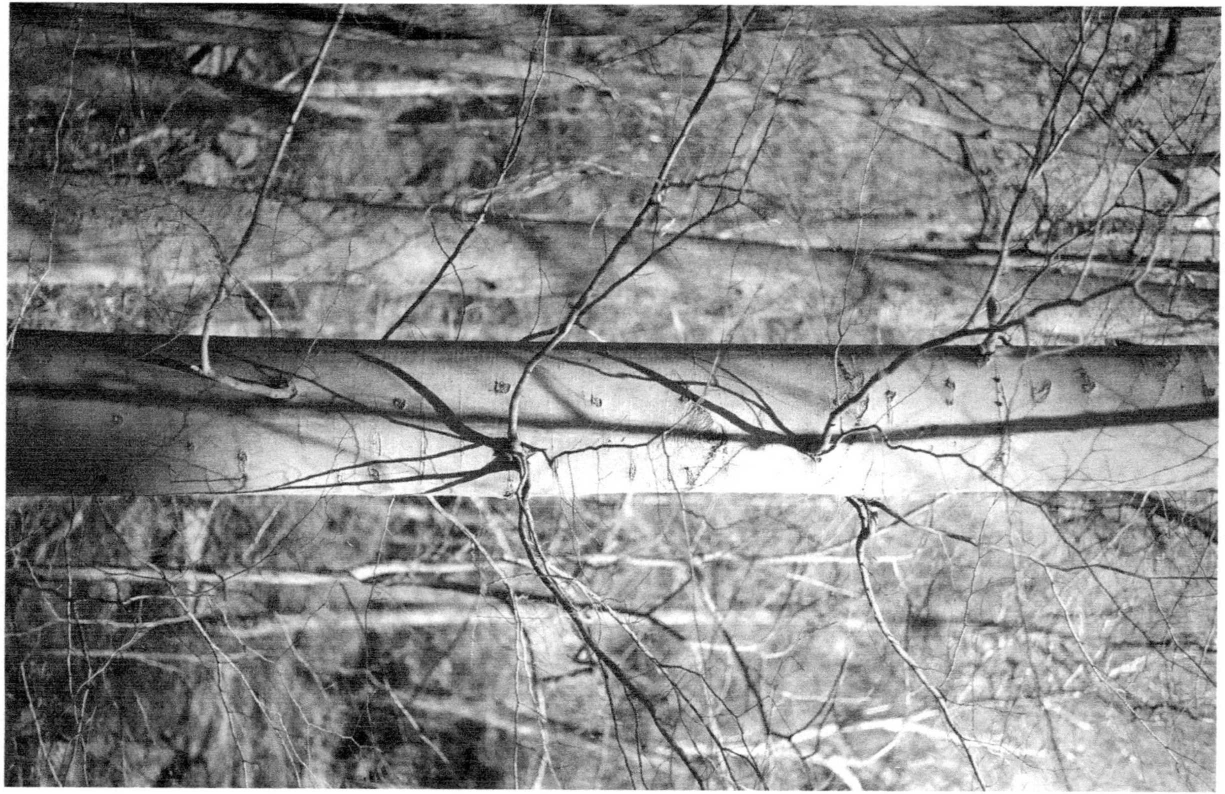

Photo: Terri Weinfenbach

FIGURE, GROUND, AND ALL AROUND

The Middle "Woods" of Terri Weifenbach

Most writers I know take lots of different gigs — to make a buck, to make a point, to give voice to projects you believe in that need vocalists. You find yourself crafting press releases, authoring books on subjects you only start to care about after hearing the size of the advance, writing promo copy for friends' websites, and countless other deserving projects in need of scribal services. Besides having logged many hours doing all of the above, one of my favorite niche assignments is writing introductions to art shows and gallery catalogs (and ghost-writing friend's artist statements). Over the years, I've done this for a number of artists and gallerists. Being so passionate about art, I'm always honored and challenged when asked to interpret an artist's work. I pride myself on telling those who express interest that I don't "do artspeak." I try to write about the art as clearly, plainly, and honestly as possible. I won't write about work I don't believe in and I won't bullshit my way around the work. Upon hearing this, only one artist has decided to give me a pass, in search of a writer, I assume, more willing to lay on the "tautological differentiations" and the "aesthetic interrogations."

When I write one of these essays, I usually read artist statements, bios, maybe a few previous pieces about the artist and the work I'm introducing, but most importantly, I try and fully immerse myself in the work itself. I live inside of it for a few days. I make it my screen savers, tape up copies of the art, stare at it before I go to sleep. And when I'm confident I've reached a certain level of saturation, I try and let the essay be an outpouring of my accumulated thoughts, impressions, and feelings. Sometimes, this method has gotten me in trouble as I've used up all of the available time for the soaking-in-it phase and have ended up doing the final piece the day before, or even hours before, the deadline.

Such was the case with this essay, done for my friend, internationally recognized fine art photographer Terri Weifenbach. Terri asked me to write this for her 2009 "Woods" show, held at DC's Civilian Art Projects. I have huge respect for Terri's work, but honestly, when I was first exposed to it, I didn't understand it. Spending more time with her, seeing more of her pieces, and learning more about her process, the work became far more interesting and accessible to me. So when she asked if I'd write the show description, I was excited by the challenge. But I was also nervous that I might not do it justice. I used up all of my allotted time cogitating the work until I had a morning to write the piece. I wrote the following and went off to a doctor's appointment, knowing that I basically only had time to do minor edits before having to deliver it that afternoon. If it needed major revisions, I was screwed. Another artist friend drove me to the doctor's and I let him read it while he was waiting. He liked it. A lot. I was off the hook! I got home, sent it to Terri, and she called up and was thrilled with it. Everyone was happy. Whew. Close one.

So far, this method of light study, heavy immersion, then shot-from-the-hip prose has worked almost every time. Two of the other art introductions included in this collection, "Techno-Temporal Mash-Ups" and "Mechanical Animism" were also (if you'll pardon the expression) brain-farted this way.

Immersive Media Note: You can see Terri Weifenbach's work in color at terriweifenbach.com. Go to her site, look at some images, then read this essay. Then look at the images again. There's a tab on her site for the "Woods" series displayed in this show. Newbie viewing tip: Thinking paintings, not photographs.

"Consider that it's next to impossible to open your eyes and deliberately stare at the world unfocused. You can hold a blade of grass in front of your nose, focus on it, and the background will blur. But you're not really seeing the background. Our brains are apparently hardwired to avoid such things." — Audubon, June 2001 profile of Terri Weifenbach

In the science of human perception, figure-ground relationships are a key to our visual awareness. We see a differentiated world because a thing is rendered distinct from the non-thing, i.e. everything else. It is the edges of objects, where they interact with the rest of the world (the background), where our perceptions actually occur. Our eyeballs make little micro-movements, constantly comparing thing to non-thing, figure to ground, so that we can perceive and organize the objects in our visual field.

This dynamic relationship between figure and ground has always been a persistent theme in Terri Weifenbach's work. Her photographs unapologetically challenge our visual awareness, provoking the normal conduct of the eye to quickly and categorically assess the visual information we take in. Using narrow depth of field, selective focus, forced perspective, and other techniques, she's confidently taken photography to a place that's both familiar and strange, a realm somewhere between painting and photography. Her work attempts to employ the color and line of the photographer's vocabulary while conveying the energy of expressionist painting. And in executing her work, she is always intent to not pull away from the subject completely while still working in an expressionist domain.

When we look at a photograph (or any work of art, for that matter), we can't help but look to the artist to tell us what we're supposed to be paying attention to, what's important, what's figure, what's ground. A dominant theme in Terri's photography has always been to subvert that perceptual desire.

In much of her previous work, Terri Weifenbach has explored urban and suburban landscapes, using her camera and restless curiosity to reveal pictures of a natural world that frequently goes unseen, unappreciated. For *Woods,* she wanders deeper into the thicket, a less-tame territory of woods; lush, overgrown spaces where density of information increases and figure-ground relationships become more problematic, especially inside of her painterly lens.

In this series, Terri has gone to the woods on the outskirts of town, both literally and aesthetically. Such woods are both inviting and somewhat unsettling places, a no-man's land between civilization and a nature untouched by human hands. It is this in-between space where urbanites and suburbanites go to dip their toes in the natural world, where kids (of all ages) go to get feral, where teenagers go to drink, smoke weed, and screw. It is a place that embodies everything from the positive associations of childhood and neighborhood woods to a scary place we see on the evening news being sniffed by cadaver dogs in search of missing persons. Elves, fairies, and sprites live in the woods. And so does the Big Bad Wolf.

Aesthetically, Terri was drawn to the woods because of the profusion of signals she found there, the density of line, the layering of color and texture, the sheer overwhelming amount of visual information. If she's played with figure-ground relationships in the past by hyper-separating the two, in this series, she teases out more of the middle ground, an aesthetic interzone between clarity and confusion, meaning and noise. There's an equanimity to a lot of these photographs. Your eye goes everywhere and nowhere, the images wash over you. They're atmospheric while still offering a clear sense of place. And a season. Gaze at them long enough and you'll also discover some "Easter eggs," familiar anchorage, pathways, fence lines, the windows of otherwise hidden houses.

There are always open questions in Terri Weifenbach's work. She hints, she teases, she alludes, but she rarely resolves. And that's okay. She leaves the final dots for us to connect. Or not. For sometimes, luscious, full-color questions are far more interesting than black and white answers.

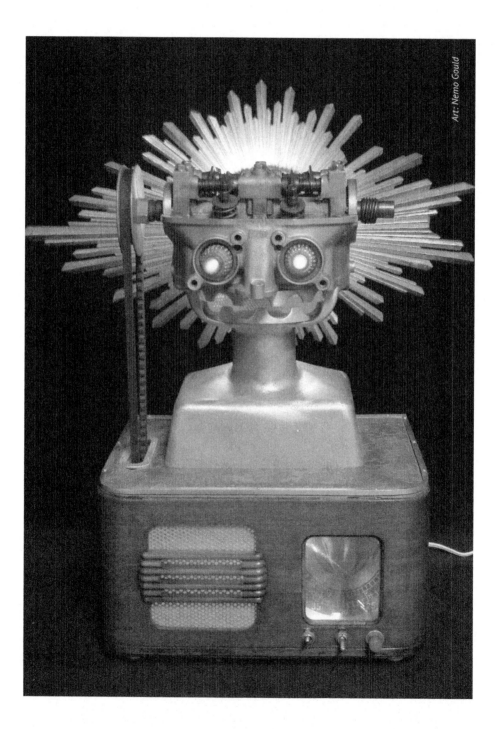

MECHANICAL
ANIMISM

Found object art (art fashioned from repurposed or junk materials) has always fascinated me. It combines my interests in art,
making/fabrication, creative reuse, and it speaks to the very
nature of creativity itself. Studies into the workings of the creative
process have shown that one key characteristic is the ability to find
meaningful relationships between two (or more) seemingly disparate,
unrelated items. This type of mind hack is a hallmark of found object
art. Combining things that don't normally go together in ways that
make them seem "natural" and believable to the viewer does funny
things to our heads, tickles our imaginations in delightful ways, and
awakens new possibilities for seeing the world.

Given my interest in this art form, I was thrilled when, in 2008,
sculptor and gallery owner Greg Brotherton and his wife Amy asked
me to write the introduction to a book they were doing, called *Device
Volume 1: Fantastic Contraption*. Published by the iconic comic and art
book company, IDW Publishing, *Fantastic Contraption* coincided with
the opening of their Device Gallery in La Jolla, CA. The show and book
included amazing work from many of today's major found object
artists, biomechanical artists, and others working similar veins. These

artists included Nemo Gould, Stéphane Halleux, Christopher Conte, Mike Libby, Wayne Martin Berger, Theo Kamecke, Greg Brotherton, and even the O.G. of biomechanical artists himself, H.R. Giger. Here is my introduction to the book. To see the art, check out the Device Gallery website (devicegallery.com) or do a Google search on the above artist's names.

The Fly

Little Fly,
Thy summer's play
My thoughtless hand
Has brushed away.
Am not I
A fly like thee?
Or art not thou
A man like me?
For I dance
And drink, and sing,
Till some blind hand
Shall brush my wing.
If thought is life
And strength and breath
And the want
Of thought is death;
Then am I
A happy fly,
If I live,
Or if I die.

— **William Blake**

LEAKY MARGINS

The great cyberneticist Gregory Bateson used to like to paint an evocative picture for his students. Imagine a blind man walking down the street. Where does the man end, he would ask? At his hand clutching the walking stick? Obviously the stick has become a necessary part of the man, he can't "see" without it. It has become part of his sensorium. So does the man end at the tip of his cane-sensor? Without the feedback provided by the environment itself — the street, the curb, the stairs — he would be equally unable to move, once again, blind. The man is, in fact, a leaky set of relationships between his mind and nervous system, the technology he uses to sense the world around him, and the world itself, which provides the feedback he needs to make his way within it.

We are all, of course, the same as this blind man. Our technology extends our senses into the world, helps us to interact with, navigate it, and we, the technology, and the world itself are all shaped by this complex and dynamic loop of interactions. This may be obvious to some, but strangely, few of us seem to grasp the extent to which we living beings leak into and enliven the seemingly inanimate technologies we fashion, or the extent to which that technology helps shape our biological world in return. The borders between "the born" and "the made" are far more permeable than many of us would freely admit. It is inside this interzone, this permeable membrane between flesh and steel, biology and technology, where you'll likely find the artists of Device enthusiastically poking their walking sticks.

POST-INDUSTRIAL SURREALISM

While a quick survey of the Device artists will clearly reveal a fascination with technology, with mechanism, as the name *Fantastic Contraption* implies, it's not a technology we can readily recognize. Much of the impact of this work comes from its ability to simultaneously appear familiar and foreign, earnest and ironic, useful yet impossible, and as both a product of science and science fiction. The effect of all this is to generate the delirious perceptual oscillations between these (and other) poles of contradicted expectations. One of the artists found in these pages, Victor Koen, in referring to some of his own art, has described it as "the formula that isn't." This self-destructing formula can be used to factor all of the work in the Device collection.

Fantastic Contraption also isn't rooted in any historical period one can recognize, or even in some rationally imaged future. This mysterious machinery has caused time to collapse in on itself, with known past, present, and countless possible futures, all smelted together, and again, the effect serves to crank up our perceptual oscillators. Adding to these heady hits are style- and reference-checks from cultural icons as diverse as Da Vinci, Bosch, Giuseppe Archimboldo, Raoul Hausmann, Hannah Höch, Jean-Pierre Jeunet, Jules Verne, Franz Kafka, H.P. Lovecraft, Salvador Dali, Lucille Ball, Rock'Em Sock'Em Robots and Robbie the Robot. And, of course, the All-Father of biomech, H.R. Giger (who himself is featured in *Fantastic Contraption*).

VISUAL DEBRIS

Another term Victor Koen uses to describe the aesthetics for a series of his digital collages (of insects, machinery, and corporatized humanity) is "visual debris." This captures another leitmotif amongst the Device artists. Everything seems grist for the mill, potential raw material, for these artists. Everything from the literal mixed media, found objects, and repurposed technologies incorporated into the pieces, to the ideas, issues, and cultural conversations they seek to encapsulate — it all ends up suspended in the amber of the work, like so many ancient mosquitoes. This is a collection that is deeply rooted in superb, almost old world, craftsmanship. It is work that is supremely confident in itself, while at the same time, remaining surprisingly fluid and defiant of tidy interpretations. The fact that one can even make this many broad statements — as if this body of work was the product of a school or a movement — while the art, the media and techniques used, and the artists themselves are so incredibly diverse, points to something extraordinary and exciting here.

"Contraptions" are more often the products of garages, machine shops, and sketchy basement labs rather than artist studios. Feasting your eyes on the sepia-toned, rusty robots world of Ash Wood, the crazed kinetic sculptures of Nemo Gold, the borged insects of Mike Libby, the sacrilized circuitry of Theo Kamecke, the meticulously detailed figures of Stéphane Halleux, the Frankensteinian cameras of Wayne Martin Belger, and the reanimated domestic machinery of Device co-founder Greg Brotherton, one can't help but imagine these artists being as comfortable in the garage, the lab, and the shop (not to mention the dank corners of the backyard), as the artist's studio.

So, if you're ready, it's time to let your nervous system get leaky, to give yourself over to a techno-surreal funhouse mirrorworld where teddy bears become telephones, watches morph into winged beetles, motherboards become monoliths and sarcophagi, antique sewing machines sprout spider legs, and guns chamber humanoid rounds. You haven't entered the Twilight Zone, but you have stepped inside the no less heady, surreal, and psychoactive machinery of *Fantastic Contraption*.

TECHNO-TEMPORAL MASH-UPS

and Bringing the Tinfoil

I have to admit I was a little shocked (in a good way) when Greg and Amy Brotherton of Device Gallery invited me back to write the introduction to *Reconstructed*, the second volume in their Device Gallery series. I tried to talk them out of it. I told them I could find someone else, someone better, more famous, but they said no, they wanted me. I was flattered and I gratefully accepted the assignment.

I even ended up moderating a panel of many of the artists associated with Device (and San Francisco's Applied Kinetic Arts) at Maker Faire Bay Area in 2009. And as I write this, I'm in the middle of writing the introduction to *Device Volume III: Traveling Device*. I'm starting to feel like the court scribe for the found object/post-industrial surrealist/biomech art world. I better get busy on trying to dream up a snazzier name for this strange and beautiful little enclave of artist production.

As with the previous Device introduction, you can see some of the artists at the Device Gallery site (devicegallery.com) or search on the individual artists' names. Since this intro describes the work of many of the artists, you'll get more out of it if you look at their work beforehand.

Volume I has sold out, but Volume II is currently available from Device. These books are beautiful, inspiring, and worth getting ahold of, used if you can't find them new.

When I think about the future, all I wanna know is: when do we get to wear the tinfoil?

That statement was uttered by a friend of mine, a New York artist and fashion designer, during a conversation in the early 1990s. It floored me. It was so simultaneously funny and cynical about the future – quaint, quirky, and honest. It called to mind so many Ed Wood-worthy 50s and 60s films where everybody ran around in silver lamé flight suits with fishbowl helmets on their heads.

I was so inspired by this statement that I created a page for my art zine, *Going Gaga*, made out of aluminum foil, with this question printed on clear sticker paper and stuck to the foil page. *I* brought the tinfoil, so the future could be delivered without further delay.

This anecdote came back to me while looking at the amazing collection of "mechanical animism" assembled for *Device Volume II: Reconstructed*. The artists represented seem similarly intent on bringing the tinfoil, or at least delivering a heady dose of all of the projections, fears, fetishistic obsessions, utopian desires, and other associative baggage we have for the future we dream of (or lose sleep over).

Like the collection found in *Device Volume I: Fantastic Contraption,* the work here comes from no apparent school, no labeled movement. It will be issuing no manifestoes. It boasts no house organ. The closest we get to anything tying it all together into a discernible whole is the impressive curatorial eyes of Greg and Amy Brotherton, their Device Gallery, and this dazzling series of books.

Each volume offers a pattern recognition; each is a meditation on some aspect(s) of the collected work. The koan for that meditation is partially encoded in the name of the volume. *Fantastic Contraption* was just that, a beautiful piece of artistic machinery made of sub-assemblies from sixteen artists' sculptures, paintings, and digital work. Each piece was a human/animal-cum-machine, or a machine becoming something alive or mystical. Otherworldly. It was about biology and machinery changing state, exchanging DNA, and it all was constantly phase-shifting between the mundane and the fantastic. Although a number of the artists here are back from Volume I, and the work mines similar veins, *Reconstructed* is pleased to present a different thought for your consideration (to paraphrase Serling in *The Twilight Zone*).

LIVING IN THE MATRIX

While we were busy waiting to wear the tinfoil, looking up at the skies for the future to arrive via a pie plate held on a string by a B-movie grip, the future arrived through a rather unlikely portal: it came through our phone lines! The Internet and the digital revolution changed everything. There is probably no area of human endeavor that hasn't been significantly altered by computers, instantaneous, global communications, and personal multimedia publishing. The reverb on all of this is endless, but one wave of it especially concerns us here, in considering our koan for "reconstructed:" the acts and aesthetics of cut and paste. It didn't take netizens long to figure out that cutting and pasting didn't just apply to email messages and word processing. In a digital universe, where a copy can be cloned as perfectly as the original, any medium can be cut, copied, pasted, edited, recompiled, and reissued. The digital world is one big mash-up, a writhing, dynamic act of (re)construction.

This is nothing new to nature. Creation has always been an act of recombinism. One of the most mind-blowing, life-changing thoughts I've ever had came by way of a cyberneticist I met (who was also something of a devoted stoner). He told me to try looking at the living world as a "conversation between elements and processes, a nexus, a matrix in which these elements are held together and find expression." It sure sounded good, as did the apparent quality of whatever it was he as smoking. But one night, with my nose buried deep in a riotous bunch of spring flowers on our dining room table, I had an epiphany, I understood — actually felt — exactly what he was talking about. I understood that the flowers I was looking at were the overlapping points at which all of these feedback loops of "elements and processes" (water, sunlight, soil, photosynthesis, the genetic information being meted out by the seeds — defining the protocols by which these elements should interact) came together and "had a conversation." The result of that conversation was the deliriously beautiful and fragrant nature-art in which I had enthusiastically planted my head. I had a visceral sense of these elements recombining, constantly, dynamically, in some cosmic lambada by which nature, life, expresses itself.

While meditating on the collection of art found in these pages, I had a similar sense of almost being able to see the active entrainment of elements and processes as they came together to create the sculptural objects found here.

Look at the dense, wiry constructions of Andrew Smith and tell me you don't almost feel the electromagnetic forces by which they have seemingly assembled themselves out of the cast-off materials they've managed to draw to them. As if to drive home the temporal nature of these pieces, some of them, such as *High Rise Billiards* and *Nine to Five*, are kinetic; they are literally constantly reconstructing themselves.

Looking at a piece of Greg Brotherton's work is like simultaneously peering into a three-dimensional piece of fine art, an absurdly expensive hand-built luxury auto from some golden age that never existed, and into the fever-dreams of a 40s-era industrial designer. And that's just the first wave of impressions. The thing you can't get over is the technical virtuosity. In pieces like the Sisyphian *Pushed Around*, with its sense of movement aggressively offered, yet denied (the piece does not move), and the vertigo-inducing *Migraine Machine II*, which you'd rather didn't move (at least its subject wouldn't), but it does, we experience clever tweaks of our expectations, while the craftsmanship wows our aesthetic senses and feeds our appreciation for such stellar engineering.

Christopher Conte's work is almost genuinely scary, with such beautifully-rendered, precisely-engineered techno-sculptures calling to mind some cyborged, componentized future. Then you learn of Christopher Conte's previous day-job, as an engineer of prosthetic devices, building artificial limbs for amputees. The horrible beauty of it all kicks into overdrive, like some stim injection in a cyberpunk novel.

Rich Muller, Jeremy Mayer, Lewis Tardy, Nemo Gould, Olivier Pauwels, Paul Loughridge, and Stéphane Halleux all work a similar vein of rich techno-temporal mythology: over five decades of the robot. In speaking about the rights of digital artists to mash-up existing work to create new work – reconstruction, in other words, Mark Hosler of the audio-collage band Negativland once talked about the emergence of folk art whenever physical objects, codes, and signs reach a level of saturation where they become the available raw material through which a culture expresses itself. So, in a third-world country, aluminum from Pepsi and Coke cans and rubber from imported tires are just as likely to show up in artwork as indigenous materials – it's what's at hand. While actual robot components have barely reached the outskirts of modern, first world culture – so saturation is minimal — robot codes and signs have been thoroughly penetrating our consciousness for decades, thus becoming "folk art" fodder.

These artists have decided to use all of their creative powers to cut and paste the found objects, the future-forward household appliances, electronic components, and other everyday elements cast off from our lives, to fashion the robots we always wanted. They're bringin' the tinfoil. And they all do it in very unique and inspired ways, from the 50s-looking constructions of Rich Muller's sweet and personable knuckle-draggers and Paul Loughridge's sparky little bots, to Jeremy Mayer's incredibly-detailed typewriter recombinisms, to Lewis Tardy's quicksilvery, Art Deco-y robotic humans and animals obsessed with a need for speed. Nemo Gould's work is packed with whimsy and works on multiple levels in teasing and defying initial impressions. His art (and a lot of the work here) is usually an act of promising one thing and delivering something else, like a joke that's funny because the set-up creates a certain expectation but the payoff comes completely out of left field. A comedian once told me that, in a joke, the distance between the expectation and the payoff describes the size of laugh. In kinetic pieces like *The Performer #2* and *Re:animated*, the distance traveled is satisfyingly great.

Olivier Pauwels and Stéphane Halleux draw from a similar box of found junk, but recombine it in very different ways. Olivier's work is darker, more innervating. Although Stéphane's subject-matter is no less potentially sinister, there's a sense of wonder and pervasive charm about it all that adds a note of sweetness. He's probably heard it too many times before, but there's something extremely Burton-esque about the world Stéphane has conjured.

If much of the work in this collection trades on the reconstruction of components found in the adult world, Kris Kuksi's constructions cut and paste the contents of a child's. Army men, vehicles, dolls, plastic models, and other similar components coalesce into unimaginably dense Boschian sculptures that speak to decidedly adult themes. Not surprisingly, given these raw materials, war, death, and the depths of human suffering infuse this work. If the Devil had gone through an adolescence, these would've been his play things.

Rounding out the collection is Mike Libby's increasingly well-known (and deservedly so) cyborged, watchwork bugs, along with some newer pieces heading off in a very different direction. This recent work is represented here by *Recycled Ruins*, constructed of little paper boxes, and *Stegosaurus*, a dinosaur model built from bible pages.

Crossing Jules Verne's rivets n' brass Nautilus with Italian surrealist Luigi Serafini's cryptic visions (with a little Peter Max Yellow Submarine thrown in for good measure) might approximate the flavor of Michihiro Matsuoka's art. As with all of the artists in this collection, the quality of the construction, the obsessive attention to detail, is as impressive as the ideas being expressed.

There is something Lovecraftian about Steve Brudniak's pieces, an old (Old) world menace, a discernible chill that creeps along the walls upon which much of this work hangs. These are devices that give you the impression that, as you're looking at them, they might be looking back. Closer examination, peering into the worlds on the other side of the windows most of the objects feature, offer payoffs not anticipated – again, a twist of rusty wire that threads itself through the entire *Reconstructed* collection.

Tom Haney's folky, handcarved automata dutifully bring up the rear, with robotic wood and metal servants going about their robotic business, from behind antique glass. Are these robots made to look like humans, or do they depict humans turned into automata? Watching them in action offers up a strange feeling of both sadness at the rote drudgery of the tasks these mechanical humans are perpetually performing, but also, a sliver of hope for the nobility that we'd like to think is ever-present in the human spirit.

In the end, looking at Haney's automata, some of the other kinetic works in this collection, and the robot and cyborg sculptures, we're reminded of one of the things that attracts us so strongly to robots and personified machinery in the first place – the extent to which we identify with them. And in a world that's becoming increasingly cut and pasted, reconstructed, to the point where the cutting and pasting have come to include us (see Chris Conte's former day-job), it's only fitting that the Device artists have decided to bring the tinfoil, if for no other reason than for us to decide if we *really* want to wear it.

POST OFFICE

DOWN THE RABBIT HOLE

I've always been fascinated by all types of miniatures. When I was a kid, anytime you were allowed to build a diorama as a school project, I built a diorama. As a teen, I built HO train models and train boards, and as an adult, for years, I converted and painted 28mm sci-fi gaming minis, built tabletop gameboard scenery. Some people are content to allow their fantasy worlds to remain phantasmagorical, in their heads, or in the pages of their favorite novels, or up on the big screen. For me, I've always wanted to download those fantasies, leak the fantastic into the mundane. I want to see fantasy in the real world. This piece, which I originally wrote for *Boing Boing*, tells of two instances of such leakage.

I've since become online friends with Lea Redmond whom I write about in the piece. She was kind enough to do an original photo illustration for this essay. You can see more of Lea's enchanting world at *leafcutterdesigns.com*.

I'm a firm believer in clinging to as much childlike wonder as possible. I love it when people take it upon themselves to inject a little magic and whimsy into the lazy hind quarters of the human herd. Here are a few examples, one from my past that's stayed with me, and one, a more recent discovery.

Years ago, I was living at Gesundheit Institute, the healthcare community created by Patch Adams. A woman came to visit, an artist and crafter who specialized in miniatures and dioramas. Her work, which she shared with us one night via a slideshow, was breathtaking — these pristine little dioramas, frozen scenes from some alternative kiddiverse of talking-animal storybook characters and various human strangelings, all going about their daily Lilliputian lives within the confines of her little black diorama boxes. She stayed with us for a few days, and after she left, life on the commune went back to (ab)normal.

We had a tree in our front yard which was itself something out of storybook, a big ol' gnarly tree with a humongous rotted-out knothole on one side. One day, I was doing some work in the yard, likely grumbling over the heat and the generalized ick of a late-summer Virginia afternoon. As I passed the tree, something caught my eye, something unusual with the knothole. I peered in, and for a dizzying triple-take, all of the wistful fantasies of my childhood overtook mundane adult reality.

There, inside the dank hole, was a tiny overstuffed chair sitting on a braided rug, and next to it stood a floor lamp. Tiny pictures hung on even tinier nails on the inside walls of the hole. A family portrait. Reclining in the chair, watching TV, sat a little rabbit-man. I think he had on overalls. And he may have been drinking something. A can of carrot juice? Honestly, I don't remember the real details, and I'm sure that time and my memory have exaggerated everything.

I may not fully recall the particulars, but I'm not the least bit fuzzy on the impact. It was a simple reality hack with an extraordinary effect, a rare moment when magic winked into the world. And it worked me on several levels — the fact that she never said anything to us about it, the amount of thought and work she'd put into it (all in secret), my chance discovery of it days after she'd gone, and that brief, delicious blurring of the mundane and the fantastic — a gift given only to those of us who happened upon it.

This is all a whimsical way of introducing my most recent encounter with someone also doing the work of the fairy: Lea Redmond, the human-pixie hybrid behind the World's Smallest Postal Service. With an impossibly small-nib India ink pen, Lea writes tiny letters on tiny stationary and seals them with wax inside a tiny stamped and canceled envelope. The letter is then placed by an official World's Smallest Postal Service employee (um… Lea) inside of a tiny blue post box.

Then our ham-handed Land of the Giants reality takes over and the little magic letter is prepared for real-world mailing. It is put inside of a slide mount-like viewing envelope and then inside of a larger glassine envelope with a magnifying glass, thoughtfully included so that the recipient can actually read the letter.

You can order the letters online or you can check the calendar to see where the World's Smallest Postal Service will be setting up shop in the Bay Area. To write a letter that Lea will render in minuscule for you, you go to her site, fill out a form with what you want your letter to say (up to 12 lines) and where you want it sent. Each letter currently costs under $10. I bought a bunch of them for family and friends one holiday and everyone seemed genuinely enchanted by the whole experience. Some of Lea's other clever and sweet products include matchbox theater, recipe dice, letter embroidery kits, seed earrings that have plantable flowers and herbs inside them, and lots more fun stuff.

If you ask me, I think we need a lot more surprise knothole dioramas and little tiny wax-sealed letters in this-here junkyard world. Every time I hear about an artist 3D-printing and installing LEGO brick "repairs" to broken city stairs and walls, or an Improve Everywhere action, or a Zombie flash mob, or similar acts of "poetic terrorism," the world glows just a pixel brighter to me. We become so habituated, dutifully marching within our little life-ruts, that even the smallest of these little whacks on the side of the head can wake us up, at least for minute.

Notes:

Lea created the tiny post office diorama, seen in the accompanying photo, in a treehole in the Oakland, CA woods. The little dollhouse lamp she used was battery-powered and she left the whole scene set up and the light on. We both were tickled by the idea of trail-walkers stumbling upon it. I can almost guarantee that it was a highlight of their day. You can see a little video of the treehole post office here: *vimeo.com/83522457.*

Art: Danny Hellman

BUILDING SPACESHIPS OUT OF 5s AND 6s

A few years ago, Mark and Carla of *Boing Boing* came up with a brilliant idea. They wanted to publish a new print edition of *bOING bOING*, Issue 16. It had been nine years since the last issue had come out, and in the meantime, the *Boing Boing* blog had become hugely successful, now part of popular culture, and an internet media success story. But the new print issue would ignore all that. We would get a bunch of the original editors, authors, and artists together, revive some of our favorite columns and features, and basically act as if the intervening near-decade had never happened. We wouldn't even mention the blog, except to include the URL. I was absolutely thrilled by the idea and immediately signed on.

We quickly picked up where we'd left off and began writing our own pieces, reading and commenting on each other's, assigning and editing stories and art from others. It was such a delight to be working on *bb* and with Mark and Carla again. But after our initial burst of enthusiasm and output, the rest of our busy lives, work, and other projects overtook us – as all that is want to do. I was still in the long-arc recovery of a heart attack and heart surgery (see "Boating the Abyss") and was struggling to put the pieces of my life back together. And so, *bOING bOING* 16 remains in mid-air. It may still make planetfall one day. In the meantime, this is one of the pieces I wrote for it.

The illustration used here was originally commissioned by *bOING bOING* from Danny Hellman. It is used with kind blessings of Danny and *bOING BOING*.

"Those who regard this ritual as a mere device to invoke or banish spirits, are unworthy to possess it. Properly understood, it is the Medicine of Metals and the Stone of the Wise."— Aleister Crowley, on the Lesser Banishing Ritual of the Pentagram

I was deeply involved in the occult in my youth. At 13, I declared myself a witch and was into Wicca and Neopaganism into my early 20s. But then, I had a rather violent reaction to all such hokum pocus (and the particular flavor of weirdos that it all seems to attract). I pulled strongly to the opposite pole, toward science, rationality, and atheism (or at least agnosticism – I've never understood the idea of being science-minded and being absolutely certain that there is no God. Being 100% certain of no God seems as absurd to me as being 100% certain that there is one. Cyberneticist Gregory Bateson suggested you tie all of your beliefs, ideas, and theories with slipknots. So, to me, agnosticism is tying any negative conclusions about the existence of God with a slipknots).

Several years ago, I started writing a novel which explores, among other things, these polarities of faith and science, magic and reason. The main character, a sort of funhouse-mirror version of myself (only younger, smarter, better looking, and with lots more hair) is similarly a science/tech journalist. He too has become dismissive and cynical in all matters of faith and the supernatural. Over the course of the book, we find out that something very unnerving happened to him in his youth, something inexplicable and deeply frightening, that sent him straight into the well-defined and confident arms of scientific rationality.

As I began to write the novel, I decided it might be helpful to my creative process to reexamine some of what I'd been up to as the young wannabe magus. So, one day, I climbed up into my stale attic and found my boxed-up books on magic, the occult, and Eastern mysticism. I unearthed all sorts of dusty gems, such as my well-marked and dogeared copy of Richard Cavendish's classic *The Black Arts*. Opening it, I saw where I'd first encountered (and nervously underlined) the names *Aleister Crowley* and *Eliphas Levi*. Within these books, and in the preserved "magical diaries" I dutifully maintained at the time, I also rediscovered the foundational ritual of Western ceremonial magic: the Lesser Banishing Ritual of the Pentagram, or the LBRP.

I decided, against my embrassment and better judgment, that to truly get into the spirit of the novel, I should re-learn this ritual and begin practicing it again. I planned on having the character in the book be re-introduced to it and reluctantly begin to practice it as well, so me doing it too made a lot of sense. The fact that I felt squeamish about it, that I thought it silly to even consider, made me even more motivated to do it. "Novelists do this sort of thing," I told myself. "I'm a novelist now. It's book research, fodder for all the TV talk shows and internet podcast I'll inevitably be invited onto during my glamorous worldwide book tour." And so, I sheepishly set up a little altar (an old plant stand) in my bedroom and outfitted it with all of the "magical tools" I'd saved from my teens (dagger, wand, cup, pentacle). I began re-learning the rite.

The Lesser Banishing Ritual of the Pentagram originated with the Hermetic Order of the Golden Dawn, the hugely-influential British occult society of the late 19th and early 20th centuries. The Golden Dawn boasted such illustrious members as W.B. Yeats, Allan Bennett (often credited with bringing Buddhism to the West), Arthur Edward Waite (author of the world's most popular Tarot deck, the Rider-Waite, created with artist and fellow GD member Pamela Colman Harris), and proto-feminist and Irish revolutionary, Maud Gonne. The most notorious of GD members was the James Dean-meets-Blofeld of the occult world himself, Aleister Crowley. It is actually through Crowley's massive *Magick Book 4* (Part III), first published in 1911 (and later as the stand-alone, *Magick in Theory and Practice*, 1929), that the LBRP was first introduced to those who were not members of the Golden Dawn.

The LBRP was the basic, beginner ritual taught to all Neophytes. It was actually the only ritual taught to this beginner grade of the Order. It was the foundation upon which the rest of the GD system rested.

The LBRP is designed to be a sort of a psychic power wash for you and your ritual space, a way of mentally cleansing your "temple," preparing yourself, and tuning up the ol' cosmic radio for whatever else it is you wish to receive or transmit in the rituals you want to perform. The pentagram represents the four classical Greek elements (Air, Fire, Earth, Water), and spirit, the fifth element, the cosmic breath of life that animates the other four. All of this comprises the sacred number "5" and is represented in the symbol of the pentagram.

The hexagram, the 6, is also used in the Lesser Banishing Ritual of the Pentagram. It represents the classical planets as known to the ancients (Mercury, Venus, Moon, Mars, Jupiter, Saturn). The sun, Sol, is often depicted by a dot in the center of the planetary hexagram. The LBRP involves addressing all of the symbols and the words, sounds, numbers, colors, deities, and other concepts associated with the pentagram and the hexagram, and asserting your control over all of them. If you really get into it, it's very theatrical, like your own private Wagnerian opera where you are both performer and audience. There's a sexual component to it, too — the pentagram represents the female/procreative powers of Earth, and the hexagram, the male/solar and planetary powers. The ritual is a union of the 5 and the 6 – you're basically calling a shaft of solar/planetary power to enter the Earthly, feminine circle you've just opened up. Sword into cup. It's basically a symbolic reenactment of the cosmic bonking that makes all life possible.

The LBRP is seemingly simple on the surface, but actually rather complicated when probed more deeply. I won't go into the mechanics here, but rather, focus on what the experience feels like.

In the opening phase of the ritual (called the Qabalistic Cross), you envision yourself as part of the Qabalistic Tree of Life from Jewish mysticism, imagining yourself lighting up some of the key spheres or life-qualities (known as "sephirot") on the Tree (and in you).

For the rest of the ritual, you draw pentacles in the air with a dagger and vividly visualize them in your mind's eye; intensely "vibrate" the ancient Hebrew names for various aspects of God; invoke the angels of the four directions, seeing them in your mind's eye; and you try and put every ounce of yourself into all aspects of all this.

The whole production is extraordinarily "yang," loud and downright aggressive, something that would completely freak out your neighbors if they heard you performing it (they'd think cultists or a Norwegian black metal vocalist had just moved in next door). Luckily, I live on the end of a street and my bedroom is not close to other homes. And I do my rituals at about 2am, when nobody is likely to hear anyway.

When I first started doing the LBRP, I was a little creeped out by the idea of waving a dagger around, but after doing it for awhile, I realized that there's an important function to this: healthy respect and attention for the proceedings. You can't phone in the ritual when there are sharp objects involved and a lot of furious arm-waving and guttural shouting. There's one gesture in the ritual, called the Sign of the Enterer (or the "Sign of Horus"), where you gather up all of the "energy" in your body, pull your arms up along your sides, thrust them up towards your head beside your ears, and then, you plunge the happy dagger forward with your whole upper body, in a dramatic, thrusting lean. You really need to be fully awake and aware when doing this, lest you fillet your midsection or Van Gogh an ear in the process.

By the end of the banishing part of the ritual, you've used your dagger to carve four pentacles of blue-white light into the air, in the four cardinal directions, and you've called down the angels of each direction to stand guard over your rite. Actually, I like to think of my archangels as being well-meaning but rather lay-about deities who I have to wake up and gently but firmly eject from my templespace so that I can get some serious work done in there.

The next thing I do is not always part of the LRBP. It's a variant I found that I liked (for reasons I'll explain in a moment). I visualize a glowing hexagram above my head, and when I can "see" it, I say: "Above me, my Father." And then I visualize a blue-white hexagram at my feet and say: "Below me, my Mother." Then, I stand at attention in the center, try to "resonate" with everything I've just done and the psychic constructions I've built. I try and vividly feel all of this around me and in me, lighting me up, calling me to a kind of spiritual attention. Then, I visualize Crowley's "unicursal hexagram" (which has a 5-petaled rose, alluding to the pentagram, at its center) coruscating around my heart, and I end with the traditional statement: "And in the column shines the six-rayed star."

So what is all this shouting and gesticulating in the dark supposed to do? Well, besides it being the sort of temple-cleansing I talked about, it also has another function that I find poetically lovely (and why I like to mentally "cap" my construct with hexagrams above and below). As you inscribe the pentacles into the air, and perform the banishing, you're supposedly driving out all of the Earthly forces and influences (represented by the four elements) – and those shiftless angels, from your space (and out of your head). By doing this, you're creating a cosmic vacuum, and because, as we know, nature abhors a vacuum, extra-planetary cosmic forces rush in to replace the banished Earthly ones. Then you picture the hexagram above you and below you, sealing up your little cosmic spacecraft built from 5s and 6s. In the process of the ritual, you have built a mental construct with walls of four pentagrams, and a roof and a floor out of hexagrams. You have orchestrated a union of the forces they represent, and you have become the center of their union. YOU are the "six-rayed star." You're building a little mind ship and you're the warp core, baby!

When I was a teen witch, I loved all this stuff and I especially loved the idea that the magic circle you cast for a ritual was a space between worlds, a cosmic bubble within which you could mentally travel places or safely conjure spirits from within and you'd be protected from any negative outside forces. Although I don't really know how much of this jazz I actually believe (being "open to anything, skeptical of everything"), I like that concept aesthetically, symbolically.

Doing this ritual over these past few years, I've had some strange and powerful experiences. For instance, I've had a couple of what I call "Jesus moments," utterly ecstatic upwellings of joy, moments of profound "being-here-now" where I've felt fully and completely alive. This is the state of grace that William Blake liked to call "Eternal Delight." In this bliss-ninny state, I've found myself involuntarily throwing my arms open and craning my neck skyward (like you see Jesus freaks doing at tent revivals).

I've reached highs a few times while doing the LBRP that rival some of my better drug experiences. As I've already mentioned, the ritual is extremely intense, outward, aggressive. I quickly found myself wanting to do something "yin" to balance it, so I usually do a Hindu mantra or one of my own made-up chants in the middle of it.

The quiet that comes over me after the LBRP is impressive. You've been working so much of yourself (the gestures, the intense vibrations, all of the complex visualizations) that it feels SO good when it stops! The concentration one can achieve immediately afterwards can be powerful. As I said earlier, this ritual is usually a prelude to the "work" you plan to do. All I care to do is the chanting, some meditation, and sometimes I have my journal with me and write down ideas that come to me. To close the session, I repeat the Qabalistic Cross that opened it and I'm done.

Five years ago, I had the misfortune of having a heart attack, which led to open heart triple-bypass surgery. As you might image, this was serious, scary business. The night before the procedure, lying in my hospital bed, scared and needing to comfort myself, I was surprised by the fact that I really wanted to perform that LBRP. I did the...er..hum.. "astral version" of it, where you just imagine that you're at your altar and you internalize all of the gestures, vibrations, and chants.

There's an amazing effect of doing a ritual over and over again that I've dubbed "ritual persistence." As soon as you get into the magic circle, it's like you never left — there's a part of you that's always there, always going through those motions. It's a powerful feeling. Having done the LBRP fairly regularly for several years before my hospitalization, it wasn't hard for me to close my eyes and quickly find myself standing in my bedroom, at my altar, awash in that comforting glow of candlelight, ardently constructing my little Hermetic escape pod. I was truly surprised by the comfort this brought me, the sense of a safe, familiar place I could mentally retreat to, a little gossamer mindcraft I could leave this world in, a world which was literally about to get split open at the breast bone.

I used the astral LBRP several times during my hospital stay when things got too painful, scary, or boring. I was impressed at what a useful tool it turned out to be. If nothing else, it is a unique and powerful meditation and fantasy visualization. In fact, with all of the physical movements, the invocations, and the visualizations, you could think of the pentagram rituals as a kind of western yoga.

When I did this ritual as a teen, it never really meant that much to me. I rushed through it, mumbled the words – it always sort of felt in the way of the other, sexier mumbo-jumbo I was anxious to get to (trying to evoke some heavy metal-worthy dark deity or another, casting spells to get girls to like me, etc.). Now, the LBRP has become the only ritual I do and the only one I'm really that interested in. I've gotten more out of it than most of the other occult, Eastern mystical, or other such practices I've dabbled in over the lifetime. There's a Greater Ritual of the Pentagram, and Lesser and Greater Hexagram rituals, but I don't feel the need to "graduate" to them yet. For now, I'm happy building my spaceships out of 5s and 6s and using the poetic energies of my Gareth-powered six-rayed warp core stardrive to blast me deep into the aethers of innerspace.

Ad astra per aspera!

More info:

If you want to know more about the LBRP (and the other pentagram and hexagram rituals), a good place to start is Lon Milo DuQuette's *The Magick of Aleister Crowley*. There are also numerous resources, of wildly varying quality and usefulness (and silliness), on the other end of a Google search. One decent how-to can be found at tinyurl.com/yedsdnk

BOATING THE ABYSS

In early fall of 2009, I had a heart attack. That should've been scary enough, but in the hospital, I was told that I had major arterial blockage and needed triple bypass surgery – the next day! And, the sweaty, bug-eyed fear only dialed up from there. Miraculously, I came through my "triple cabbage" (coronary arterial blockage) and was discharged in a record four days. But shortly before I left, they'd given me a blood transfusion (a quart low 'n' all that). Unfortunately, it was improperly cross-matched blood. Turns out, I'm a mutant. OK, that's not news to anyone who knows me, but I'm apparently more of a mutant than we ever realized. Previously unbeknownst to me, I have two rare antibodies in my otherwise B Positive blood. They didn't test for these in the donor blood and I got very sick as a result, circling-the-drain sick. After getting discharged, I was rushed back to the hospital within 24 hours and came perilously close to dying. How close? Read on.

This piece is based on an email that I originally sent to my co-workers at *MAKE*, after getting my head screwed back on straight and my *final* hospital discharge papers. I've fleshed it out quite a bit (NOW WITH MORE HALLUCINATORY WEIRDNESS!) and added some thoughts with the hindsight of several years downwind from this bizarre and frightening ordeal.

"The Shaman swims in the same water the psychotic drowns in." — Joseph Campbell

On the late afternoon of August 12, 2009, I began to be repeatedly and unceremoniously flung against death's door. That I'm here telling you about it is testament to the fact that the door was in no mood to be opened that day. And for that, I am eternally grateful.

My heart attack was completely unexpected. I don't live a particularly decadent lifestyle. I eat well, drink moderately, take my Flintstones vitamins. I have no family history of heart disease. But once in the ER, scans showed that I had significant blockage in my three dominant arteries, too extensive for stents. Bypass was the only answer. They scheduled my surgery first thing the following morning. It all happened so fast, I had little time to over-think or even to be particularly afraid. The night before, as I surrendered myself to sleep, I took a moment and contemplated what lay before me. Open heart surgery is always dangerous, but my entire sternum and ribcage are fused, calcified from a lifelong battle with arthritis. I knew there was even more risk for me in this operation. But I decided to unreservedly embrace my fate. I would cross this Abyss and face whatever perils presented themselves along the way. As corny as it may sound, I decided, whatever the outcome, I was going to face it with a smile on my face and a song in my blocked and broken heart. Lying there, I took a quick mental inventory of my life, my great blessings, and the overwhelming richness of my life experiences. Overall, I was happy with how my life had played out, whether this was the end of the piece or just a rather dramatic middle movement. If this was the curtain call, I decided I wanted to be ready to graciously take my bow. I went to sleep that night in an odd state of contentment. The next morning, I practically zippity do-dah'd my bony ass into that operating room.

It seemed like it was only seconds later and I was in the ICU, post-op. I could hear people, from an echoey, dream-like distance, but I couldn't open my eyes for the life of me. I'd made it through, but I wondered if I hadn't made a big mistake. Unable to open my eyes, as hard as I tried, I feared I might be in some sort of a coma. My chest was in excruciating pain, like it was piled with cinderblock. I have never been more physically uncomfortable in my life. Later, my family and friends who were in the room said my skin was the exact color as the bleached-white bedsheets. I looked like a ghost. And I felt like one. I hung, helpless, in this state for what seemed like hours.

But once I was fully awake and able to communicate, things seemed to rapidly change, became oddly charmed. The pain subsided quickly (helped by a constant drip of IV pain killers) and I started to perk up almost immediately. And it just got better and better from there. I could actually feel this acceleration. Hospital staff were complimenting me on how good I looked, how my color had returned. They were telling me that I might be one of the fastest patient recoveries they'd seen. I was discharged in four days (it's normally at least five). I thought: "Wow, they've got this bypass business down. Open heart surgery isn't so bad." I was elated to get out of there, anxious to start my cardio rehab, and get on with my life.

Then, suddenly, everything went pear-shaped. I got home on Saturday night. I felt okay, weak, but fine. On Sunday, without knowing it, my life began draining away. My son Blake says I became lethargic, distant, answering questions I wasn't asked, rattling off weird paranoid fantasies. Yelling at him, even accusing him of plotting to kill me. My skin turned otherworldly colors, orange and gray. Blake invited a doctor-friend, Steve, over. Steve took one look at me and quickly called 911.

The next week was the most bizarre chapter of my life. Due to the bad blood reaction, I became psychotic. They never figured out exactly why. I lived in several parallel realities at the same time, teased out the most elaborate plots and machinations. And I "enjoyed" the most intricate, hyper-vivid hallucinations. Little did I know, cast adrift now within my fevered brain, but during the first ten hours or so back in the ER, I was fighting for my life. Once they realized the blood was the issue, they were scrambling to find more, properly cross-matched blood. It took over 9 hours. In the meantime, Gareth the meat puppet had become a lifeless rag doll. My hematologist later told me that I had the worst blood values she'd seen in her career. "For all intents and purposes, you should be dead," she told me during a follow-up visit.

My friend Alberto said, when blood finally arrived, just in the nick of time, it was like that stereotypical scene in a movie where cheers and high-fives go up all around. My boat across the Abyss had came that close to sinking. While they'd been trying to find blood, there'd been another drama going on. My blood pressure was so low, they couldn't find a pulse or a vein to establish an IV. They spent hours poking and scanning my lifeless limbs in search of IV sites. Blake saw some of this and said it was utterly horrifying. They ended up having to go in through my jugular — they literally cut and sewed an IV port into my neck. I screamed so intensely (they obviously couldn't sedate me in such a perilous state), I saw kaleidoscopic images of bright crystalline daggers of purple light shooting out from my eyeballs. It was pain beyond imagining. (In the midst of it, I remember thinking, as a sort of Note to Self: "Hey, I didn't know that purple was the color of excruciating pain.")

Once I got the proper donor blood in me, physically, I started to quickly turn around, But the psychosis was only starting. I had to spend another week in the hospital as they tried to get my blood back on track and get me mentally stable. I would be in the hospital for another week.

The whole experience was transcendently strange. Within the course of a few weeks, I felt as though I'd lived in several distinct sci-fi universes. The bypass was pure cyberpunk. I turned myself over to futuristic flesh mechanics, meat-hackers, and they'd engineered a new heart for me. Arlington has a very modern hospital, but it was built in the 1980s, and has something of an 80s futuristic, now retro-futuristic, feel to it. They took me apart and put me back together in short order. It felt almost like it wasn't a huge deal, "post-human" medicine at work. The hospital is very computerized. Most of the tests and X-rays come right to your bedside and most of the test equipment is networked and handheld. Your body stays covered with "dermatrodes" and is wirelessly connected to monitors at the nurses' station where a graphical display shows your glowing vitals 24/7.

The horrifying trip on the bad blood was like mainlining a Philip K. Dick novel. I suddenly found myself in a creeped-out reality of multiple universes and fractal levels of paranoia. I was certain that international, perhaps even intergalactic, conspiratorial forces were assailing me. I experienced layer upon layer of the most bizarre and hi-def hallucinations. I was convinced that an Asian crime syndicate, involved in international child trafficking, snuff porn, and counterfeit medicine, was responsible for giving me some sort of spacetime-altering hallucinogen disguised as post-operative antibiotics.

Whatever actually triggered the psychosis, it was amazing in the detail of the visuals it produced. It was as if the hallucinated things were right there in the room with me — they weren't vague, ghostly apparitions, but tangible people and objects, as real as anything in our meat world. But I knew that they weren't from around here. I spent one week living in multiple realities and staring into the very clockwork mechanics that animate our universe (at least the universe in my fevered imagination).

Two weeks after my initial ambulance ride to the hospital, on a bright Sunday afternoon, I found myself home again, the P.K. Dick realities fading in my rear-view mirror. But things had now turned positively post-apocalyptic Zombie Town. I remember it so vividly. It was almost as if I awoke from a bad dream. I suddenly find myself standing in my kitchen in a pair of ratty cut-offs and an olive drab work shirt, the only things I'd found clean when I got home. The most violent, rainbow-colored bruises (if there are rainbows in hell) and pin-pricks dot my body where they'd pestered me for IV sites. A huge bandage is covering my chest (where, what now seems like a lifetime ago, I'd been cranked open with Frankensteinian purpose). The IV wound on my neck still shows where they'd sewn on a dual-port plastic access panel. My legs and feet are bluish-gray and swollen to Elephantine proportions (they're not exactly sure why that happened either). My left foot and lower leg are wrapped in bandages and there's a hose coming out of some hardware bandaged onto the side of my calf. The hose run up my thigh to a satchel slung over my shoulder which houses a "wound vac," a Cronenbergian device that's sucking the blood from the site on my lower leg where they'd harvested the vein for my bypass. It's making a very unpleasant, irregular clacking and clicking sounds, like some mechanical, vampiric insect is feeding on me. When I'd been rushed back to the hospital, loopier than Charlie Sheen on a bender, they'd taken a freakishly large vertical eye-shaped biopsy from the vein site to see if I'd acquired an infection. That led to the need to wear the vampire vacuum for, they said, up to a month (it ended up being three months). I look down at myself and think I look convincingly outfitted for a prize-winning Halloween costume contest, or as an undead extra in a horror film! What on Earth (or dimensions beyond) has happened to me!?

[Nightmare Prevention Pro-Tip: Do NOT Google "wound vac."]

The hallucinations I had during my week of blood-poison looneytunes were so intense, elaborate, and prolific, I can't possibly recount them all here. After I got out of the hospital, I recorded over five hours of me recounting them. Here are a few from the highlights reel:

One of the more curious gems I smuggled back from my Buckaroo Banzai adventure in the 8th dimension was the shocking discovery that the constituent building blocks of everything (at Virginia Hospital Center, anyway) are koosh balls, and to a lesser extent, 50s wrought iron lawn furniture. Thanks to the spacetime tweaker drugs given to me by that dastardly Asian crime syndicate, I'd apparently acquired the ability to see through walls, furniture, hospital test equipment, everything. And inside it all lurked squiggly blue koosh balls, like so many inanimate *Star Trek* tribbles. Needless to say, I was both tickled and a tad deflated. I guess I was hoping for something with a little more *matter gravitas.*

The alternate material, wrought iron lawn furnishings, was more interesting, but far less common. I decided that was because it couldn't be packed in as tightly as koosh balls. I remember taking note of a few wrought iron pieces I'd spotted through my x-ray vision, thinking they might look good in my yard, and wondered if and how one could extricate them from the bedrock of matter.

And where did all the koosh balls come from, you must be wondering? In the late 1970s (in my head), a new Atlanta-based shipping company, called Next, made a dramatic stab at the burgeoning overnight shipping market. Their novelty give-away was the festive blue koosh ball. ('Cause when you think overnight delivery, who doesn't think of a tendrilly squish-toy?) They had zillions of them made, and when the company failed disastrously, they had some tribble troubles of their own. What I can't tell you is how they found their way into the fabric of reality.

I also began to obsess over a little-known 80s new wave film, called *Two Toma-hawks*, directed by a pair of movie-making twin brothers. *Two Tomahawks* was a rockumentary about the Native American teen new wave music scene on reservations in the southwest. It was these teens that began selling turquoise jewelry to pay for their futuristic fashions, their clubbing, and their big-haired synth pop bands. The turquoise jewelry business took off, and some of these kids became very wealthy, eventually getting involved in heavy drugs, organized crime, the usual dirty deeds. By some strange twist of fate (and mad free association), one of these teen turquoise jewelry moguls resettled in my home town of Chester, Virginia, and some of my high school friends had appeared in the film. The only problem with all of this is that there is no such movie, no such twin brother directing duo (wait, but one of them was a childhood star!), and as it turns out, the growth of the turquoise jewelry craze of the 1980s had nothing to do with Flock of Seagulls-coiffed Native American teens.

My main crazed narrative centered on the reason why I'd been sent back to the hospital in the first place — that dastardly intergalactic, tainted-antibiotic, drug trafficking and kiddie porn/sex slave crime ring. I apparently had some information in my brain, thanks to a chemical signature in the drug they'd given me, that could help law enforcement – DEA, Customs, Interpol, the Men in Black – track down the bastards that had almost killed me (and likely harmed or killed countless others).

As part of my treatment, several times a day, a nerdy guy, whom I was sure I recognized from an old PC ad in an early *Byte* magazine, wheeled in a device with a tank and a face mask. As I talked to him about the good ol' days of the PDP-11, CP/M, dBase II, and other lumbering creatures from the computer

Jurassic (he seemed strangely intent on making pretend he knew nothing of what I was talking about), he'd strap on the mask and crank up the aerosol inhalant. As soon as I'd breathe in the gas, I would get the most intense and vivid hallucinations. And each time, they were the same: My visual field was split in half horizontally. The top half was a video screen tinted in a fuchsia hue. It was obvious to me that I was looking at some surveillance camera feed that looked onto a housing block in some sketchy Asian neighborhood. Information in Asian ideograms and a timecode appeared at the bottom of the feed. The bottom half of my "mind screen" was similarly set up, but I somehow knew that it was of a crime-ridden street in a Mexican slum. The color-tint on this video was sepia-tone and the info (with a timecode) was in Spanish. I assumed that what they wanted me to do was to look at these surveillance feeds in my mind, which were somehow attached to the sale of the poisonous spacetime-altering antibiotics, and try to relay any actionable "intel" I might find. After about three days of these treatments, I finally asked the former *Byte* PC nerd-model turned hospital technician if the images I was seeing were actually encoded in the aerosol or if it was just a substance designed to trigger my own memories of these events. He looked at me like... well, like I was nuts, and said: "It's basically water vapor. It's just to hydrate your lungs." Looking mildly alarmed, he gathered up his rig and quickly wheeled it from the room. I started to wonder whose side he might *really* be on (and why he'd decided to switch careers, from computer modeling to nursing).

Many nights, as I phased between sleeping and waking, I'd have the most fruit-loopy visions, my brain fevered by temporary insanity and the nightly Dixie cups of festive-colored painkillers and sleep aids they fed me. I would dog-paddle my way right up to the edge of sleep, with dream images leaking into waking reality. At any given moment, I could be off on some rickety train of thought, and the next, I'm watching a couple fucking up against the door jam of a Tolkien-themed pub in the UK (where all of the graffiti is in High Elvish). Or ethereal female elves would appear in a mind-borne informercial for the new Galadriel Tequila. (I was so convinced that there actually was a Galadriel-brand Tequila, even after I was sane, that one of the first things I did when I got home from the hospital was to Google it.)

Everything in my mind was eventually overtaken by the infection of conspiracy. I was convinced that the hospital staff was part of some global cabal of kicks-seeking caregivers doing unforgivable things to patients. The funny thing was (in retrospect), they were all centered around the idea that the staff was bored shitless and using the internet and webcams to connect with other hospital workers so that they could all entertain themselves. The "games" they played were elaborate, the conspiracies and dramas I cooked up around them even more so. One of the more horrifying of these games was called The Scab Orchestra.

A big part of being in the hospital, a very unpleasant part, is the various daily pains of being stuck with needles, having bandages and adhesive strips yanked off, being catheterized (and un-catheterized), and having wounds dressed. I was convinced that an international hospital workers union, in some quest for cruel kicks, was recording these procedures on webcams and composing the video'd hoots, yowls, ouches, and screams of patient pain into video orchestral pieces that they shared with each other over the Internet. Appalled, I tried to take mental notes of as much of all this as I could and was already mentally accepting my Pulitzer, knowing what a huge *exposé* this was going to be, one that I planned to write as soon as I got out of the hospital.

I was also busy mind-writing another headline-grabber about another evil nurses' game, a drinking and drugging game. Patients would agree to play and they'd then have to take a certain number of hits on a hash pipe or shots of... you guessed it, Galadriel Tequila. If you failed to complete the required number in the first round, you had to take penalty shots or hits (of the opposite drug you'd initially chosen) for a set number, and then switch back. So, for example, five shots of tequila and three penalty hits of hash. There was some sort of prize offered, and for me, it had something deliciously unholy to do with that elvish barmaid back at the Tolkien pub. But I realized, as nurse Sheila dutifully delivered my hash pipe and shots of Middle Earth spirits, that the game was rigged. The hash was so potent, as was the booze, that no one could likely make it to the lucky number without having to take the penalty hits and start over. And apparently part of the initial agreement was that you couldn't stop, once you started, until you won. So, if you didn't win by the first or second round, you were pretty much done for. I was convinced I was going to die, drugged to death by my night nurse. I remember lying there thinking what a waste it was that I had lived such a wonderful life, had overcome crippling arthritis, and a heart attack, heart surgery, blood poisoning, and now temporary insanity, only to die because of a pointless drinking game. Mercifully, I passed out before the International Nurses Cruelty Cabal could torture me any more with Lebanese blonde and Elvish hooch.

There are so many other twisted tales I could share: How Virginia Hospital Center was a giant origami-like structure that folded up each night. How Adobe Corporation had funded the construction of the hospital and had built Flash movies, like Talking Heads' *Stop Making Sense*(!), into the very walls of the building. How one of the nurses was in love with me, and I was sweet on her, but she was a white supremacist and that was a deal breaker. (One night I apparently also told her that she had bugs crawling all over her face, but she was so beautiful, that it didn't matter.)

The most astonishing aspect of all of this is how sane I was in the midst of my insanity. I was conscious of the fact that I was crazy. It was like being in a dream and seeing yourself from on-high. Most of it was more curious and entertaining than scary and I even had the detachment to think: "This is going to make for some really crazy story material!"

Of all of this, the spookiest part was the fact that I interacted with people that I knew didn't exist, but they had all of the convincing characteristics of physicality. They looked as flesh and blood as you or I. I guess most of us have this Hollywood-driven idea that when crazy people hallucinate, what they see is somehow phantasmagorical – there, but not there, or not completely; a sort of ghostly holographic projection of one's imagination. This was not the case at all. These phantasms looked and acted real, so I interacted with them, we carried on conversations.

The other surprising, and frankly, sad thing is how quickly the incredible high that comes with feeling like you've just walked away from a catastrophic accident faded. That morning, headed toward the OR, I was proud of myself. I felt brave, and strong, and fully alive. I was ready to move towards the next challenging phase of my life. Or into oblivion. The initial four-day recovery was almost spooky in how good I'd felt, how rapidly I'd recovered. Then the madness came. That was a very hard and scary ordeal, but again, I came through. By then, I felt that I had earned my battle scars and showy chest medals, that I really had crossed the Abyss, passing through the perilous darkness to the other side.

Jean Cocteau used to talk about going through phases of "molting" and coming out the other side as a different kind of being, more evolved, more beautiful. I felt like I had done that. I'd faced death, I'd crawled through the wreckage of my mangled heart. I'd fought off invading forces deep within my own blood. And on the other side, I got to LIVE! To experience the simple joy of drawing breath! To absorb daylight. To hug my blessed son (over and over again). I felt fully, expressively, sacredly ALIVE!

But then, the impolite realities of life slowly began crawling back – work pressures, loneliness, money worries, all the rest of it. I held my survival over death up like a shield to deflect all of this – you can't harm me, you many-tendrilled monster of mundane reality, I've boated the fucking Abyss! I've seen the kooshy watchworks of reality! I've performed in the Scab Orchestra! I've survived the Galadriel drinking game! This held the beige at bay for awhile. But slowly, my old life began to return.

I certainly believe that I learned a lot from my ordeal. And I feel as though I confronted (and overcame) many demons: heart disease, madness, death, heinous hospital food. The cock-eyed optimist in me would like to think that I'm tougher now, that I learned a lot about human frailty and the nature of madness. In the aftermath, and the fading euphoria, I was reminded that no matter how much you overcome or how reinvigorated you might feel as a result, it doesn't secure your ongoing strength and happiness. Abyss-crossing and demon-slaying are daily, dynamic processes. Every night is that night before surgery. My ongoing "hero's journey" challenge is to have the courage to zippity-do-da my ass every morning toward whatever trials life decides to throw at me.

Let's just hope there are no more intergalactic drug and kiddie porn cartels to battle in my future. That last takedown darn-near killed me.

YOU'RE ON!

I wrote this essay especially for this collection. And I always saw it as the last essay in the book. It's painfully personal and that probably says something too about the ride this book has been for me and how much of me has been revealed within its pages – and how it perhaps made sense to end on such a note, a note about letting go. I've never been one to substantively edit expressions of my experience – comes with being a writer and an extreme extrovert, I suppose. One of the reasons I did this book on my own imprint was that I wanted to collect my work and tell my story in the way that I wanted it to be told, with little thought to shelving categories or market expectations. For good or ill, I feel like I've done that.

It's safe to say that the impact of my 22 year marriage to Pam Bricker, and her tragic death, have come through in these pages. Anyone who's lost a spouse knows how difficult it can be. Losing someone after a very close and satisfying marriage of over two decades presents another level of challenge (especially when the wheels came off so dramatically at the end). Trying to learn from those experiences, to integrate them, and then to move on, is yet another challenge that every widowed person faces.

Perhaps against my better judgement, I decided to finally go back to a Thievery Corporation show. I hadn't been able to bring myself to see the band in concert since my wife Pam had died in 2005. She'd been a singer in the band and toured the world with them. She sang on such well-known songs as their *Garden State* soundtrack hit "Lebanese Blonde," the title track to *Mirror Conspiracy*, and the very haunting, posthumously-released "The Passing Stars." Pam had even been a part of that musical tribe before Thievery existed, first appearing on Eric Hilton's 1996 Exodus Quartet album, *Way Out There*.

[The almost eerie thing about Pam's involvement with Thievery was the way that association seemed to almost be wished into existence. One of the many gratifying aspects of Pam's annual late-summer gigs on Nantucket, which ran for over 25 years, was the discussions she and I would have on the long car rides to and from Massachusetts. The trip each year was like a creative pilgrimage for both of us and we spent much of the time in the car discussing our respective careers and brainstorming how we could improve our work and personal lives. One summer before she hooked up with Eric Hilton, on the ride home, we were talking about the tragic lack of interest in classic vocal jazz (what Pam was doing most of at the time). By the end of the discussion, we had articulated an ideal career path for her. She needed to find a group of ridiculously talented, market-savvy young musicians who could use her jazz vocals in some new, creative, potentially commercial way. Soon after getting home, purely by coincidence, Eric asked Pam into the studio, and her relationship with what would eventually become Thievery began. We would often joke about how perfectly this met the fantasy we'd imagined on that car ride, like we'd conjured it into existence.]

I had seen Pam play with Thievery for the last time in November of 2002, as they came off of their world tour. That show was part of an absolutely magical four days, starting with them landing in DC on Thanksgiving day. Pam had arrived on our doorstep with fellow Thievery vocalist Emiliana Torrini in tow (perhaps best known for singing "Gollum's Song" on Peter Jackson's *Lord of the Rings: The Two Towers* soundtrack). Emiliana, who is from Iceland, had never had a traditional American Thanksgiving dinner and she was anxious for one. I'd never cooked a Thanksgiving dinner before, and was a different kind of anxious, especially now that we had a famous dinner guest pulling up to our table. But the meal turned out surprisingly well (beginner's luck?) and the rest of the evening was as charming as anything I could imagine. After dinner, the three of us sat around drinking red wine while the two of them shared Thievery tour stories and Emiliana regaled us with tales of working with Roland Orzabal of Tears for Fears on her record *Love in the Time of Science*, and touring with Tricky and Dido. Emiliana is one of those captivating presences that you can't help but immediately crush on and don't soon forget.

The next night we went dancing at the Rumba Cafe with the Thievery crew. That Saturday, the band played their 9:30 Club gig (the last time I would ever see Pam perform), and Sunday was her return to what she called her "artistic residence" at U-Topia, the U St. "art bar" where she'd played most every week for years. Thievery members showed up for that, too. Another American custom that Emiliana wanted to experience was a high school prom, but not any era prom, specifically an 80s prom, "with big poofy-foofy sleeves," she insisted. So, on that Saturday afternoon before the 9:30 show, Pam and I had gone to our local Goodwill and bought several jewel-toned satin dresses with puffy sleeves and we threw Emiliana a prom night at U-Topia. I wore an iridescent acetate Zoot suit that a friend of mine had bought in a rural West Virginia thrift store. It's an absurd garment that you have to see in person to truly wrap your mind around. Those almost Fellini-esque four days with Emiliana and the rest of the band really endeared them all to me.

Fast forward to 2012, seven years after Pammy's passing, and here I am finally deciding to see the band again. When I'd gone to see them before I'd had gotten my hip replacement, I had been in a wheel chair. I remember being really touched by members of the band carrying my chair up and down the stairs so I could hang out with them in the 9:30 Club dressing rooms. I was nervous to see how they would regard me now.

For this 2012 show, they were coming off another big tour and had sold out the 9:30 Club for three nights. The show was spectacular — fun, exuberant, and featuring Thievery's usual parade of vocalists, from Roots and Zeebo, the two Rastas who've been with Rob Garza and Eric Hilton from the beginning, to LouLou, Sleepy Wonder, Sister Pat, Frank Orrall, and Natalia Clavier, who now sings Pam's signature tunes. Sadly, Emiliana has her own busy solo career and no longer tours with them.

The band was as gracious and welcoming to me as always, but as soon as I stepped into the club, I began to wonder what the hell I was doing there. How could I have expected to see Thievery, minus Pam, and not be emotionally wrecked by the experience? Especially seeing them in the same place that I had the last time, the last time I'd ever laid eyes on my wife on a stage? It was everything I could do to not flee the building.

I eventually managed to do a decent job shaking all of this off and enjoying myself as best I could. But by the end of show, I found myself in a very haunting tableau that took my breath away. Right before the band's first encore, I'd gone upstairs to try and find a wife of one of the bandmembers. I ended up on the dressing room balcony. It was empty as everyone was already pressing their way into the dressing rooms for the after-party. On this darkened, empty balcony, I peered over the railing just in time to see Natalia, the woman who now sings Pammy's tracks, taking the stage to perform "Lebanese Blonde," Pam's most famous tune with the band. Nat was dressed very similarly to how Pam had been that night in 2002, she even had a similar hairstyle. Suddenly, I realized that, ten years ago, I had been in the *exact* same spot, then sitting in my wheel chair, looking down at my wife singing the exact same song.

I had talked to Pam from the road, late into that 2002 tour, and she'd told me about how she thought she was finally finding her place in the band, her role onstage. She was doing more patter (talking to the audience between tunes), and feeling comfortable with it. And that night in 2002, I had witnessed, sitting in this balcony, a level of confidence and stage presence I'd rarely seen in her. There was an inspired grace about her that night. She sounded amazing, as always, but I saw her much more open, relaxed, and expressive onstage. I even thought her physical presence, her gestures, were so perfectly, confidently sexy. I remember being so proud of her. I had seen her on stage hundreds of time, but I don't think I'd ever seen a more confident and moving performance. And sitting there in '02, I'd reflected on those charmed last few days, with Emiliana and the band, how magical they'd felt, how absurdly rich our life seemed.

And here I am, in 2012, and all these years and dramatic changes later, and I find myself back on that balcony. But I might as well have been looking onto the band from a balcony on the moon. The disconnect of seeing and hearing someone else performing Pam's song became horrifying. I literally felt chills, the hairs on my neck standing up, as if the ghost of Pam was making herself known. I thought I might be having a panic attack. The spookiness of it all was too intense; I recoiled from the railing like I'd suddenly acquired a fear of heights. I raced from the dressing rooms and down the backstage stairs.

I found Roots and Zee at the bottom of the stairwell. With hugs and bro-fists exchanged, they began telling me how much they loved Pam and missed her, how they thought about her all the time. Roots was saying that the casual voice lessons she'd given him on the road had really improved his vocal performance, and as a result, he felt like she was with him whenever he's onstage. It was a touching reunion, and I felt all the more comforted by their kindness, given the unnerving moment I'd just had on the balcony.

As the three of us huddled around on the stairs, all of a sudden, the stage door blasted open. Giant sound waves from of the rest of the band came crashed over us. The stage manager yelled: "Guys, you're ON!" Roots and Zee leapt up and ran toward the door as he handed them their wireless mics. They had to start singing before they even topped the stage as they shot across it, launching into "Richest Man in Babylon" (one of Thievery's popular tracks). "There is no guidance in your kingdom, your wicked walk in Babylon. There is no wisdom to your freedom, the richest man in Babylon." The crowd went apeshit.

I'd bolted after the two of them through the stage door and gotten to the side of the stage almost at the exact moment they'd taken the front of it. I got to see and feel the waves of energy pouring towards them from a reaching, screaming, and leaping audience. It was unreal. To go from this quiet, sweetly human exchange on the stairs to, seconds later, a joyous riot of music and celebration (being generated and orchestrated by the two people I'd just been talking to) took the top of my head off. It's a moment I will remember for the rest of my life.

And then, suddenly, an internal calm settled over me, one of those slow-mo life moments. Everything around me was in loud, dramatic motion, but my insides had found a peaceful, reflective pause.

I felt like Pam was there again. I smiled. I imagined her smiling back. I saw Roots onstage and thought about her being up there with him, within the power of his voice as he sang, high-fived the front row, and pulled women onstage to dance.

I looked out into the crowd and saw frenzied joy on people's faces. The night had been emotionally challenging, but I was glad now that I'd made the effort, that I'd faced down the ghosts I'd found lingering in this hall. I realized that I had just let a little more of Pam go a few minutes ago upstairs. And I was letting more of her go now, smiling and happy, floating up to the rafters, propelled by the high-spirits in this room and the soundwaves that she had once helped generate herself.

It has been a slow, steady scrabble away from the wreckage of Pam's awful death, but I've made the climb. And I'll keep climbing. We all will. For we should never be afraid to exorcise the lingering ghosts of our past, but we should also never let go of those parts of the dearly departed that gave us the strength to climb in the first place. And that taught us how to sing.

APPENDICES

GARETH'S TIPS ON SUCKS-LESS WRITING

Or: Everything I know about writing, I boosted from other writers and editors.

I first started working on this piece in 1997 but didn't actually post it online until 1999. I'd just released my book, *Jamming the Media*, a guide to all forms of 90s DIY media, when I started brainstorming a list of writing tips. By 1999, blogs (followed by podcasting a few years later) were offering a degree of easy and ubiquitous DIY media-making I hadn't foreseen just two years earlier (at least not in the forms they took). With all of the new media creators settling this promised land of Web 2.0 (there's content-gold in them-there hills!), I wanted to create a basic good-writing tips sheet.

Over the years, I'd picked up so many great craft-of-writing ideas and hard-won words of wisdom from fellow writers, editors, and other word nerds. When I finally published the first version of this piece, it struck an immediate chord. It was widely linked to and covered on *Boing Boing* and some popular writing sites. It even ended up being taught in several college creative writing classes. One second year class at Purdue still uses it.

One of those 90s classes even created an early blog to talk about the class, my sucks-less tips, and for students to share their own writing tips. My favorite comment on that blog came from a student who said (about me): "He sounds really young. And cynical." I liked the "young" part. Reading over this now, I do sound rather cynical. I was reading too much Warren Ellis and his *Transmetropolitan* comic at the time, so I was perhaps channeling some of his gonzo exuberance. I even ended the piece with a paraphrase from Spider Jerusalem, Transmet's butt-kicking journalist, followed by a picture of him filing a story from the seat of a public commode while screaming at his editor on his cell phone. It's actually a photo of a collectable statue. That glorious statue sits on a shelf in my library, perpetually pooping and yelling and filing stories. There may be another writing tip or two in that.

[Original Intro:]

I've been working on this, in dribs and drabs, for a few years now. The original idea was to share some tricks of the writer's trade with the bloggers on my tech site, Street Tech (*streettech.com*), many of whom were new to regular writing. I violate some of my own "rules" here. The piece is a bit long-winded and even more than a bit redundant, but I decided that, in this context, it was OK. For instance: "Garage Band Writing Style," "Shitty First Drafts," "For God's Sake, Have Fun!," and "Writers Write!" are all in a similar vein, only expressed in slightly different ways. One may speak to you where another doesn't. Anyway, consider this a work in perpetual beta.

I've always thought that it's important to honor one's teachers. Good teachers impart the knowledge and practical wisdom that makes a difference in the way we work, live our lives, and more fundamentally, the way we perceive the world around us. They inspire us. Unfortunately, at least in my case, I'm not talking about teachers from my formal education (with a few exceptions). Over the years, it's been those foot-slogging the muddy, bloody trenches with me — fellow editors and writers — who've taught me the most about the writer's craft. When

I look at my work, I can see them lurking about within it. Whatever success I've had as a writer, I owe a great deal of it to them. So without further ado ...

PRECIOUS LESSONS LEARNED

✎ Split Your Writer and Editor Heads

The first book I ever bought about writing was called *Writing with Power*. It was largely forgettable and engendered in me a life-long suspicion of how-to-write guides, which BTW, seem to permanently appear on "What to get writer boy?" holiday gift lists.

> **Note to Beloved Family and Friends: I'm all set on the how-to write books. If I haven't figured it out by now... Oh, and could you hold off on more blank journals, too? I now have a small library of them, a small, blank library. And, as much as I'd like to think otherwise, I don't have that many profound thoughts, and when I do, I have plenty of paper, what with the blank library and all. Need gift suggestions? Liquor is always good. Writers love to drink.**

But I digress. *Writing with Power* wasn't a complete waste of my lunch money — it contained one core concept that changed my early life as a writer: When writing, don't try to edit as you go. Say what you want to say, unencumbered by the constant commentary from the fussy editor that floats about in your head. First step: Get it all down. Then, you can have at it. Keep what works; bug-zap the rest. By separating writing and editing functions, you can convince yourself that you're just doing a first draft. This way, you often end up with better-than-expected material. When I read this book, personal computers weren't even a gleam in Turtleneck Steve and Mr. Bill's eyes (yes, I'm THAT old. Shush!). Way back then, it was difficult to type and retype multiple drafts without the burning desire to edit as you went. Word processing suddenly changed all that.

> **This memo just in from the Profound Thought Department: *Mondo 2000* was the first magazine I worked for where the entire writing process had become electronic. For my first writing job, as a columnist for *Communities* magazine, I'd write on a legal pad and then type up the final version (or several drafts and a final). As the Computer Sciences Editor for *The Futurist*, I would write my articles on my trusty Apple IIe, print them out, and then get on the DC Metro and travel from Arlington, VA to Bethesda, MD to physically deliver my manuscript. With *Mondo*, I would pitch the editors via email, write the piece on my computer, and email them the article.**

It was while proudly looking at my first printed piece in the magazine that it hit me: The characters I was looking at, printed there in full color, on slick paper amongst the bright colors and cyberdelic swirls of that pioneering techno-culture rag, were the very ones I'd first committed to bits. I had started with my brainstorm, my "shitty first draft" (see below), and cut/pasted/added/edited until I was satisfied. Then I'd fired it off in an email, which got packetized and datagramed and sent down dozens of pipes, finally arriving across the country in San Francisco. Editors had further tweaked my keystrokes and sent them on to the art department, who'd laid them out in a graphics program and finally sent them to the printer to be shot onto printing plates. Looking at the magazine, I was looking at the very characters that had come out of my head, through my nervous system into my keystrokes and onto my computer. Such a far cry from the pre-digital world of scratching your ideas into paper, hammering them into more paper, usually multiple times, sending them to a typesetter, having them re-keyed in again, cut into plates, etc.

Today, they don't even manually photograph and process metal printing plates anymore. It's all done digitally within the press itself. The fluidity allowed by "word processing" frees you up to really write from the hip, and the irony is that, what comes out is often better, thanks to this freedom. It's much closer to a direct connection between the writer's fingertips and the printed page. Nearly every time I look at a piece of my writing in a magazine, I feel the electronic lineage of those characters on the page. And, of course, in ebook publishing that distance is even shorter. Coming soon: From my nervous system to yours.

✗ Throw Out the First Waffle

One of the things I noticed when I first started getting my work published was how often my introductory paragraphs got unceremoniously tossed into the trash by delete-happy editors. I once heard the phrase "throwing out the first waffle" used to describe divorce in a first marriage. I've come to think of these intro paragraphs as the first waffle(s) of writing. Writers, especially newbies, often waste this first paragraph (or two or three) dancing around their subject, gobbling up precious column real estate, awkwardly warming up themselves and their readers. When you're done with your initial draft, take a hard, dispassionate look at those first few paragraphs. See if they're necessary. Be harsh. Which brings us to:

✗ Apply Occam's Razor

A friend of mine, Andrew Lawler, a science and technology writer who was an editor at *The Futurist*, *Science*, and *Space Business News*, taught me this one. When it's time to switch from your writer's hat to your jaunty editor's chapeau, carefully scrutinize every word in your piece. Ask yourself: is this necessary? Is this the simplest, most straight-forward way of saying this? If not, toss or revise! You'll be amazed at how many words you can trash. (Then sit on the piece overnight — no, not literally! The next day, whip out that happy, happy razor again. You'll be surprised how many more flabby words you'll find lazing about before you, sucking up perfectly good electrons and laptop battery life).

And now a word about sitting on your work: I cannot stress how much your piece will improve if you can let it marinate for a good 24 hours OR MORE. You need distance from the work, perspective. The longer you wait, the more perspective you'll gain. Stephen King, when he finishes a book, puts it in a drawer (and IMMEDIATELY starts in on the next book – but he's not human). He waits at least two weeks before he starts editing. And knowing to split writer and editor heads, he's done NO going back and reading/editing the manuscript while writing it. Two weeks is a luxury for most writers, but the worst thing you can do is take all of the time up to the deadline writing and then quickly editing and sending off (or publishing) your work. When you read the published piece in a few days/weeks, you'll hate yourself for all of the glaring mistakes, clunky word choices, too-late ah-ha moments, etc. So, do yourself a favor, leave time and SIT ON IT!

Critical note to Newbies: Never, EVER find yourself saying the following in email to an editor: "I know you only asked for [your assigned word count goes here], but here's [your outrageously flabby, up all night buzzing your brains out on coffee and energy drinks till you've lost all restraint and perspective word count goes here]." Editors are busy, over-worked people, often tightly-wound, Type-A personalities with little patience for sloppy, logorrheic writing. Getting the piece at least in the neighborhood of the assigned word count is your job, not theirs. If they have to spend tons of time wrestling that anaconda o' prose of yours into the allotted space, you may not get invited back onto their dancefloor.

✒ Don't be Redundant. Really. Don't.

Sometimes, you learn what not to do by watching others. I have a friend (who'll remain nameless) who's a supremely funny and talented writer, but he often slips into repeating himself. He constantly repeats concepts and sentence structure. When you constantly repeat concepts and sentence structure, you end up writing about 50% too much material, just like my funny and talented writer friend does. I've learned my lesson well from him, not to repeat concepts and sentences endlessly. He's really funny and talented though. He really is.

More on this: I find, when editing writers, that they'll often use the same primary noun over and over again in successive sentences. So, if they're writing about a 3D printer they'll use "3D printer" in every instance. A good writer can come up with creative ways to avoid over-using the primary/proper noun. So the "3D printer" can also sometimes be "the printer," "the desktop fabricator," "the wannabe Star Trek Replicator," "the glorified computer-controlled glue gun," whatever. I'm being silly here, but you get the idea. Free your mind. Mix it up.

⚡ Damn the Cliches!

Many, many years ago, I contributed to a book for Time-Warner. My editor was big on cliché busting. I'd never realized how many clichés I relied upon until she pointed them all out. So, in order to weed out those moldy chestnuts, keep your eyes peeled and your ear to the ground. Then, your work will be as fit as a fiddle and fresh as a daisy.

⚡ Read it Out Loud

The late William Safire suggested that you read your work out loud. Writing is not the same as speaking, but they each have (when done well) a lot to do with rhythm and satisfying word flow. If your writing sounds good when spoken, it's likely to read well on the page. It's definitely a good idea to read all dialog out loud, especially if you're new to writing it or struggle with getting the voice right. Aloud, you'll find all sorts of words, sentence structures, and rhythms that just aren't natural to speaking.

> Tangential to this: Brian Eno says that he has certain people he sometimes imagines looking over his shoulder, hearing his music, reading his words, a kind of virtual Greek chorus of critical voices. I do this sometimes and it can be helpful. The trap is not wanting to change what you need to say because you want to please each of those voices. Do that, and your work will end up as invigorating as luke-warm bath water. Stephen King says you should designate someone you know, whom you think represents the consumer of your work, as "The Reader," and write to that person. He or she doesn't even have to know. In his case, it's his wife, and she eventually does read the drafts, but he always keeps her in mind when he's composing and directs everything he creates at her. Again, this can be a trap, but can also serve as a useful compositional trick.

⚡ Giving Good Headline

Writing great heds (headlines)/deks (subheads) is an excellent way of framing the concepts of your piece and adding another level of wit and humor to your work. I hardly ever do proper outlines. I usually come up with a general concept, create the lede, hed, and deks, then hang my story from there. Which leads us to:

✗ Know How to Get In and Get Out

A friend of my dearly-departed wife, a TV news "crime and grime" reporter in DC, was trying to give her some advice on "patter" (what a performer says to an audience between tunes). He shared an old TV journalist's tip: Know how to get in (how to set up what you're going to say, your "lede") and how to get out (how you plan on finishing). Then you're free to bullshit your way through the middle. If you stumble, or run out of things to say, you can jump to your closing. The same thing basically holds true in writing. Once you know how to set up your piece (with a great attention-seducing lede) and how to end it (with an equally clever and compelling wrap), much of your heavy lifting's done. The rest is mainly filling in the who-what-where-when-why and providing some painterly descriptions of your subject.

✗ "Write Like Yourself, Only More So"

This motto comes from science fiction author Rudy Rucker who has called what he writes "transrealist" fiction. Rudy takes real situations and people from his life and exaggerates them in his novels. He believes this creates a more honest, grounded, textural fiction, even when dealing with out-of-this-world subjects. Even though I don't write much fiction, this concept appeals to me since I usually write non-fiction in a personal, first-person style.

Writing in a first-person, conversational style is a mixed bag. Some people like it, others don't. Some writers are good at it, others aren't. If you write this way, be careful not to come off sounding condescending, or overly chatty. Aim for smart, friendly, funny, unpretentious prose.

> **More on this:** My approach to writing is based on the editorial policy of the old *Whole Earth Review*. "Write like you're writing to an intelligent but uninformed friend." This style may not work for, or appeal to, everyone, but it's worked for me.

> **Even more on this:** If you write in a conversational style, be careful not to make it TOO conversational. Limit sentences that begin with "And," "So," "Well," "OK." Also avoid opening qualifiers that wimp out your point: "In my opinion," "I think," "If you ask me," etc. "Adverbs of degree" are another type of weakening qualifiers used in conversation that don't work well in text — words like "just" ("I just think that I've lost all faith in my creator and humanity."), "pretty" ("Sex with you last night was pretty good."), and "fairly" ("I'm fairly sure that this sentence will communicate my point.").

⚡ Writers Write!

Mike Gunderloy, founding editor of the iconic zine review guide *Fact-sheet Five*, used to say that, even if you aren't a writer to begin with, after cranking out a million words or so, you're a writer! Gunderloy himself was a prime example. He wasn't much of a writer when he started F5, his now-legendary "zine of zines," but he sure as hell was by the time he called it quits millions of words later. By then, he had truly mastered the art of short-form, concise, and spunky media review and criticism.

⚡ Writers are Makers

In the early days of working for *MAKE*, at events where people stood up to say what they made, I would say: "I make magazines and books about people making things." People would laugh, but I meant it sincerely. Writing is a kind of making, a form of idea engineering and communication. When I edited the "Lost Knowledge" issue of *MAKE (Volume 17)*, steampunk artisan Jake von Slatt (who was writing a project article for me) called one night, excited, because he'd realized that writing is just another form of making — designing, engineering, constructing. Indeed. A piece of writing has structure, it needs structural integrity to hold up under its own weight. It has design, it has sub-components that need to fit together properly, there are frequently construction problems that require troubleshooting and tinkering to get the contraption of your piece to run. A written piece is like a little thought machine that you build and then it gets run in the reader's mind and delivers a powerful idea (if built properly). It can be helpful to some writers to think of the craft of writing in these physical terms of making.

⚡ Speling Counts (So Don't Grammar)

A lot of readers out there don't give a jot how clever you are if you have the grammatical chops of Dan Quayle. Computers have been a boon to the language-impaired, thanks to spell- and grammar-checkers, but these tools can't help you if you don't use them. It astonishes me how many articles I get from writers — allegedly pros — who haven't bothered to spell- or grammar-check their manuscript. This is NOT the way to an editor's (or an intelligent reader's) heart.

⚡ Sometimes, the Best Things You Write, You Write by Mistake

Several of my most reproduced pieces came from rants I posted on The Well BBS that I had no intention of ever publishing beyond that forum (one post even became the words that opened Billy Idol's notorious 1993 Cyberpunk record!). I was posting on the fly, as part of a written conversation. Unencumbered by my "editor head," I got something out of me that I may not have otherwise. Keeping a journal of your thoughts on anything (not just the daily details of your life), or engaging in good online conversation, are great ways of learning how to write with freedom and immediacy. You'll be surprised how much turns out to be useable material.

> More on this: Your next big idea may occur to you at any time, so always keep a pen and notebook handy. (I have these tools by my bed, my chair in the living room, in my basement workshop, by my toilet, in my shirt pocket, etc.) Write down what comes to you, DON'T tell yourself that you'll remember it! You won't. I've had brilliant brainstorms (at least that's what I've told myself) in the middle of the night, and being too lazy to write them down, have tried to memorize them before floating back to Slumberland. Next morning: Nada. Zippo. Not a clue (except the memory that, whatever it was, it was a zinger). Once you get in the habit, you'll automatically reach for the pad even before the thought has finished forming itself.

> Even MORE on this: If getting up, turning on the light, and jotting things down is too much, or there are other situations where writing is not convenient, get a cheap digital voice recorder or a recording program for your mobile phone (if it doesn't already have one). You can also use Evernote. com, the free, Web-based note-taking program that allows you to take audio notes, text notes, even photographed "notes." I record my dreams at night (yes, I sleep with my phone. Don't you?) and they're already uploaded to my Evernote account before my feet hit my bunny slippers in the morning.

✒ For God's Sake, Have Fun!

The awesomely talented Sean Carton taught me to loosen up and have fun with my writing. He worked with me on the Mosaic Quick Tour books (the first book about the Web, I'll have you know). He is such a relaxed, fun, conversational writer. He inspired me to try and relax more at my keyboard. Don't be afraid to flirt with your readers. Tapping into a flirty, cocky, humorous style, again, without condescension, has a lot to do with being relaxed as you write. That, and not caring too much about the outcome. Which brings us to:

✒ Garage Band Writing Style

Writing is something that anyone can do, and do well, IF you know how to get out of the way of yourself. And then, how to massage what comes out into something that can communicate powerfully with others. A lot of the really talented magazine writers and editors I've worked with over the years started out in zine publishing, the writer's equivalent of punk rock. Along with "writing like yourself," and "having fun," toss "writing like you don't give a shit" into your toolkit. Shoot from the hip, write from your gut, put some passion into it! Write what excites you. Don't be afraid to break the rules or piss on statues. The results may suck, but they might not, and you might be onto something fresh and exciting. Elvis Costello was a punch card drone at Elizabeth Arden Cosmetics when he saw the Sex Pistols on TV. He thought (paraphrasing): "Fuck this. I can play better than these louts. If they can be rock stars, I can too!" There are plenty of big name writers out there, with all of the questionable talent you need for this kind of "if s/he can do it, I can too!" inspiration (I'll resist naming names).

More on this: One of my writing teachers (and "life editors") is Peter Sugarman (with whom I did Beyond Cyberpunk!, and who co-founded the website Street Tech with me). Peter and I have very different writing styles, but the emotional power and directness with which he writes have always inspired me. He seems to have a nearly direct link between his guts and his keyboard. He reads a lot of comic books and admires their poetry and economy of words. He's obviously been influenced by the genre and the immediacy and brevity of his writing reflects it. I've tried to let this approach inform my own.

Develop a Thick Skin

My first professional gig was as the Computer Sciences Editor for *The Futurist.* I was nervous about the job and didn't feel like I was getting enough pats on the back from my editor. One day, I confronted him. His answer, although maybe something of a cop-out, did contain a valuable lesson. He said: "You're here because we wanted the best. We hire people who are good at what they do. I expect great things from you and you deliver."

This was, of course, the kind of recognition I was looking for, but it also reminded me that the writing world is a fast and furious business. Editors can't always (and rarely do) hold your hand or pat your back. Being hired, THAT'S their big vote of confidence. Editors don't have time to respond to every email message and phone call. You have to be self-motivated, low-maintenance, and above all, thick-skinned. You're mainly going to hear from them when they DON'T like what you've done. And honey, when they tell you how badly they think you screwed up, they're not likely to mince words.

Then there are the nasty letters to the editor and the hate mail and web comments from readers. You have to suck all this up, too. Again, most likely, you'll only hear from people who think you stink. But that only makes it sweeter when you get mail from readers who say that what you wrote changed their lives, or saved their lives, or set them down a brilliant career path, or whatever. These messages may be few and far between, but when they arrive, they make all of it (dealing with surly type-A editors, readers from hell, inadequate pay) worthwhile.

✏ Editors: Give 'Em (Part of) What They Want

One of my awesome writer/editor friends, who should probably remain nameless (*sneeze* *Mark Frauenfelder*) shared this one with me many years ago, after I'd suffered through a couple of endless rounds of "Frankenedits" on several *Wired* features. I was always under the impression that, when an editor sends back a manuscript bleeding profusely with red ink, you have to make every change they suggest or insist upon. Mark says "Nah." Pick the two or three big changes, especially the ones you agree with, make those, and then any additional changes that are easy. Then send it back and say that the edit suggestions were really great, insightful, and you're really happy with the piece with the new changes you've made. Nine times out of ten, that will be it. You're done! (Of course, telling you this might be a little like revealing stage magic secrets. I probably just violated some sort of writer's Fight Club rule. Sorry, Mark, sorry fellow indolent wordsmiths).

✏ Watch Out for Mixed Metaphors

One of the things I've worked hard to cure myself of is the use of mixed metaphors. "Like a rock, standing arrow straight" or however that Bob Seeger ode to the Chevy pickup goes, is a prime example. Sure you can force the fit, but it's just lazy writing. A rock might be tough, hard, long-lasting, but one doesn't tend to associate chunks of geologic aggregate with lean and supple arrows. By the way, Bob, rocks don't really charge through gates, either.

✏ Take it "Bird by Bird"

One of those writing how-to books I got as a gift, and initially shelved with the others, was Anne Lamott's *Bird by Bird*. Since a writer-friend I love and respect had given it to me, I figured I should at least give it a whiff (after months of feeling guilty about not doing so). The book turned out to be extremely inspirational. It's filled with hysterical stories about the craft of writing and the art of living from someone who lives an unconventional, paint-outside-the-lines life. The central premise concerns getting over your laziness about writing. As mentioned above, "writers write," but often, this only happens when they can trick themselves into doing so.

The title refers to an incident when Anne was a child. Her brother had waited until the night before a school project on birds was due to start work on it. He sat at the kitchen table, with a blank pad of paper and a pile of bird books, overcome by the immensity of his task. His father sat down, put his arm around him and said, "Bird by bird, buddy. Just take it bird by bird." This has become Lamott's way of tricking herself into writing. She tells herself that she's only required to write a small amount each day, one "bird." No matter how busy, how distracted, how depressed, surely there's time for one measly paragraph or character description or scene outline? Of course, once you sit down to bang out that one 3x5's worth of text, you end up producing two or three or more. But you always tell yourself you're gonna take it one non-intimidating chunk at a time. Bird by bird, buddy.

✓ Shitty First Drafts

One of Lamott's other "tricks" (which we've already covered above in "Split your writer and editor heads," "Garage band writing style," and "For God's sake, have fun!") is to perfect the art of the "shitty first draft." Get over yourself and just get it out! Tell yourself it's your goal in life to craft shitty first drafts, that you LOVE your shitty first drafts, that shitty first drafts are your amigos. Amaze yourself by the impressive quantity and quality of the shit you can squeeze out. Bow to the Buddha in that shit! Nobody but you ever has to see these unholy early drafts. Lamott says her career might be over if readers saw some of hers. But it's this rough, let 'er rip copy that she's crafted into numerous and inspiring best sellers.

✓ Keep it Naughty AND Nice

I also highly recommend Connie Hale's *Sin and Syntax: How to Craft Wickedly Effective Prose*. I swear my writing literally improved with each chapter. The book is about the balance between sin (breaking the rules, writing with courage, being fresh and creative) and syntax (knowing and applying the rules when appropriate). The book mainly reads like a post-modern Strunk and White and is a good reminder of what you learned (or should have learned) in school. Connie, the former Copy Chief at *Wired*, uses a dizzying array of real-world examples (from the Bible to press releases to rock lyrics) to illustrate bad writing that follows the rules and good writing that doesn't.

✓ Tell the Truth, the World Has Too Many Liars!

This is my final tip (then I'll go away and let you get to work). Here in our sucks-more 21st century, where most journalists have become corporate spokesbots, media politicians skewing the news based on what polls and focus groups tell them their "demos" are interested in hearing (and what their advertisers will support), more then ever, we writers need to tell the truth, at least as we understand it.

When I was a teen and dreamed of becoming a writer, I had this romantic notion of the writer as rebel, a L'enfant terrible who sat at a typewriter, with a pack o' smokes and a bottle o' Jack, and bled truth onto cotton weave. Over the arc of my career, age, familial responsibilities, and a bothersome bottom line may have worn down some of my own edge, but I still try to do an honest day's work, and write with as much honesty, authenticity, and passion as I can muster.

Given the current state of things, as I watch too much of our future being flushed down the craphole, I'm wanting to sharpen some of that edge back on. One of my inspirations? A comic book character, Spider Jerusalem. Spider, the "hero" of Warren Ellis' brilliant *Transmetropolitan* series, is a Hunter Thompson-esque bitraker who beats the streets of a sprawling city in an indeterminate future. His laptop has become a dangerous weapon in his fight against government corruption, corporate crime, and social apathy. He is journalist as superhero (albeit a flawed, drug-addled, vigilante one). If you're a writer who (like me) needs a Doc Marten in the behind every now and again to remind you why you got into this game in the first place, read Transmet!

I even bought myself a Spider Jerusalem action figure. Half-naked, fully tattooed, he sits on my computer, along with his assault laptop and two-headed, chain-smoking mutant kitty, keeping me honest. A lovely collectable statue of Spider (sitting on a toilet) perches like a gargoyle on the shelves of my library, too. Corny? Maybe. Childish? That, too. But Spider is here to remind me how I can, right now, reach through this computer and grab you by the head, the throat, the heart, or the nethers. How? With the power of my words, 'cause in this closing sentence, I'm here to remind you that…

I AM A FULLY-ARMED, GODDAMN PROFESSIONAL JOURNALIST!

CYBURBAN MYTHS

I edited *Wired*'s "Jargon Watch" column for the first twelve years of the magazine's existence. Even though this was the early days of the web, way before social media, the content of the columns frequently ended up spreading through email and being posted on websites and bulletin boards. At one point, someone collected terms from a number of my columns and began circulating them in an email. It contained no attribution or mention of *Wired*. Friends and colleagues would get this document, think it was a collection of new slang that would be interesting to me and would email it to me. The list quickly went viral and floated around the Internet for years, right alongside the "$250 Neiman Marcus Cookie Recipe," the "Save NPR" email petition, and other persistently viral (frequently hoaxed) messages.

But the truly interesting thing is that nearly every time I found one of these emails washed up in my inbox, it had a different title attached to it. It was like some weird information age Rorschach test where everyone who looked at the list needed to come up with a slightly different subculture who spoke this strange new language (geeks, dot-com office drones, Gen Xers, new media mavens).

Several times, the list was credited to Scott Adams (creator of *Dilbert*), and in one instance, it was ascribed to a contest that the *Washington Post* had done asking its readers to coin new terms. Sadly, no one ever credited it to *Wired*, or to me. Or, at least no one ever bothered sending me any properly attributed versions.

The unattributed list even ended up in the *Washington Post*. John Schwartz, then at the *Post*, excerpted it in the "Cybersurf" column and then did a very charming apology the next week (starting off with: "Hey Gareth, I'm sorry!"), after I sent him an email. *Post* columnist E.J. Dionne published it a few weeks later, in his *Washginton Post Sunday Magazine* "Chattering Class" column. He was not as gracious as John. I sent him an email and never got a response or apology and there was never a correction in the paper. *The Microsoft Newsletter* also published the list. I went ahead and added *The Washington Post* and *The Microsoft Newsletter* to my resume.

The most interesting outcome of all this is that I got a call from Richard Roeper, the columnist and movie critic. He was doing research for a book on urban legends and wanted to cover online legends, email hoaxes, and the like. I guess since my list so frequently got caught up in the same drift nets as the other viral emails, he thought it was relevant. Like me, he thought the shifting nature of the document's title was particularly interesting. I don't think anything about the list ever made it into his book.

Below is a list I started keeping of all of the titles of the emails. This isn't even all of them. I had a longer list at one point but its bits are slowly rotting away in a drawer somewhere, on a disk from some long-lost storage technology. Following the titles is the original email.

```
Generation X Office Lingo
Cyberspeak for the Highly Strung
Office Lingo
Office Jargon for the 21st century
Silicon Valley Geekspeak
New Lingo
Cubonics
New Media Speak
Microserf Glossary
Technology-Inspired Lingo
The New Dilbert Vocabulary
The Language of the Cube Farm
Office Terms of the Late 90s
New Office Words
New Words for the Next Century
New Words for the New Millennium
Modern Day Office Lingo
New Age Office Terminology
Life in the Corporate World
```

New Hacker Lingo
Latest terminology used by the modern day worker...
Dilbert Neologisms
Office Terminology by Scott Adams
Terms to Add to Your Vocabulary in the Early 00s Office
Environment
Geek Terms for the Late 90s
GenX Dictionary

Mouse Potato
The online, wired generation's answer to the couch potato.

Blamestorming
Sitting around in a group discussing why a deadline was missed, or why a project failed, and who was responsible.

Dilberted
To be exploited and oppressed by your boss. Derived from the experiences of Dilbert, the geek-in-hell comic strip character. "I've been dilberted again. The old man revised the specs for the fourth time this week."

Body Nazis
Hard-core exercise and weight-lifting fanatics who look down on anyone who doesn't work out obsessively.

Cube Farm
An office filled with cubicles.

Ego Surfing
Scanning the Net, databases, print media, and so on, looking for references to one's own name.

404
Someone who's clueless. From the World Wide Web error message "404 Not Found," meaning that the requested document could not be located. "Don't bother asking him . . . he's 404, man."

Elvis Year
The peak year of something's or someone's popularity. "Barney the Dinosaur's Elvis year was 1993."

Idea Hamsters
People who always seem to have their idea generators running.

Keyboard Plaque
The disgusting buildup of dirt and crud found on computer keyboards.

Ohnosecond
That minuscule fraction of time in which you realize that you've just made a BIG mistake.

Perot
To quit unexpectedly, as in "My cellular phone just perot'ed."

Prairie Dogging
When someone yells or drops something loudly in a "cube farm", and people's heads pop up over the walls to see what's going on.

SITCOMs
What yuppies turn into when they have children and one of them stops working to stay home with the kids. Stands for Single Income, Two Children, Oppressive Mortgage.

Starter Marriage
A short-lived first marriage that ends in divorce with no kids, no property and no regrets.

Stress Puppy
A person who seems to thrive on being stressed out and whiny.

Swiped Out
An ATM or credit card that has been rendered useless because the magnetic strip is worn away from extensive use.

Tourists
People who take training classes just to get a vacation from their jobs. "We had three serious students in the class; the rest were just tourists."

Treeware
Hacker slang for hard copy documentation or other printed material.

Uninstalled
Euphemism for being fired.

Xerox Subsidy
Euphemism for swiping free photocopies from one's workplace.

Flight Risk
Used to describe employees who are suspected of planning to leave the company or department soon.

Seagull Manager
A manager who flies in, makes a lot of noise, craps all over everything and then leaves.

CLM (Career Limiting Move)
Used among microserfs to describe ill-advised activity. Trashing your boss while he or she is within earshot is a serious CLM.   (Also known as CLB - Career Limiting Behavior)

Salmon Day
The experience of spending an entire day swimming upstream only to get screwed and die in the end.

Chainsaw Consultant
An outside expert brought in to reduce the employee head count, leaving the brass with clean hands.

Percussive Maintenance
The fine art of whacking the crap out of an electronic device to get it to work again.

Adminisphere
The rarefied organizational layers beginning just above the rank and file. Decisions that fall from the adminisphere are often profoundly inappropriate or irrelevant to the problems they were designed to solve.

Assmosis
The process by which some people seem to absorb success and advancement by kissing up to the boss. You will all be measured on this at some point in your career.

THE BORG COLLECTIVE

This book was an experiment in doing as much of a book's production process myself as possible, from crowdfunding to overseeing every aspect of production (and subsequent promotion and sales). I wanted to really get my hands dirty. And man, did I get FILTHY! The rewards during the funding and production phases have been great (the extent of the financial rewards remains to be seen) and I'm thrilled to have undertaken the project.

Saying this was an experiment in DIY might create the impression that I did it alone. Far from it. I oversaw it all, but there were many sous chefs in the kitchen, principle among them were Blake Maloof (project management assistance, design, graphics, production help), Gillian BenAry (editing and art consulting), Michael Lee (production management, design, and layout), Katie Walker Wilson (design and layout), Greg Brotherton (design), Jeremy Mayer (art), John Bergin (art), and the other artists who contributed illustrations to the project (see "Artist Bios"). A huge and very special thanks to video artist Rob Parrish who did an amazing job on my Kickstarter video. His good spirits and generosity got the book off to a great start. And a great thanks to my 11th hour line editors: Chris Chen, Peter Sugarman, Phyllis Klein, Tom Burtonwood, Caitlyn Dorsey, and Andrew Lewis.

Friends and supporters who went above and beyond the call of duty during my Kickstarter campaign and during the book process include: Mark Frauenfelder,

Kent Barnes, Daniel Rehn, Steve Hoefer, Andrew Lewis, Alberto Gaitán, Mark Dery, Daniel Carter, Jeri Ellsworth, Phyllis Klein, Peter and Colleen Sugarman, Virginia Vitzthum, Jonathan Monaghan, Stacia Cosner, Steve Roberts, Andrea Pollan, William Barker, Shannon Wheeler, Lea Redmond, Darick Chamberlin, Shawn Wolfe, Danny Hellman, Bart Nagel, Chip Wass, Libby Buloff. And those who helped with KS reward fulfillment: Blake Maloof, Jessica van Brakle, Judy Willard, Maggie Duvall.

I'd like to also thank all of my pals at Maker Media (past and present). It has been so inspiring working with all of you over the years and calling you friends. Thanks for all of your continued support.

A special shout-out to David Culkins and Simone Davalos of RoboGames. It was their generous donation that finally took me over the top to my $15,000 KS project goal. I still owe one of their robots a kiss on the mouth. But NO TONGUE!

KICKSTARTER BACKERS

The Kickstarter campaign for *Borg Like Me* launched on July 17th, 2013. It was one of the most exciting and challenging things I've done in ages. Putting the campaign together took a month of work and running the thirty-day campaign took most everything I had. I tell people that it was like grabbing onto the tail of a comet and that's not much of an exaggeration. It was as exhausting as it was exhilarating. I got so much love, support, and general good will during that process. And, of course, pledges. I had sort of stumbled my way into the process, creating the video, setting up the web page, and creating all of the backer rewards. Without knowing a lot about what I was doing, I managed to get a lot of things right and a few things wrong (e.g. I had way too many items in my reward bundles which became a nightmare to process and mail). I was beyond thrilled to have achieved the trifecta of Kickstarter staff support; being chosen as a Staff Pick in the Publishing category, a Staff Pick on the front page of the site, and one of three campaigns chosen for their weekly "Projects We Love" mailing. In the end, I had 476 backers and raised $20,776.

I can't thank my backers enough. You all were so kind and generous and I received so many social media shout-outs, emails offering help and encouragement, and other bolstering gestures of support. I really felt a tremendous amount of love and respect, which made the hard work far more bearable and the entire experience so gratifying. It was all definitely an experience I will never forget.

Cue the *Borg Like Me* credit roll. Hugs and high-fives to you all.

A special shout-out
to my most generous
backers:

Kim Haas
Dan Woods
Dieter Ceelen
Blake Maloof
Trenton Wynter Brown

Mary Corzine
Michael Castor
Mark Adams
Christopher T Palmer
AnnMarie Thomas
Pam
Jake von Slatt
Liz Martin
Jake Spurlock
Goli Mohammadi
Gary Honig
Jonathan D. Sousa
Anna Kaziunas France
Matt Wagner
Jody Culkin
Len Cullum
Marko Manriquez
Christos Liacouras
Ryan Peterson
Jeremy Blum
Kipp Bradford
Jon Cole
Claire Packer
John Abella
Alan Bloom
Nancy Calvert-Warren
Mike Maurer
Jennifer Arnett
Mike Fisher
Melissa Asher Morgan
Chaz Carlson
Tim Gottleber

James O'Dell
Bill Casti
Nicola Beddow
Robert Carlsen
Hal Gottfried
Kathryn Rowe
Jon Andrews
Jason Babler
Jimmy DiResta
David Scheltema
Matt Silver
Cyberoptix/Bethany
Shorb
Brian Judy
Tod E. Kurt
Sean Carton
Kevin Segall/Collector's
Shangri-La
Natasha Reatig
Sean Michael Ragan
Tim Tate
Nick Normal
Peter Wiggin
Skip Lancaster
Tom Burtonwood
Steve Hoefer
Christel Davies
Michael Jason
Shawn Connally
Shay Brog
Laurie Stepp
Brad Barr
Andrea Pollan
Mark Frauenfelder
Jeannine Mjoseth
Christopher Carnelian
Eric Weinhoffer
Kent Barnes
Nathan Loofbourrow
Maggie Duval
Micah Solomon
Cathie Arquilla

Judith D Willard
Ross Vann
James Bridson
Brian Jepson
Rachel Lovinger
Josef Szuecs
Stefan Antonowicz
Jeri Ellsworth
Daniel Rehn
Tony Evans
Alden Hart
Ted Hall
Angus Hines
Bryce Lynch
John Bagby
Rob DeMartin
Chris van Gorder
Jose R. Cordero Ladner
Rodger Boots
Ryan Moran
Julia Pelosi
RoboGames
Don Russell
Dave Arney
Rob Myers
Alberto Gaitán
James Leftwich
Richard Gould
Matt Richardson
Christie Uhler
Gregory Hayes
Jason Naumoff
Paul Leonard
Chris Connors
Mike Pechner
Tom Igoe
David Lang
Richard Brull
I-Wei Huang
Bill Young
Sheena Stevens
Ryan Kunde

Bruce Schreiner
John Ulaszek
David Pescovitz
Dondi Lyons
Sandra Pruzansky
Dave Kellar
Sparkle Labs
Edward Iglesias
ShopBot Tools
Martha Barbour
Jon Lebkowsky
Eric Brown
Courtney Lentz
Robert Loring
Jillian Pichocki
Laura Cochrane
Heather Cochran
Daniel Carter
Jackie Steven
Callie Oettinger
R.U. Sirius
Kathleen Ryan
Pam Grossman
Katy Dunn
John Willis
Lisa Doan
J.J. Larrea
Jim Donaldson
Katherine Morgan
Rob Vincent
Linda Hesh
Sabrina Merlo
Miranda Mager
Fran Reilly
Miriam Cross-Cole
Philippa Hughes
Richard Nagy (R.I.P.)
Mitchell West
Mary Kranz
Jacqueline Loustaunau
Craig Couden
Tim Lillis

Matt Dibble
John Park
Dean Putney
Ross Hershberger
Marian Weiss
John Bergin
Thomas Lee
Stefanie Fedor
Eri Gentry
Mike Daren
Alex Wawro
Monique Priestley
Jeff Berg
Jon Malis
Rob Giseburt
Byrons' Telescope-
Burning Man Team
Kathryn Cornelius
Laurie Barton
Louise Glasgow
Andrea E. Janda
Bridgette Vanderlaan
Andrew Lewis
Steve Hernandez
Matt Mechtley
Evil Mad Scientist
Laboratories
Janice Marks
Bre Pettis
Rita J. King
Steve Davee
Robert Patterson
Pierce Presley
Jason Gollan
Keith Woeltje
Mike Zeitz
Marc Parsons
Janine Tursini
Karlee Vincent
Joel Westerberg
Paolo Tabaroni
Mark Hartsuyker

Marcus Escano
Biruk Woldu
Donald Melanson
Matthew Griffin
Stefan Jones
Gareth Wilkins
Rusty Blazenhoff
Eric Siegel
Robert Cashin
Bree Kalb
Steven Smethurst
Rody Douzoglou
Mary Rotman
Mrs Giggles
Carolyn Weaver
Lisa Cherkasky
Sara Winge
johngineer
Jessica
Chriss Peter
Joseph Thibault
Jimmy "JR" Ray Tyner III
MaryAnne Glazar
John Pallister
Andrew Taylor
Danny Pettry
Lee Walter Mothes
Jesper Michaelsen
Branka Tokic
Shannon Wheeler
Jenni Brammall
Kristin Whetstone
Miffi Maxmillion
Gillian BenAry
Arwen Griffith
Anthony May
Andy Holtin
Nathaniel Johnstone
Alasdair Allan
Gary McGraw
Todd Burks
Rachel Lewett

Shing Yin Khor	Marque Cornblatt	Mark Mordarski
Rich Vander Klok	Christine Mallia	Geoff Hogg
Don Coleman	Philippe Van Nedervelde	Stephen Mack
Paul Spinrad	John Baichtal	Cory Clines
Will Kreth	Jonathan Korman	Burkhard Grosche
Lewis Fulwiler	Matt Mets	Barbara Lewis
Katie Wilson	Travis Good	Patrick DiJusto
Allison Lonsdale	Brady Forrest	Dave Davies
James Moore	Jonathan Hitchcock	Sylvia Egger
Scott Fitzgerald	Robert Forbes	Jason Kofke
Matthew Hawn	Terry H. Romero	Daniel Young
Shawn Wallace	Marty McGuire	Jeffrey McGrew
Vamsi	Anton Olsen	Jeremiah McCarty
Vincent Rossi	Matthew A. Dalton	Paige Totaro
Scott Austin	Bob Gourley	Mike Grusell
Kent Reynolds	Phil Grossblatt	Remco de Korte
James Husum	Apollo Lemmon	Lang Thompson
Michael Fagan	Norman Sohl	Karl Endebrock
Sangwoo Han	Theron Trowbridge	Stephanie Walker
Daniel Southwick	Juliane Gross	perrie iles
Casey Rae-Hunter	Michael Chiasson	Paul Szymkowiak
Diana Eng	Paul Havig	Ashley Simpson
Sindre Ø	Matt Billings	Ben Gokel
Alan Swithenbank	Gareth Kennerley	Barry Rittberg
Susan Eder	Joshua Ellis	Costa
K.A. Moylan	Paul Cutler	Will Sanborn
R Siggs	Tim Slagle	M. Eric Carr
Zetetics	Lucinda Rose	David Schweikart
Chris Gilroy	Pol Moragas	Eric P. Kurniawan
kicklix	Delbert Saunders	Calle de Blok
Kathy Ceceri	Elise Ackerman	Colin Day
Rob Donnan	David McFadzean	Jiri Suchomel
Sherry Huss	Matthew Peterson	Gerard van der Woud
Adam Ware	Mark Dery	Adam Houston
Mary Beth Williams	Flexline Designs	Jamie Gaughran-Perez
Bruce Sterling	Kenneth Richards	Jonathan Ward
Bruno Boutot	Jason McNinch	Joe Torre
Cory Doctorow	Jim Wisniewskij	sharoninavolvo
Meg Allan Cole	Roy Christopher	Dennis
Michael Carroll	Alan Cheslow	Thornn jones
Meredith Yayanos	Richard Kadrey	Rachel Hobson
flashthedog	Suzanne Huston	Seric

William Claydon
Julie Hudy
Bilal Ghalib
Ross Waldron
Garin Hiebert
Rachel Horvath
Sergey Milanov
Martin R Rothfield
Steve Silberman
Dustyn Roberts
Phoenix Perry
Eric Hervol
Jon Singer
Peter Sugarman
Steven Roberts
Christian
Phyllis Klein
Joe Thibeault
Hans Moen
Chrtis Nikoloff
Matt Jones
Jeff Kroll
Mark Sherman
Bob Knetzger
Dave Nuttycombe
Rachel Kalmar
Miika Oksman
kgroocock
Eric Mesa
Jen Edwards
Thomas Bourke
Harriet Cavanagh
Thien Vu
Ziv Kitaro
Morgan Winter
Charalampos Doukas
Gordon Meyer
Marianne Petit
Gustin Johnson
Mircea
Thomas Izaguirre
Tino Dai

Rui Pereira
Erik Sund
Brandon Mechtley
Ryan Gates
Julia Stoops
Ellen Chenoweth
Isaac Wedin
Deepak Mehta
Ross Hendrickson
Jason Griffey
Laura Ellis
Micha Savelsbergh
Kamil Sliwowski
Jim Cavera
Jan
Libby Bulloff
Michael Silva
Aaron Levitz
Beth Trombley
Evan G. Phillips
Jimmy Samsara
Niki Corradetti
Sophi Kravitz
Franck Yvonnet
Griff Maloney
Jen Shannon
Jesper Anderson
Marcus Verduchi
Anne Graham
James Huckenpahler

THE ARTISTS BEHIND THE BORG

I've had the pleasure of working with some truly amazing, inspiring artists over the years, at both the mainstream magazines I've written for, and through the labors of love of the zine scene. Many of them have remained some of my dearest friends. Rather than doing traditional bios, I thought it'd be fun to share some anecdotes about us working together, how we met, etc.

The names of the artists are followed by the titles of the pieces in the book to which they contributed art. Please visit their sites and support their work. They contributed to BLM out of friendship, and to support this project (after I didn't reach the art goal in my KS campaign). I am forever grateful for their support, generosity, and friendship. I owe you all a debt of gratitude. And a round of Pink Ladies.

William Barker (Chapter Zero: The Launch Party) – William is best known for creating Schwa, a universe not unlike our own populated by paranoid, drone-like stick figure humans and their alien overseers. Schwa art and products were darlings of the zine world in the 1990s and landed William a Chronicle Books contract, an AOL online gaming deal, and animation interest from (Colossal) Pictures. After raking in surprising quantities of dough for a fringy art project, William retreated to the deserts of [redacted], going off-road, off-grid and living like a Hunter S. Thompson character for awhile (I once had a phone call with him while drunken neighbors were joy-firing guns in the background). William has resurfaced in the last few years and is currently running alaVoid *(facebook. com/alaVoid)*, a store for "21ˢᵗ Century Far-Edge Art."

James Huckenpahler (By This River) – James makes pretty and ponderous pictures on his laptop. His current work-in-progress, "Allegories," is an illustrated history of the federal city. He's a member of FURTHERMORE, a very cool research and development lab for visual culture and sustainable art communities in DC. Like me, he is also a fellow of Provisions Research Library, and currently serves on the advisory board of Transformer, one of the more tenaciously badass art galleries in DC. James and I run a mutual admiration society and I was thrilled that he agreed to create an original piece for this collection. *(superluckyland.com)*

Mark Frauenfelder (Journey to Kooktopia) – If you've read this far, you already know plenty about my relationship with Mark. When I was looking over the BLM essays, I was struck by how much of him is shot through almost everything; how closely our life paths have remained since the day we met. Besides being an amazing writer, editor, businessperson, and dad, Mark is also a gifted artist. I was so happy to be able to lift a piece from his stash to use in the book. *(boingboing.com)*

Danny Hellman (Below the Clown, Boating the Abyss, Building Spaceships Out of 5s and 6s) – The piece that Danny did for "Below the Clown" in *bOING bOING* #5 was the first time that any artist had ever illustrated an article for me, so Danny has always had a special place in my heart. I can't thank him enough for finding that original art, re-screening it, and contributing two additional pieces. Danny Hellman: the man, the mensch. *(dannyhellman.com)*

Shannon Wheeler (Please Captain, Not in Front of the Klingons) – I first met Shannon at an epic *bOING bOING* after-party in my hotel room at Austin's ArmadilloCon in the early 90s. That crazy party still lives large in my memory. That night, Shannon gave me copies of *Too Much Coffee Man* and I've been a huge fan ever since. Besides *TMCM* (genius), check out his recent collaborative re-telling of the Bible (with author Mark Russell), *God is Disappointed in You* (also genius). *(tmcm.com)*

Steven Raymond (No-Tech TV Interactive) — I worked with Steve at *STIM*. Besides being the founder of that very innovative early web magazine, Steven is also a talented artist and I was so bowled over when he did the original online illustrations for "No Tech TV Interactive." My plan was to reprint all of them in the book, but alas, the original hi-res files have been lost, so I had Blake Maloof "upconvert" one of them in Photoshop to use here. This gives you some idea how lovely the others were.

John Bergin (Tears in the Rain) – John and I go back. Way back. We began exchanging zines in the early 90s (my *Going Gaga* and his *Brain Dead*) and have remained friends ever since. I was so inspired by John's many talents (fine artist, illustrator, animator, musician, the list goes on) that I once wrote a story about an artist/musician who's utterly dark and depraved, but the beauty with which he renders his work is so profound, it refuses to scare, alarm, disturb anyone. His talent has actually become an impediment to the totrured artistic self-expression that he's attempting. That's always been John Bergin to me. I even found *The Penis Object* a thing of beauty. You don't want to know about *The Penis Object*. Check out John's amazing feature-length, award-winning animated film, *From Inside* (frominsidemovie.com), which he created almost single-handedly. *(johnbergin.blogspot.com)*

Stéphane Halleux (Apocalyptic Bone Dancing, Is There a Cyberpunk Movement?) – I first met Stéphane while doing a piece about the art of steampunk for *Wired*. I immediately fell in love with his work. Stéphane is the only Academy Award-winning artist in this group (as far as I know). While we were working on this book, *Mr. Hublot*, the animated film by Laurent Witz and Alexandre Espigares, based on Stéphane's characters, won the Oscar for animated short film. Proud to know him. *(stephanehalleux.com)*

Jeremy Mayer (Cover art, Borg Like Me) – I first discovered Jeremy's work in one of those viral "Holy crap! Look at this!" posts that spread through social media like a Hollywood hills brushfire. Jeremy sculpts the most amazing pieces exclusively out of typewriter parts. Exclusively. No bolts, glue, added wire, or welds. If it doesn't come from a typewriter, it doesn't go into the work. I was so touched that he graciously agreed to let me use two of his pieces for this book. *(jeremymayer.com)*

Scott Beale (Makers vs. The Blob) – If ever there was an Annie Leibovitz of the maker movement, it's Scott Beale. Scott has been such a great friend to the movement, covering nearly every flagship Maker Faire in the US (SF, NY, Austin) and I'm sure some of the local Faires. Scott is also the big cheese behind the highly-recommended Laughing Squid website. There are many things to love and appreciate about Scott. For me personally, he's one of the few photographers who consistently takes pics of me that don't make me want to burn my face off with battery acid. For this, I am eternally grateful. *(laughingsquid.com)*

Howard Hallis (Darkside Rocketeer) – When I was doing research on Jack Parsons for my "Darkside Rocketeer" piece in *MAKE* (Volume 13), I bumped into Howard's amazing faux comic book cover of Parsons's life. It was too good not to include in the article. Or in this book. Thankfully, Howard agreed to both. *(howardhallis.com)*

Terri Weifenbach (Figure, Ground, and All-Around) – World-renowned Terri Weifenbach is one of my favorite art photographers and I'm honored to know her as a friend. I was gobsmacked when she asked me to write the introduction to her "Woods" show for DC's wonderful Civilian Arts Project. That intro is reprinted here. Cheap B&W printing doesn't do Terri's work justice. Go to her site (after reading my essay) to get the full effect. *(terriweifenbach.com)*

Nemo Gould (Fantastic Contraption) – Nemo is, hands-down, one of my favorite found object artists, and at this point, I know MANY such artists. I knew Nemo from my work at *MAKE* (where he's something of a regular), but I got to know him more through Device Gallery, where he's appeared numerous times. What I love about Nemo's work the most is the great sense of humor and irony with which he infuses it (and it's frequently hidden, or delayed, like a comedian's punchline). Nemo is a humorist working in found-object kinetic sculpture. *(nemogould.com)*

Greg Brotherton (Techno-Temporal Mash-Ups) – Like Stéphane Halleux, Greg and I first met when I was doing the piece for *Wired* on steampunk. Greg's work is not exactly steampunk, but he was traveling in similar circles and mining similar tropes. The *Wired* piece led to me being asked by Greg and his wife Amy to write the introduction to the first book collecting art from their Device Gallery (devicegallery.com) in La Jolla, CA. That book was called *Fantastic Contraption* and it certainly lived up to the "fantastic" part. Greg and Amy have asked me to write introductions to the other two volumes in the Device series, Reconstructed and Traveling Device. The introductions to the first two volumes are included in this collection (Mechanical Animism and Techno-Temporal Mash-Ups). *(brotron.com)*

Lea Redmond (Down the Rabbit Hole) – I was enchanted by the work of Lea Redmond the very first time I saw one of her tiny hand-calligraphied letters. Everything she does has a sense of childlike wonder and playfulness about it. She thinks and creates in unique ways that I wish we saw much more of. *(leafcutterdesigns.com)*

Blake Maloof (Los and Orc icons, incidental art) – Blake Maloof, my beloved offspring, is an artist and game designer. When he was four years old, a friend saw him drawing at his Playskool desk and said: "Oh, look, you're going to be an artist." He shot her the dirtiest look and growled: "I already AM an artist!" And he has never wavered from that self-identification. He currently works for the game design studio, Toys for Bob, in Novato, CA.

Kathryn Rathke (Bio illustration) Kathryn originally did the illustration of me for a column I was writing in *MAKE*. I was stunned when I saw it. I think that image completely captures me. From now on, I want Kathryn to be my court caricaturist. Rather than posting pics of myself on Facebook, from now on, I'm just going to have her sketch all of my selfies. *(kathrynrathke.com)*

Art: Kathryn Rathke (kathrynrathke.com)

Gareth Branwyn

For over 30 years, writer and alt.culture chronicler Gareth Branwyn has written about DIY media and technology, fringe culture, art, and the internet. He was an editor at *Mondo 2000*, a contributing column editor for *Wired* for 12 years, an editor at *bOING bOING* (print), and the co-creator of the seminal hypermedia ebook, *Beyond Cyberpunk!* Gareth also wrote the first book about the web, *Mosaic Quick Tour: Accessing and Navigating the World Wide Web*, and co-authored *the Happy Mutant Handbook*, with the editors of *bOING bOING*. He has written or edited over a dozen books. Most recently, he was the Editorial Director of Maker Media/*MAKE* magazine and has been one of the people spearheading the growing "maker movement" of DIY enthusiasts.

To learn more about Gareth and his work:

Mind Bone, *blog.garethbranwyn.com*
Sparks of Fire Press, *sparksoffirepress.com*